POLITICAL RHETORIC, POWER,
AND
RENAISSANCE WOMEN

D1027693

SUNY Series in Speech Communication
Dudley D. Cahn, Jr., editor

POLITICAL RHETORIC, POWER, AND RENAISSANCE WOMEN

Edited by
Carole Levin
and
Patricia A. Sullivan

State University of New York Press

Published by
State University of New York Press, Albany

©1995 State University of New York

For information, address the State University of New York Press,
State University Plaza, Albany, NY 12246

Production by Christine Lynch
Marketing by Dana E. Yanulavich

Library of Congress Cataloging-in-Publication Data

Political rhetoric, power, and Renaissance women /   edited by Carole
    Levin and Patricia A. Sullivan.
        p.   cm.—(SUNY series in speech communication)
    Includes bibliographical references and index.
    ISBN 0-7914-2545-2 (alk. paper).—ISBN 0-7914-2546-0 (pbk.   :
  alk. paper)
        1. Women in literature—History. 2. European literature—
  Renaissance, 1450–1600—History and criticism. 3. Women—Europe—
  History—Renaissance, 1450–1600. 4. Politics and literature.
    I. Levin, Carole, 1948–   . II. Sullivan, Patricia Ann.
    III. Series.
PN56.W64P65   1995
809'.93352042—dc20   94-32811
                                                                  CIP

10 9 8 7 6 5 4 3 2 1

"*Rhetorica*" [Lady Rhetoric] from Gregor Reisch, *Margarita Philosophica*
(Freiburg, 1503), reproduced from the Collections of the Library of Congress.

For Ruth
"we were sisters long before it was the fashion"
and for Ray
"we were partners long before it was the fashion"

CONTENTS

LIST OF ILLUSTRATIONS

ACKNOWLEDGMENTS

It was a great pleasure for us to edit this collection. One reason this project proved to be such a joy was because of how wonderful the authors were with whom we worked. For Carole, it was bringing together scholars whose work she had long admired. For Pat, it was getting to know a new group of great people. They were all hardworking, patient, generous, and fun. The excellence of their work speaks for itself. We appreciate that Lee Cahn, our series editor, asked Carole and then Pat to do a book for his series, and we hope he is as pleased as we are by this collection. We are grateful also to the people with whom we worked at SUNY Press, especially Priscilla Ross. We would like to thank James Schiffer, Helen Sterk, and William Covino for their careful reading of the manuscript. We especially thank Ruth Elwell for her care and expertise in doing the index.

A number of these essays were originally presented at the Patristics, Medieval, and Renaissance Conference at Villanova University. We thank Thomas Losoncy, conference co-chair, for all of his support. We are also very grateful for the support we have received from SUNY at New Paltz, especially from Gerald Sorin and Adelaide Haas, our department chairs, A. David Kline, Dean of Liberal Arts, and William Vasse, Vice President for Academic Affairs. We also want to express our appreciation to the other members of the New Paltz Medieval and Renaissance group, Karin Andriolo, Kit French, Dan Kempton, Yu Jin Ko, Todd Quinlan, and Michael Willis.

Carole also wants to thank the students of her class on the history of European women, who talked through with her many of the issues of the introductory essay. Ann Simonds and Adam Schenkman also were very helpful in refining some ideas. She also thanks Amos Lee Laine for his support of this and many projects. Thanks are especially due to the Carney family, Sandy, Jo, Alex, Julie, and Annie, for their warmth, love, and hospitality during frequent research visits. Carol Brobeck, Rick and Casey Gershon, Jo Margaret Mano, Joe Silvestri, Martha Skeeters, and Lynn Spangler support the scholarship, and much

much more. Pat Sullivan, dear friend and colleague, is a model collaborator; working with her was a joy.

Pat also wants to thank Ray Miller for making all aspects of her life more meaningful through his love and support. She is grateful to Carole Levin, a constant source of inspiration, for the opportunity to collaborate on this project. Carole is a special friend and colleague whose generosity is unbounded. Her parents, Eathel and Joe Sullivan, as well as her grandparents, Daisy and Pearl Nicholson, deserve thanks for fostering early interests in rhetoric and political communication. Steve Goldzwig and Lynn Turner facilitated this project through friendship and their efforts as provocative and diligent coauthors on other projects.

Aprill.

From Edmund Spenser, *Shepheardes Calendar*, Illustration to the April Eclogue.
By permission of the Folger Shakespeare Library.

Politics, Women's Voices, and the Renaissance: Questions and Context

Carole Levin and Patricia A. Sullivan

In 1558, the Scots reformer, John Knox, published his *First Blast of the Trumpet Against the Monstrous Regiment of Women.* Knox was horrified to think of such women as the Scottish Queen Mary Stuart, her mother, Mary of Guise, and Mary I of England actually being so forward and inappropriate as to claim the power to rule. Knox vehemently described female rule as blasphemous against God. "I am assured that God hath reveled to some in this our age, that it is more than a monstre in nature that a Woman shall reigne and have empire above a Man. . . . howe abominable, odious, and detestable is all such usurped authoritie." Knox argued that God not only ordained that women were barred from authority, but given their essential nature they would be incapable of wielding authority if they illegitimately usurped it. Yet women, by their very nature avaricious, deceitful, cruel, oppressive, and proud, sought domination over men, and some men foolishly gave it to them. "To promote a Woman to beare rule, superioritie, dominion, or empire above any Realme, nation, or Citie, is repugnant to Nature . . . it is the subversion of good order, of all equitie and justice." Men must "acknowledge that the Regiment of a Woman is a thing most odious in the presence of God . . . she is a traitoresse and rebell against God . . . they must studie to represse her inordinate pride and tyrannie to the uttermost of their power." Knox claimed divine authority for his views. "By the Holy Ghost is manifestly expressed in these words, I suffer not a woman to usurp authority above the man. So both by God's law and the interpretation of the Holy Ghost, women are utterly forbidden to occupy the place of God in the offices 'foresaid, which he has assigned to man, whom he hath appointed to be his

1

lieutenant on earth. The apostle taketh power from all women to speak in the assembly."

Knox was not only responding to the specific Catholic women rulers, Mary I, Mary Stuart, Queen of Scots, and her regent mother, Mary of Guise, for whom his tract was aimed, but more generally to the enormous social, political, religious changes in the sixteenth century that allowed women to gain some measure of power.

In the late fourteenth, early fifteenth century, the French author and poet Christine de Pizan had begun to speak as a woman, to give voice for women. Educated by her father, and then left a widow with two young children by the age of twenty-five, Christine began to write for consolation, but also to make a living. Critics now see her as one of those writers who helped bridge the transition between medieval and Renaissance. She imagined a world of women, a city of ladies, and explored who would be their heroes, what were the roles available, how could they deal with the problems for women in the public arena. By the sixteenth century, in part through the accident of female birth and early male death, women were to achieve power in startling new ways. One result was not only changes in some women's behavior and how they expressed themselves, but changes in how the larger society perceived women's roles and nature.

In early sisteenth-century England, Henry VIII, as the second generation of the new Tudor dynasty, believed that England's stability depended on his having a son to succeed him. When his first marriage to Catherine of Aragon produced only dead babies and a daughter Mary, Henry decided to have his marriage annulled. Catherine was in many ways a model queen. She was pious, strong-minded, and fiercely loyal to Henry. But she believed that if God had given her and Henry no sons this meant Mary should reign, which was a point of view anathema to Henry. Pope Clement VII's refusal to grant this annulment led in the late 1520s and early 1530s to Henry's eventual break with the Church of Rome.[1] Though Henry originally had political and dynastic motives, the English Reformation caused great changes in the course of the sixteenth and seventeenth centuries in how people regarded their religious beliefs. And the Reformation came to have significant effects on how women were valued and on their status.

Henry's passionate attraction and second marriage to Anne Boleyn, would eventually turn to hatred when she produced a daughter, Elizabeth, and miscarried a son. The first wife, Catherine, was thrust aside, her marriage pronounced annulled by Henry's Archbishop of Canterbury, Thomas Cranmer. Catherine never recognized this annulment, and in 1536 signed her last letter to Henry, in which she told him what she desired above all things was to see him once again, "Catherine the Queen." Only a few months later, Henry dispatched his second wife as well, this time to the executioner's block, accused of adultery and treason. Henry's third marriage gave him the son, Edward, he so craved. Jane Seymour, however, died of complications due to childbirth. Though he married three more times, these later unions produced no children. Henry's will, which had the force of Parliament behind it, placed his daughter Mary and then his daughter Elizabeth as successors to the realm should Edward die without heirs. Despite all his care, England might well have a queen.

Though for Henry the original motives for his break with the Church were political, in the 1530s some of those closest to him, particularly Cranmer and Thomas Cromwell, his Principal Secretary, had encouraged a real religious reformation. For some women, this religious change allowed them to see other ways to reconceptualize their lives. One especially was Anne Askew, who was known from her adolescence for her enthusiasm and commitment to Protestantism. In 1540, when she was twenty, her father arranged a marriage for her with a wealthy landowner, Thomas Kyme. It was not a happy marriage, since Kyme was still a believer in the old faith, while Anne had become a committed and ardent Protestant. Anne, convinced her husband was doing all he could to prevent her from worshipping as she believed, left him. She claimed her marriage was not lawful in the eyes of God, and went to London to seek a divorce. In London she became a visible part of a Protestant prayer circle. Conservatives attacked her and attempted to use her to discredit Henry's last wife, Catherine Parr. Askew's sense of self was so strong it did not waver even when she was tortured and finally burned to death in 1546 as a heretic. Early the next year, Henry himself died, leaving England to his one son.

Yet despite Henry's great concern that England be ruled by kings, in 1553 at the age of fifteen his son Edward VI died. After an attempted coup to place yet another female, Henry's grand niece Lady Jane Grey, on the throne, Henry's two daughters, Mary and Elizabeth were to rule for the rest of the century. Mary attempted to follow a more traditional path. She married her cousin Philip of Spain and desperately hoped for a child. The country's disillusion over this foreign and barren marriage, as well as the horror over Mary's burning of three hundred Protestants, were lessons not lost on Elizabeth when she became queen in 1558. Across the channel in France the early death of Henry II in an accident in a tournament in 1559 meant that the queen mother Catherine de Médicis was powerfully involved in governing until her death thirty years later. At the end of the seventeenth century as well, James II's daughters Mary (with her husband William III) and Anne were to again to be queens in their own right. Women in positions of power had great impact on the age.

Such changes in the political structure also caused people to examine in new ways earlier powerful women, such as Isabel, French wife of Edward II, who in the early fourteenth century led a rebellion against her husband, and with her lover ruled for her young son Edward III, until he wrested power away from her. In the seventeenth century, women, such as Elizabeth Cary, Madeleine de Scudéry, Margaret Cavendish, Margaret Fell, Bathsua Makin, Mary Astell, and Aphra Behn as well as men were writing about both specific powerful, political women and about changing ideas about women in the public arena. Knox's trumpet was being blasted over a stormy and changing landscape.

Aimed at Catholic rulers, Knox had the bad timing of having his work appear only a few months prior to the beginning of Elizabeth I's reign. Though in no way arguing for the overthrow of the twenty-five year old Protestant Elizabeth, who succeeded to the English throne from her sister Mary in November 1558, Knox was committed to the proposition that for a woman to be the head of government was "monstrous." In the "apology" he sent Elizabeth he stated, "I can not deny the wreiting of a booke aganis the usurped Authoritie, and injust Regement of Women; neither [yit] am I myndit to retract or call back any principall point, or propositioun of the same, till treuth and verritie do farder appeir." Knox would not have considered himself to be primarily a political theorist; what mattered to this Calvinist preacher was "true" religion. But in the sixteenth century, politics and religion were completely intertwined.[2]

Knox's horror over women's rule and the power women might exert was echoed over four hundred years later in the 1992 elections. The Rev. Pat Robertson, who has run in the past for the Republican nomination for President and who may well make another attempt, warned of the dangers of a proposed equal rights amendment to the Iowa Constitution. Passage of such an amendment was part of the "feminist agenda," an agenda Robertson claims to be "a socialist, anti-family political movement that encourages women to leave their husbands, kill their children, practice witchcraft, destroy capitalism, and become lesbians."[3]

Knox and Robertson, in their image of women, their horror over women in politics, their use of religious rhetoric as an argument against powerful women, their perception that powerful women are on the offense against nature, uncannily echo each other—and also evoke comparisons between powerful, gifted, politically engaged women of the Renaissance and of our own age, and the fears caused by each.

This collection examines the political rhetoric of a number of powerful women of the Renaissance, at male rhetoric about such powerful women, at drama and fiction by both male and female authors that consider women and political context, and how historians—then and now—have evaluated powerful women. Our collection begins with an essay about Christine de Pizan and her fifteenth-century look at powerful women and ends with an essay about seventeenth-century rhetoricians and how they viewed and reshaped the Renaissance in terms of giving power to women. The essays in between consider women in the sixteenth and seventeenth centuries, mostly English, though with some French examples. We also contextualize these examples where appropriate into modern issues as well. Our approach in this collection is deliberately multidisciplinary, as is obvious from the range of disciplines represented by the authors—history, literature, rhetoric—because we believe that a meshing, an interweaving, of different disciplines enriches our subject matter. As a result of our meshing of disciplines, we use the term political rhetoric in the broadest sense. This collection examines the rhetoric used by powerful women, the rhetoric used about them, and their representations in histories and dramas written during the Renaissance by both women and men. The use of all of these disciplines and texts allows us to learn much more about the Renaissance, the place and status of women, and the use of political rhetoric. Just as today the enormous social changes have meant re-evaluation of women's roles and gender relations, so, too, was the Renaissance a time of great social, intellectual, cultural, and religious change.

In the Renaissance—as in any period—most women belonged to family units and had roles as wives, mothers, daughters, and widows. Both within the household and often beyond it women were workers. Religion played an important role in women's lives and in the conceptions by both men and women of what woman's nature truly was.[4] There were also, of course, some exceptional women who found more public arenas for their gifts and ambitions. This book, by its nature, not only focuses more on such women but also attempts to place them within the context and understanding of other women's lives. The

Renaissance was a time of women in public roles—of queens—and also a time when many women, thousands of them, were also accused and sometimes executed for witchcraft. Sometimes the accusation of witch was used against a powerful woman—such as Anne Boleyn or Catherine de Médicis—though most who were actually executed were of lower social, economic status, of the powerless rather than powerful. And just as accusations of witchcraft were used against powerful women, so, too, were comments about their sexuality.

The distinction between a "good" woman and a "bad" one was used to control women in the home, but also in the public arena. While for men, the conception of honor was concerned with physical demonstrations of courage, such as on the battlefield or the joust, and with keeping one's word, for women honor was inextricably tied up with their sexuality—not only their actual behavior, but also their sexual reputation. Even if a woman were chaste, if she behaved in such a way that she was thought not to be, she was dishonored; and her male kinsmen were dishonored with her. The easiest and most successful way to destroy a woman was an attack on her reputation for chastity.[5] Such belief systems made it difficult for women to move into the public realm with an articulate voice. As Ann Rosalind Jones suggests, "Female silence was equated with chastity, female eloquence with promiscuity."[6]

And this is still true today. During the Anita Hill-Clarence Thomas Senate Judiciary Committee Hearing in 1991, John Doggett, a character witness for Thomas claimed that Hill was a spurned woman. He noted: "She was having a problem with being rejected by men she was attracted to." Senator Alan Simpson [Republican, Montana] shook his head and expressed outrage concerning Hill's sexual appetite, exclaiming, "Watch out for this woman." When interviewed by a reporter, Senator John Danforth [Republican, Missouri], a Thomas supporter, identified a disorder associated with power and lust. He smiled and said, "There is a specific disorder relating to how people perceive authority figures and possible sexual interest by authority figures in them."[7]

Clearly, for a woman to speak with an articulate voice in the public arena makes her the object of worry and the butt of jokes, and makes those around her worry about their vulnerability. A Republican consultant, after evoking a promise of anonymity, told a network newscaster about efforts to damage Hillary Rodham Clinton's credibility before President Bill Clinton seeks reelection in 1996. The consultant referred to "the rumor machine" that he was activating against Hillary and claimed that stories about an "either nonexistent or all too active" sex life would discredit her. As Elisabeth Perry points out, when Hillary Rodham Clinton asked people to use all three of her names, "the charges flew. Ambitious feminist. Power mad. Who is in charge here?" Perry then goes on to ask, "If, on the brink of the twenty-first century, the wife of the President of the United States still cannot perform in an authoritative role without questions being raised about the appropriateness of her behaviour, how could the women of the 1920s have stood a chance?"[8] We might ask even more, what about the women of the Renaissance?

Elizabeth I, who ruled England from 1558 to 1603, was a well-beloved, and in many ways a successful, monarch, but throughout her reign, and especially at moments of national crisis, the English records are peppered with people arrested for slandering the queen, and questioning her chastity. People named her supposed lovers, and accused her of bearing—and killing—illegitimate children.[9] Elizabeth's own mother, Anne Boleyn, was literally destroyed, beheaded on Tower Hill in 1536 when Elizabeth was less than three years old, for accusations, most probably false, that she was an adulterer who had taken five lovers, one of whom was said to be her own brother.[10]

Just as Anne Boleyn's reputation proved to be so damaging to her, Catherine de Médicis, widow of Henry II and mother to Francis II, Charles IX, and Henry III, was also known in France as a manipulative, Machiavellian poisoner who orchestrated the murder of thousands of Protestants. Yet women who stayed within the framework of approved behavior, such as Catherine of Aragon or Mary II, also did not find it easy to be in the public life. All of Catherine's virtues were cancelled by her failure to have a son. Mary II was also childless, and her obedience to her husband sometimes made her appear a faithless daughter.

Women in positions of power often carefully constructed the rhetoric they used to justify that power. Elizabeth elaborately crafted her rhetoric on the issue of whether she would marry. She rhetorically created for herself a family as she ruled England alone. But Elizabeth and other women had less control over what was said about them both in their own lives and later. Especially in the last part of Elizabeth's reign, her Privy Council was extremely concerned about anyone whose statements seemed to threaten the Queen's legitimacy. In 1587 and again in 1592, a woman named Anne Burnell came before the Privy Council for her claims that she was the daughter of the King of Spain. In 1592, the Council ordered her whipped through the streets of

London to punish her and warn others. Burnell's case is only one of a number of examples that demonstrate the significance of gender in the different reactions to power in the Renaissance. Examining the rhetoric used by powerful women, by both men and women about such women, and the literary and dramatic weaving together of the themes represented by their lives can tell us a great deal about gender and power in the Renaissance, and also about how these themes echo in our culture today.

The essays in this collection are wide-ranging in considering issues around Renaissance women and political rhetoric. Some deal with specific historical individuals and their rhetorical strategies. Other essays consider how other people both at the time and later regarded some powerful women. And still others look at specific authors, both male and female, and analyze their presentations of powerful women, and gender relations within political structures. Together these essays bring us to a greater understanding of questions of gender and power in the Renaissance, and, by extension, in our own age as well.

In Christine de Pizan's "*Cité des Dames: Toward a Feminist Scriptural Practice*," Daniel Kempton explores Christine de Pizan's efforts in carving out space for her voice as a female author at the end of the Middle Ages, the beginning of the Renaissance. Kempton argues that de Pizan's *The Book of the City of Ladies* and *The Treasure of the City of Ladies* reveal three modes of a medieval woman writing. The first mode is "writing like a man/clerk" within the library. The second mode is self-reflexive and confronts the challenges of "writing like a woman" on the margins of discourse. The final mode constitutes feminist consciousness-raising as de Pizan addresses the material conditions that marginalize women in the City.

One woman whose place on the margin was deadly was Anne Boleyn. Retha Warnicke's essay asks us to rethink history from a feminist perspective as she argues for a gendered approach to studying the image and representation of Anne Boleyn in Tudor England. "Conflicting Rhetoric About Tudor Women: the Example of Queen Anne Boleyn" suggests that literary conventions in early Renaissance England constrained biographical accounts of Anne's life. Contemporary religious and social beliefs, including attitudes about gender roles, informed the approaches of her biographers, all of whom were male. They saw the Queen as a fallen woman—a harlot executed for sexual crimes. Warnicke concludes by proposing that analysis of conflicting rhetoric about Anne's appearance, sexuality, and death must be framed in terms of Tudor gender relationships.

Anne Boleyn's daughter Elizabeth ruled for forty-five years as Queen. She, too, had to deal with the expectations for appropriate behavior for women. In the early years of her reign, the pressure on her to marry was intense. Ilona Bell's analysis of Elizabeth I's marriage speeches at the beginning of her reign counters the popular Petrachan image of the "virgin queen." In "Elizabeth I—Always Her Own Free Woman," Bell turns to Elizabeth's rhetoric to argue that the Queen refused to succumb to partriarchal pressures to marry. She insisted that she had the capability and authority to rule England alone. Furthermore, Elizabeth's words expressed female desire and freedom of choice. In refusing to marry for convenience or political gain, Elizabeth revisioned marriage and political power from a female standpoint. She rejected the notion of courtship as duty and argued that she would resist marriage until a man appeared who pleased her.

Lena Cowen Orlin also argues that Elizabeth I subverted patriarchal expectations during her reign. In "The Fictional Families of Elizabeth I," Orlin examines Elizabeth's rhetoric on family relations to suggest that the Queen was "ever her own mistress." Elizabeth's rhetoric reveals that she recognized the constraints she faced as a ruler—her family's history, her birth order, her gender—and strategized to turn those constraints to her advantage. Because she lacked traditional family relationships, Elizabeth embraced the opportunity to rhetorically transform the kingdom into her family. Through familial tropes, Elizabeth became wife to the kingdom, mother of the people, cousin to the nobility, and sister to foreign princes.

In "Dutifully Defending Elizabeth: Lord Henry Howard and the Question of Queenship," Dennis Moore discusses one response to Elizabeth's rule and rhetoric. As Moore notes, the prevailing conceptions of womanhood in the sixteenth century echoed Knox in arguing that women were not suited to serve as rulers. *A Dutiful Defense of the Lawful Regiment of Women* (1590), written by Elizabeth's cousin Henry Howard, represents one rhetorical response to the debate over queenship. Although *A Dutiful Defense* was never published, it was circulated in manuscript. Moore argues that scholars have erred in overlooking the treatise; it provides a window on Elizabethan reasoning concerning female rule.

Just as there were many responses to Elizabeth, so, too, were there to her contemporary, Catherine de Médicis, Queen Mother of France during the sixteenth-century wars of religion. In "The Blood-Stained

Hands of Catherine de Médicis," Elaine Kruse argues that misogynistic attacks on women—from Catherine to Marie Antoinette to Nancy Reagan to Hillary Rodham Clinton—reflect patriarchal discomfort with female power. Women have been cast as "other"—defective males—in efforts to exclude them from roles in public life. The charges against Catherine, that she was a Wicked Queen, dangerous foreigner, evil woman, and political manipulator constitute a patriarchal litany that greets women who seek to exercise political power.

"Expert Witnesses and Secret Subjects: Anne Askew's *Examination* and Renaissance Self-Incrimination" analyzes one autobiographical response to misogynistic rhetoric. Elizabeth Mazzola proposes that the autobiographical account of Askew, a sixteenth-century Protestant martyr, represents a voice that refused to be marginalized or repressed by the authorities who charged her with heresy. *Examinations*, the first person account of her trials, indicates that Askew *chose* silence in refusing to "play the game" as defined by her accusers. She understood the line of reasoning used by her accusers and declined to supply them with answers to their questions. Instead, she responded with questions to them that provided her with the opportunity to explain her beliefs.

We know about Anne Askew in large part because of her arrest and trial. In the Tudor period we hear the voices of two other more obscure women, Mary Baynton and Anne Burnell, whose actions, statements, and beliefs led to their arrests. Carole Levin analyzes their rhetorical strategies in "Mary Baynton and Anne Burnell: Madness and Rhetoric in Two Tudor Family Romances." In the 1530s Mary Baynton claimed to be Henry VIII's eldest daughter Mary and actually convinced people to give her money as a result. Over fifty years later, Anne Burnell was convinced that she was the daughter of Philip II of Spain. These delusions and/or impostures gave these lower-class women a voice, though at great cost.

A number of essays have considered actual queens. Jo Eldridge Carney's "Queenship in Shakespeare's *Henry VIII*: The Issue of Issue" explores the representation of queenship in Shakespeare's play. Analysis of *Henry VIII* and Samuel Rowley's *When You See Me, You Know Me*, a literary source for Shakespeare's play, reveals circumscribed patriarchal definitions of queenship. Queens, including Catherine of Aragon, Anne Boleyn, and Elizabeth, are critical to dramatic events, but do not exercise political influence as rulers. Queenship is associated with pageantry, superiority to other women, and reproduction. All the queens share the obligation to produce an heir to the throne—preferably a male heir.

Gwynne Kennedy examines Elizabeth Cary's efforts to make a revision in the meaning of wifely submission and queenship. *The History of the Life, Reign, and Death of Edward II* is probably the first prose history written in English by a woman. "Reform or Rebellion?: the Limits of Female Authority in Elizabeth Cary's *History of Edward II*" analyzes Cary's ambivalent responses to Queen Isabel, Edward's wife. The focus of the history gradually shifts from Edward to Isabel and reveals conflicting judgments about female authority. Although the *History of the Life, Reign and Death of Edward II* suggests that women have the right to protect their own interests in a household, it also implies that Isabel, as a servant of the commonwealth, had a responsibility to uphold the political order by obeying her husband. "Wits, Whigs, and Women: Domestic Politics as Anti-Whig Rhetoric in Aphra Behn's Town Comedies" also centers on a female writer's ambivalent responses to female authority. Arlen Feldwick accounts for apparent contradictions between Behn's feminism and her political convictions. Although Behn's commitment to the Stuart monarchy and its patriarchal rhetoric appears to undercut her commitment to feminism, Feldwick argues that these seemingly disparate threads are reconciled in the playwright's philosophical opposition to the Whigs. The author concludes that a Restoration woman, even a progressive Restoration woman such as Behn, could not visualize true female autonomy.

In some ways paralleling Warnicke's argument about Anne Boleyn, William Spellman identifies problems with biographical accounts of Mary II—accounts that fail to recognize the presence of female autonomy. In "Queen Mary II: Image and Substance During the Glorious Revolution," Spellman revises the history of the joint monarchy of William and Mary. He argues that patriarchal scholarly biases have eclipsed the role of Mary in the reign. Although many scholarly accounts depict Mary as obedient and submissive, Spellman argues that such views overlook the period of time when the Queen exercised executive authority. He concludes by urging scholarly awareness of patriarchal biases in primary texts, biases that inform historical accounts.

In "The Politics of Renaissance Rhetorical Theory by Women," Jane Donawerth answers Joan Kelly's famous question with the assertion that yes, women did have a Renaissance, or at least, that in the seventeenth century women appropriated Renaissance ideals, especially the rebirth of classical rhetorical education, to argue for the education of women. In using the myth of the Renaissance to their advantage, female rhetoricians spoke of women's rights to education

and speech as rights that had existed in the past, and could be re-
claimed. A new rhetorical theory was generated in the seventeenth
century in works by Madeleine de Scudéry, Margaret Cavendish, Margaret Fell, Bathsua Makin, and Mary Astell.

In the fifteenth century, Christine de Pizan began to articulate the
rhetoric of a feminist consciousness as the new age of the Renaissance
was emerging. Two hundred years later the women rhetoricians looked
back to the Renaissance and saw the changes women had made. Actual women—Anne Boleyn, Mary Baynton, Anne Askew, Anne Burnell,
Elizabeth I, Catherine de Médicis, and Mary II had attempted to rec-
reate models for women in the political realm. Both male and female
authors—Henry Howard, Shakespeare, Elizabeth Cary, and Aphra
Behn—also explored these issues. What we see in all of these essays
is both the triumphs but also the difficulties for women who wanted
a powerful, articulate voice. The difficulties—the cultural as well as
personal ambivalences—are still with us today.

Notes

1. Henry VII had acquired a dispensation from the pope so that his son
Henry could marry Catherine, since according to Leviticus it was against
Biblical law for the two to marry. By the 1520s, Henry may well have believed
that the fact he had no living male heirs was divine punishment for breaking
this Biblical law. Historians A. F. Pollard and J. J. Scarisbrick have argued that
for Henry it was indeed, at least in part, a matter of conscience. A. F. Pollard,
Henry VIII (1902; new edn. London: Jonathan Cape, 1970), p. 143. J. J. Scarisbrick,
Henry VIII (Berkeley and Los Angeles: University of California Press, 1968),
p. 152.

2. John Knox, *Works*, ed. David Laing (Edinburgh: James Thin, 1895), IV,
pp. 366–67, 369, 375, 415, 380, 353.

3. *New York Times*, 30, Aug 1992, p. E3.

4. See Margaret L. King, *Women of the Renaissance* (Chicago and London:
University of Chicago Press, 1991), and Retha Warnicke, *Women of the English
Renaissance and Reformation* (Westport, Conn.: Greenwood Publishing, 1983),
for a thorough discussion of women's roles during this period. On the subject
of women and religion, particularly valuable is Patricia Crawford's *Women
and Religion in England, 1500–1720* (London and New York: Routledge, 1993).
See also, Margaret P. Hannay, ed., *Silent but for the Word: Tudor Women as
Patrons, Translators, and Writers of Religious Works*, (Kent, Ohio: Kent State University Press, 1985).

5. For a discussion of female honor in the Renaissance, see especially, Linda Woodbridge, *Women in the English Renaissance: Literature and the Nature of Womankind, 1540–1620* (Urbana and Chicago: University of Illinois Press, 1984), p. 53. For a discussion of the impact of Protestantism on the concept of honor, see also, Mervyn James, *English Politics and the Conception of Honour, 1485–1642* (Cambridge: Cambridge University Press, 1986). It is also useful to look at proverbs about women in the Renaissance to see the linking of sexual misconduct and generally dishonorable behavior. Morris Palmer Tilley, *A Dictionary of the Proverbs in England in the Sixteenth and Seventeenth Centuries* (Ann Arbor: University of Michigan Press, 1950), pp. 741–49.

6. Ann Rosalind Jones, *The Currency of Eros* (Bloomington: Indiana University Press, 1990), p. 1.

7. Mary Douglas argues in *Purity and Danger: An Analysis of the Concepts of Pollution and Taboo* (1966; reprint, New York: Routledge, 1992) that "unchaste" or "dirty" behavior has been associated with transgressions against the social order. In *Difference and Pathology: Stereotypes of Sexuality, Race, and Madness* (Ithaca: Cornell University Press, 1985), Sander Gilman explores the relationship between maintenance of the social order and stereotypes. He notes that "when systems of representation are used to structure the projections of our anxiety, they are necessarily reductive. Often the very appeal to a set system of images is a sign of the observer's awareness of the absence of difference. . . . The anxiety present in the self concerning its control over the world directly engenders a need for a clear and hard line of difference between the self and the Other" (27).

8. Elisabeth Perry, "Why Suffrage for American Women was Not Enough," *History Today*, 43 (September, 1993), p. 41.

9. See Carole Levin, *"The Heart and Stomach of a King": Elizabeth I and the Politics of Sex and Power* (Philadelphia: University of Pennsylvania Press, 1994), for a thorough discussion of these rumors and their significance.

10. As well as Retha Warnicke's essay in this collection, see her book length study, *The Rise and Fall of Anne Boleyn* (Cambridge: Cambridge University Press, 1989).

Bourgeois and Common Women Seated Before Three Virtues. By permission of the Beinecke Rare Book & Manuscript Collection, Yale University.

Christine de Pizan's *Cité des Dames* and *Trésor de la Cité*: Toward a Feminist Scriptural Practice

Daniel Kempton

The *Livre de la Cité des Dames* begins in the scholar's *celle* (room, hermitage). As the scene opens, the *je* who narrates the text is, as usual, sitting alone, "surrounded by books on all kinds of subjects" (3), intent upon the "sentences de divers aucteurs" (616), to which "long and continual study" has been devoted (10).[1] Here is the medieval scene of writing par excellence: writing based upon reading. Yet an unexpected element is quietly insinuated by the grammatical form of the past participle *avironnee* (surrounded), which modifies *je*: the scholar is a woman. She is, in fact, the fictional representative of Christine de Pizan. Notwithstanding the improbability of this vocation for a woman in the fifteenth century (its impossibility in principle), Christine de Pizan was a scholar of remarkable accomplishment who had traveled far on the *chemin de long estude*. Her writing draws upon ancient philosophers and poets, the Vulgate Bible, church fathers, clerical authorities, Italian humanists, and French "translators" (adapters, commentators) of the Latin tradition. By 1405, the date of the *Cité*, her body of work was extensive, including verse romances (e.g., *L'Epistre au Dieu d'Amours*), a collection of moralized stories (*L'Epistre d'Othea*), a translation and gloss of the pseudo-Senecan *Formulae honestae vitae*, a biography of Charles V (*Le Livre des fais et bonnes meurs du sage Roy Charles V*), and two lengthy allegories on political and philosophical themes (*Le Livre du chemin de long estude* and *Le Livre de la Mutacion de Fortune*).[2] These are authoritative and impeccably canonical texts, indistinguishable, but for the signature, from those written by her clerkly, or courtly, peers.[3] Christine de Pizan was, in her (self-conscious) phrase from the *Chemin*, a "fille d'étude":[4] a woman schooled in the medieval library (which was a male preserve) and thus (paradoxically) enabled to write.

In the *Avision Christine* and the *Mutacion de Fortune*, Christine de Pizan outlines an autobiography: She recalls that she was "naturally inclined to scholarship from birth" (ca. 1364), and though obliged to marry, she was free after the death of her husband in 1390 to return to the scholar's "solitary and tranquil life," which "naturally pleased [her] the most."[5] The *fille d'étude* was her authentic identity, the destiny of her original nature. During childhood this natural inclination was nurtured by her father Thomas de Pizan, who was a scientist and philosopher—a "master of knowledge."[6] Because of social custom, however, she had limited opportunities for formal education. Nevertheless, she managed to gather together some few scraps and fragments of her father's knowledge and, possessed of this intellectual patrimony, eventually grew to resemble her father in everything, except her sex.[7] Most of all, she shared his love of learning: "Ah learning: sweet, savory, and honeyed thing, supreme and pre-eminent among all other treasures! How happy are they who taste you fully!"[8] The daughter could never taste it *fully*. But she considered the small portion of her father's "very rich treasure" which she had inherited, in addition to the learning she subsequently acquired, to be the "only wealth that was rightly her own."[9] Like her father, she capitalized on this wealth to make her way in the world, dedicating her knowledge to the service of princes: "I presented them with some new things from my books. . . . These they willingly saw and by their grace joyfully received like kind and gentle princes, and more I think for the novelty of a woman who could write (since that had not occurred for quite some time) than for any worth there might be in them."[10] As the reward for her studiousness, Christine de Pizan enjoyed success and renown, and the mystique of novelty.

This story of the *fille d'étude*, who is also her father's daughter, contains certain tensions and problems, which are more or less denied. It anticipates the biography of that figure whom Adrienne Rich calls (in the twentieth century) the "special" woman—a biography that is, up to a point, the story of Rich's own life and career as a poet:

> My own luck was being born . . . into a house full of books, with a father who encouraged me to read and write. So for about twenty years I wrote for a particular man, who criti-

cized and praised me and made me feel I was indeed "special." . . . And then of course there were other men—writers, teachers—the Man, who was . . . a literary master and a master in other ways less easy to acknowledge.[11]

By the time she wrote these words (ca. 1970), Rich had dispelled the aura of "specialness" she had formerly cherished, in her father's house, through the university, into marriage. She now saw the "special" woman as a "daughter of the father-principle," who allows herself to be "lulled by that blandishment about being 'different,' more intelligent, more beautiful, more human, more committed to rational thinking, more humorous, more able to 'write like a man.' "[12] The "special" woman labors under an illusion induced by the Man, an illusion of freedom (of self-realization, of self-expression), whereas she has in actuality "los[t] touch with her own innate strength" and "suffer[ed] [a] separation from other women, and thus from herself," from her true nature.[13] The illusion is powerful, and is exposed as illusion only by something on the order of a crisis: "we have known that men would tolerate, even romanticize us as special, as long as our words and actions didn't threaten their privilege of tolerating or rejecting us and our work according to *their* ideas of what a special woman ought to be."[14]

For Christine de Pizan, the crisis was precipitated by the *débat* on the *Roman de la Rose* (1401–1403).[15] The threat she posed to masculine/ clerical privilege was to call into question one of its exemplars, Jean de Meun: the *fille d'étude* presumed to pass judgment on the master and his book. The substance of her critique was that the language of the *Rose* was "dishonorable" and its teaching "reprehensible," or, more exactly, that such evils were dangerously intermingled with authentic eloquence and truth so that "malice [lay] concealed in the shadow of goodness and virtue."[16] Of special concern to her was the sanction the *Rose* gave, under the guise of doctrine and the aegis of Jean de Meun's authority, to an assault on women, in the real world as well as in the realm of theory; she asked: "Who are women? Who are they? Are they serpents, wolves, lions, dragons, monsters, or ravishing, devouring beasts and enemies to human nature that it is necessary to make an art of deceiving and capturing them?"[17] Her critique was written in series of open letters to prominent men of church and state (Jean de Montreuil, Provost of Lille; Gontier Col, First Secretary and Notary to the King; and Pierre Col, Canon of Paris and Tournay). The letters these dignitaries wrote in reply leave no doubt about the

extent to which Christine de Pizan had violated their idea of what a
fille d'étude ought to be. Gontier Col affected an arch tone of paternal
concern:

> ... since I love you sincerely for your virtues and merits, I
> have ... exhorted, advised, and begged you to correct and
> amend your manifest error, folly, or excessive willfulness which
> has risen in you, a woman impassioned in this matter, out of
> presumption or arrogance. ... I pray, counsel, and require
> you ... please to correct, retract, and amend your aforemen-
> tioned error with regard to that very excellent and irreproach-
> able doctor of holy divine Scripture, high philosopher, and
> most learned clerk in all the seven liberal arts. It is astonishing
> that you have dared and presumed to correct and criticize
> him. ... Confess your error, and we will have pity on you,
> will grant mercy to you, and will give you salutary penance.[18]

Jean de Montreuil stated his contempt more directly, comparing Christine de Pizan to "Leontium the Greek whore ... who dared to criticize the great philosopher Theophrastus."[19] The *fille d'étude* did not,
in this instance, escape her sex. In the eyes of the "disciples" of Jean
de Meun, as they styled themselves, she was first of all a woman and
a victim of distinctively feminine vices: willfulness, passion, presump-
tion, carnality. Christine de Pizan came to understand that the *débat*
on the *Rose* was not only (not primarily) a contest of interpretation
but also a contest of power, in which she spoke from a disadvan-
taged (because gendered) position: "you [Gontier Col] seek in every
way to minimize my firm beliefs by your anti-feminist attacks."[20] She
was undeterred, however, in her quest for membership in the fraternity of scholars; her livelihood depended upon it. If the crisis of the
"special" woman was not (could not have been) as decisive for Christine de Pizan in 1400 as for Adrienne Rich in 1970, it was not without
consequences: namely, the *Cité des Dames* and its sequel, the *Trésor de
la Cité des Dames*.

An analysis of these books of the *Dames* will occupy us for the rest
of the essay. Gender having become visible (unavoidable) as an issue,
Christine de Pizan took up the defense of women as her theme and
cause. We will review this thematic content (the representation of
women), but we will give particular consideration to the ways in which
the texts—texts of a medieval writer who identifies herself as a
woman—conform to and break from clerkly paradigms of writing. It
is my thesis that Christine de Pizan deploys writing of two different
kinds: writing as knowledge and writing as political practice.

II

The initial episode of the *Cité des Dames* is a fictionalized reprise of the personal crisis.[21] As we have observed, the scene opens upon Christine[22] at work in her *celle*. It is evening, and, weary from her day's research, she sets aside the scholarly "livre" (616) she has been reading and picks up a "petit livret" of verse to browse through for relaxation before going to supper. A contrast is established. The little book (*livret*) is meticulously differentiated from those weighty volumes (*livre*) with which Christine is habitually surrounded: it is a strange book which does not belong to her, having come into her hands, along with some others, by chance; a frivolous book of satire, written by a *poete* not an *aucteur*, and intended, not for edification, but for the amusement of an idle moment. The *petit livret* is Mathéolus's notorious diatribe against women and marriage, his *Lamentations*. Secure in her identity as a scholar, Christine can risk irony, and afford a smile, at the little book's expense: she has heard that it speaks reverently of women. Next morning, however, in the hours normally devoted to study, she turns her attention again to the *Lamentations*, and it then appears in a more ominous light, hardly amusing to her and "of no use in developing virtue or manners" (3). Moreover, its subject is "not very pleasant for people who do not enjoy lies." Impatiently, she puts the offensive book down, but it has already set in motion a train of thought.

Christine starts to wonder why so many different men, solemn *clercs* and others, past and present, have been so ready to write "wicked insults" about women:

> Not only one or two and not even just this Mathéolus . . . but, more generally, judging from the treatises of all philosophers and poets and from all the orators . . . it seems that they all speak from one and the same mouth. They all concur in one conclusion: that the behavior of women is inclined to and full of every vice. . . . I could hardly find a book of morals where . . . I did not find several chapters or certain sections attacking women, no matter who the author was. . . . Like a gushing fountain, a series of authorities ["moult grant foyson de autteurs," 619], whom I recalled one after the other, came to mind, along with their opinions on this topic. (4–5)

The memories are relentless (one after another), and their implication is irresistible: Mathéolus speaks for *all* men (philosophers, poets, orators, scholars) on the topic of women (on Woman as *topos*). The satirist's diatribe cannot be excluded from the Library; on the contrary, it finds a privileged place inside as a touchstone for a previously inconspicuous, or unacknowledged, theme (*sentence*) recurring throughout the Canon in one book after another: the vices of women. The *fille d'étude* is thus involved in a formidable paradox. She has gratefully accepted the Library's store of knowledge for her patrimony—her proper inheritance, a treasure that is "rightly *her own*"—but she now discovers that this paternal treasure "negates," as Rich puts it, "everything she is about."[23] She is that "special" woman who "writes like a man," yet she is unable to recognize herself in the writing of men.

What response is possible? At first Christine assents to the Man's demonized image of Woman and attempts to maintain her identity as *scholar*—her identification *with* scholars—by means of a radical excision: a repudiation of her identity as *woman*. Chapter one ends with a "lamantacion" (621) on Christine's part that is worthy of Mathéolus himself for rhetorical excess and anti-feminism; the last line: "I considered myself most unfortunate because God had made me inhabit a female body in this world" (5). The *je* here is evidently not identical with the "corps femenin" (621) it inhabits; the *je* is a man (in mind, in essence), whose misfortune it was (so a *clerc* would think) to be born into the prison of a female body.[24] Though shorn of the prerogatives of the "special" woman, Christine clings, at least, to the status. Almost at once, however, it will be necessary for her to confront the bad faith implicit in this response and, indeed, in her initial acquiescence as a youth to the illusion of "specialness."

Christine is left stupified ["en etargie," 619] by her painful discovery and the shame of her sex. But as she sits brooding over these melancholy thoughts, a ray of light falls on her lap, and she looks up to see standing before her three crowned *dames* with radiant faces, who have mysteriously entered her *celle*, though the doors were firmly shut (6)—a *coup de théâtre*, which will "awaken the dead." The first of these Ladies, *dame Raison* (reason), announces that she and her sisters, *Droitture* (rectitude) and *Justice* (justice), have come, providentially, to offer Christine instruction and consolation. They appear as an alternative to the authority of masculine scholarship. *Raison* holds up to the *fille d'étude* a mirror of self-knowledge so that she can see her true qualities and her alienation from her sex. The Lady tells Christine she is acting like a fool, giving heed to what she has read in others' books and forgetting what she knows by the sheer fact of being a natural woman ["femme naturelle," 618]. It is necessary for Christine to return to herself ["Or te reviens a toy meismes," 625] and trust in "the certainty of [her] own identity" (6) ["la certaineté de son estre," 623].

Moreover, *Raison* declares that it has been predestined for Christine, owing to her "great love of investigating the truth" (10), to defend women against their many assailants by building a walled city (writing a book) "where no one will reside except all ladies of fame and women worthy of praise" (11); a safe refuge, closed to all men and to "those women who lack virtue" ["a celles ou vertu ne sera trouvee, les murs de nostre cité seront forclos," 630]. This new city/book ["nouvelle cité," 638] will be a massive compilation of hagiographic stories about women, drawn from classical and Christian history and organized as an architectonic whole: that is, the stories will be arranged systematically in three tiers of ascending virtue (parts one, two, and three of the text, each associated with one of the allegorical *dames*) and grouped around numerous points of thematic coherence (for example, women who held political power, contributed to the arts, defended their parents, acted courageously, offered wise counsel, displayed constancy in marriage, guarded their chastity, suffered martyrdom). The *Cité* will stand forever in contradiction to, in refutation of, the diatribe of *clercs*—a legend of good women. Christine fears that the strength of her feeble woman's body ["foible corps femenin," 638] is insufficient for such a task, but it is precisely her natural body upon which the entire project relies.

To begin construction/composition of the *Cité*, *dame Raison* summons Christine from her *celle*:

> "Get up, daughter ["fille," 639]! Without waiting any longer, let us go to the Field of Letters ["champ des escriptures"]. There the City of Ladies will be founded on a flat and fertile plain, where all fruits and freshwater rivers are found and where the earth abounds in all good things. Take the pick of your understanding ["la pioche de ton entendement"] and dig and clear out a great ditch wherever you see the marks of my ruler ["les traces de ma ligne"], and I will help you carry away the earth on my own shoulders."
>
> I immediately stood up to obey her commands and, thanks to these three ladies, I felt stronger and lighter than before. She went ahead, and I followed behind, and after we had arrived at this field I began to excavate and dig, following her marks ["son signe,"] with the pick of cross-examination ["la pioche d'inquisicion"]. (16)

Christine follows *dame Raison*, as her *fille*, to a new site: the *champ des escriptures*. This relocation is suggestive of a fundamentally different relationship between the scholar and canonical scripture. A field must be *worked* to be useful (for agriculture, for architecture). While confined to her *celle* (the *celle des escriptures*), Christine read passively, in the mode of learning, and wrote with a conservatorial intent, faithfully transcribing the already-written; on the *champs des escriptures*, however, she begins to read skeptically, in the spirit of critical inquiry, and to write with a revisionary intent. Wielding the *pioche d'inquisicion*, Christine leaves her mark on the Field: the inscription of new *traces* and *signes*; erasures where old scripture has been dug up and cleared away. It is the distinctive mark of the *femme naturelle*.

Specifically, what this means is that Christine rewrites the source material in accordance with her own idea of feminine virtue, an idea derived from reason and nature. She deletes the hostility toward women that infects Boccaccio's *De claris mulieribus* (a collection of stories about famous pagan women), which is her main source for parts one and two;[25] and she underscores positive aspects of women's character that are irrelevant to Vincent de Beauvais's *Speculum historiale* (an anthology of Christian saints' lives), which is her main source for part three. Christine's adaptation of sources has been explored in detail by modern academic criticism, and the results of these studies, running to hundreds of pages, might be grafted onto the present essay at this point.[26] Let us mention but two examples: Semiramis, Queen of the Assyrians, and the Roman martyr Saint Christine.

For Boccaccio, Semiramis is an equivocal figure. He extolls her military conquests and skillful governance of the Babylonian Empire but counterbalances the praise with an invective against her sexual conduct and incestuous marriage to her son Ninus: "As if he had changed sex with his mother, Ninus rotted away idly in bed, while she sweated in arms against her enemies."[27] Semiramis's feminine vice undermined masculine sexual/political authority and threatened to disrupt the (patriarchal) social order, which is the natural order. For Christine, however, Semiramis is a purely exemplary woman and model for her own literary activity, the first woman in history to be a builder of cities: "this lady, Semiramis, reinforced and rebuilt the strong and cruel city of Babylon, which had been founded by Nimrod and the giants . . . and built several new cities and fortifications and performed many other outstanding deeds and accomplished so much that greater courage and more marvelous and memorable deeds have never been recorded about any man" (39–40). Christine translates only half of the source story, editing out Boccaccio's preoccupation with the queen's sexuality and his paranoid fantasy of emasculation. She squarely addresses his principal charge against Semiramis by arguing that the incestuous marriage was a bold political maneuver to consolidate power, and she tacitly omits the sensational event with which his (male-centered) version of the story inevitably concludes: matricide.

Christine's revision of the saint's *vita* is more subtle but no less telling.[28] In Vincent, Saint Christine, having been inspired by Christian faith at the age of twelve, refused to worship the official Roman gods. Her mother pleaded with her to honor the obligations of family and religion—"My only daughter, have pity on me who nursed you with my breasts: why do you worship a strange god?"—but the child repudiated her worldly parents and averred a higher spiritual lineage: "Why do you call me daughter. . . . Do you not know that I have my name from Christ my savior?"[29] Hearing this, the mother gave her daughter up and denounced her to Urban, the father. Outraged by her stubbornness, Urban beat his daughter in the public square, but Saint Christine remained steadfast in her faith and, after further ordeals (which constitute the major portion of the narrative), suffered a glorious martyrdom. Christine preserves the essential (generic) design of the saint's life but makes one significant change by deleting the mother from the story so that Urban alone is the parental antagonist representing the authority of family and state. The mother is thus absolved of responsibility for tempting the saint and condoning her torture, and the daughter of responsibility for turning against the maternal breast that nursed her. So adjusted, the *vita* of Christine's patron saint and eponym presents an unambiguous picture of feminine, as well as Christian, virtue.

In this way, through a critical rewriting of scholarship, story/stone by story, Christine builds and perfects the "nouvel royaume de Femenie" (815). The book is a literary tour de force, whose artistic merits are reduplicated in the sumptuousness of its autograph manuscripts.[30] We should not underestimate, however, the ideological limitations imposed on the project by its historical context and by the isolation of Christine de Pizan as a woman writer. Need it be said that the virtuous citizens with which the *Cité* is populated are, in truth, not women but traditional (perennial) images of Woman?—a "dream" of Woman, in Rich's phrase, correlative to the "terror," which together haunt the books written by *men*.[31] During the Middle Ages, it was a dream of the virago first of all, the exceptional woman who is not womanish but who has, like Dido, the physical and intellectual characteristics of a man ["l'appellerent Dido: qui vault autant a dire comme *virago* en latin, qui est a dire celle qui a vertu et force de homme," 775].

The *virago* has the *vertu* of the *vir*, of course—a tautology that rigorously denies the worth of women themselves. It was also a dream of the faithful wife (Griselde), the obedient daughter (Drypetina), the diligent helpmeet from Solomon's proverbs—the "femme forte" (765), whose love is unconditional. The *femme forte* is the substratum of society, at once essential and negligible, who sustains the public world of men with her tireless domestic service, providing bread, clothing, solicitude (or, like Carmentis, an alphabet), and asking for nothing in return for herself. Ultimately, it was a dream of the virgin martyr, the bride of Christ and handmaiden of Maria "Royne celeste" (976). The virgin martyr is the woman disembodied, a *femme celeste*—asexual, untouched by desire or pain, not of the flesh (Saint Martina's wounds pour forth milk and sweet scents, 225). She is a salvific star to men (218), and to women an inspirational example "for ending their lives well" (240) ["bon exemple de bien finer leur vie," 1010]. The legend of good women, no less than the diatribe against bad, is an aspect of the clerical *topos* Woman, written *within* the tradition of medieval misogyny (but written insidiously rather than overtly).[32] *As images*, that is, as objectifications belonging to someone else (the male author/theorist), both the "good woman" and the "bad woman" are dehumanizing, alienating, oppressive. But they are perhaps not equally so. We know that the image of the bride of Christ, for example, was susceptible to appropriation during the Middle Ages and that it empowered certain groups of women (cloistered nuns, mystics) to some degree, insofar as a bride of Christ avoided becoming the chattel of a man. And, in the Renaissance, the image of the virago was efficacious for women governors and heads of state, such as Elizabeth I of England. The appropriation of the "good woman" was an important, if *provisional*, act, and a necessary first stage in the evolution of a feminine scriptural tradition.

Nevertheless, we must concede that the *Cité des Dames* is written/built under a cloud of mystification. The principles and tools vital to the success of the enterprise—reason and nature—are themselves products of medieval culture rather than transcendent entities, exterior to clerical writing, as supposed. From our vantage point we can see that *dame Raison* and her sisters, despite their otherworldly trappings, are spokesmen for the status quo, who do not hesitate to endorse the gender arrangements specified by the medieval church: "God did not ordain that men fulfill the offices of women, and women the offices of men. . . . [but] ordained man and woman to serve Him in different offices and also to aid and comfort one another, each in their ordained task, and to each sex has given fitting and appropriate nature and inclination to fulfill their offices" (31). Each sex has its proper, divinely ordained nature, which is exactly suited to its social office, as that office has been instituted by God. On this matter, there would seem to be no disagreement with Boccaccio. Furthermore, *Raison* asserts that the "natural condition" of Woman is to be "simple, tranquil, and upright" (18) ["sa propre condicion naturelle qui doit estre simple, coye et honneste," 643], and that the bad woman is a "monster in nature" ["la mauvaise femme . . . si comme monstre en nature," 642]. In other words, which perhaps could not be spoken in the fifteenth century, the *femme naturelle* is identical with the image of the "good woman," which is a *fiction*. The standard by which feminine virtue is judged does not originate, as *Raison* claims, in a feminine nature; it has (always already) been determined in advance by the *clerc*. We should not be surprised, therefore, that the citizens of the *nouvel royaume de Femenie*, though liberated from misogynistic opprobrium, continue to reflect traditional patriarchal values. Ideological independence is not easily wrested from the situation of textual dependence.[33]

This is especially so when the critic of ideology aspires to make a contribution to the textual tradition herself, bequeathing something to posterity that, while innovative, is still recognizable as scholarship by those who frequent the *champs des escriptures*, namely, *clercs* and other (male) ideologues. In this aspiration we may detect a trace of nostalgia for the *fille d'étude*. Christine is not content merely to score the Field disruptively with her *pioche d'inquisicion* but aims to erect thereon a "beautiful" City of Letters, an edifice "of perpetual duration" (11) that conforms to the rules and *telos* of architectural (scholastic) workmanship. It is a monument to the virtuous Woman, certainly, but also, as *dame Raison* indicates in her Boethian justification of the project, a monument to Universal Learning: all worldly things are "transitory . . . and disappear with time" (88), but "la science tousjours dure" (764). Learning endures forever, as does the fame of that person who is possessed of *science*.

III.

But perhaps we (modern academics, experts in literature) have been overly concerned with the hagiographic content and architectural structure of the *Livre de la Cité de Dames*—its most spectacular (recognizable) features, to be sure. At the instigation of Christine's allegorical guides, we have focused upon the text as *book* and as *city*, as a timeless utopia located nowhere, nowhen on the Field of Letters. There is, however, another kind of writing that appears intermittently throughout the text (in parentheses, digressions, asides), about which we have so far had nothing to say. Let us look once again at the opening scene of the narrative when the three *dames* first approach Christine in her *celle*. We have observed that *Raison* advises Christine—setting her on her somewhat problematic course— to trust in her "natural" being (as goodness) against the scriptural testimony of *clercs*. But at the same time, the *dame* invokes another resource for Christine to draw upon, and write about, in her defense of women: her actual lived experience in the social world. For example:

> As for the attack against the estate of marriage—which is a holy estate, worthy and ordained by God—made not only by Mathéolus but also by others and even by the *Romance of the Rose* . . . it is evident and proven by experience ["prouvee par l'experience," 624] that the contrary of the evil which they . . . claim to be found in this estate through the obligation and fault of women is true. For where has the husband ever been found who would allow his wife to have authority ["maistrise," 625] to abuse and insult him . . .? I believe that, regardless of what you might have read, you will never see such a husband with your own eyes. (7)

What Christine has seen with her own eyes and what she knows *par l'experience* (however holy *Raison* believes the marital estate to be in theory) is that *maistrise* in marriage is always on the side of the husband; such power as the wife may enjoy, such claim upon the husband and right to autonomy, she enjoys at the sole discretion and pleasure of the husband. The issue here is not the moral character of the wife— whether she is good or bad—but the real conditions under which wives live. The central project of the *Cité*, the defense of virtuous women, is thus interrupted, if only momentarily, by a concrete historical observation, which has no textual source and no argumentative stake in the clerical dispute *pro et contra mulieribus*. Many pages later, on a different architectural tier (part two), *dame Droitture* reiterates her sister's observation and goes on to spell out the consequences:

> How many women are there actually, dear friend—and you yourself know ["tu meismes le sces," 818]—who because of their husbands' harshness spend their weary lives in the bond of marriage in greater suffering than if they were slaves

["esclaves"] among the Saracens? My God! How many harsh beatings—without cause and without reason—how many injuries, how many cruelties, insults, humiliations, and outrages have so many upright women ["maintes bonnes preudesfemmes"] suffered, none of whom cried out for help ["qui toutes n'en crient pas harou"]? And consider all the women who die of hunger and grief with a home full of children, while their husbands carouse dissolutely or go on binges in every tavern all over town, and still the poor women are beaten by their husbands when they return, and *that* is their supper! (118–119)

But this is not the worst of it for the wife. After adding ten more *exempla* from Boccaccio to the City, *Droitture* turns her attention again to real women from the contemporary world (as opposed to Boccaccio's mythologized figures):

Similarly, I know other women—whom I shall not name, since it might displease them—whose husbands are so perverse and follow such a disordered life that these women's parents wish that their sons-in-law were dead . . . but these women prefer ["aiment mieulx," 841] being beaten and living ill-fed in extreme poverty and subjugation with their husbands rather than leaving them, and they tell their friends, "You gave him to me; with him I will live and with him I will die." (133)

These passages have been quoted at length because they are unrepresentative of the whole and therefore nearly imperceptible, or unrecognizable. They are "notes," if we might so distinguish them from *science*, jotted down in the margins of the book (graffiti on the walls of the city), which concern the material conditions of the medieval woman's life—the social, political, economic, psychological reality of it. Another incidental remark: "how often would our contemporary pontiffs deign to discuss anything with some simple little woman ["une simple femmelette," 662], let alone her own salvation?" (30). Christine documents a violence against women that is pervasive and institutionalized (as marriage), and she begins to speak a resistance to that violence, stating that women do not want to be neglected, beaten and humiliated, or raped: "I am therefore troubled and grieved when men argue that many women want to be raped and that it does not bother them at all to be raped by men even when they verbally protest. It would be hard to believe that such great villainy is actually pleasant for them" (160–161). These historical annotations are not made from the perspective either of *clerc* or of Woman as natural entity (which is, at any rate, a mystification) but from the perspective of a woman who is herself a member of society; the intention is not to commemorate the virtuous Woman (who is the legendary exception) but to describe the lived experiences that all French women share (even the *femmelette*). Christine's graffiti and marginalia are expressions of identity (solidarity) with women as a group (though her own particular marriage had been a happy one); the notes might be thought of as a form of consciousness-raising, a halting answer to an unuttered cry—"*harou.*"

Catharine MacKinnon defines consciousness-raising as the "collective critical reconstitution of the meaning of women's social experience, as women live through it. . . . This approach stands inside its own determinations in order to uncover them. . . ."[34] Consciousness-raising is the "feminist method" and a "political practice." In the twentieth century, this critical reconstitution has found "women's powerlessness . . . to be both externally imposed and deeply internalized."[35] This double oppression was perhaps even more pronounced in the Middle Ages, as Christine's domesticated wives illustrate: they are beaten by their husbands but prefer ("love better") being beaten to leaving. The goal of the feminist method is to bring such deeply internalized oppression to consciousness; the goal of the feminist practice is to intervene in the external mechanisms responsible for oppression, with an eye toward social change. If actual social change—revolution—was beyond the scope of Christine's project in the first years of the fifteenth century, the preliminary feminist work of consciousness-raising was not. She shows women that the problems they experience in marriage are not of their own making, or peculiar to them as individuals, but are systemic to the patriarchal family, in which the husband enjoys absolute *maistrise*.

Beyond this, Christine suggests that women's very desire for (heterosexual) love, whether legitimated by marriage or not, is a major source of their oppression, for this desire is not a natural impulse (of their own) but an institutional requirement within marriage and, outside of marriage, the product of an erotic art that men control and use for themselves. One of the impressive architectural features of part two is a set of *exempla* dealing with virtuous women who were constant in marriage: Griselde, from Petrarch via Philippe de Mézières's *Livre de la vertu du sacrement de mariage*;[36] Florence, empress of Rome, from Gautier de Coinci's *Miracles de Nostre Dame*;[37] the wife of Barnabo, from Boccaccio's *Decameron*. These women patiently endured every outrage committed against them by their husbands, who claimed to be acting in the name of righteousness for the sanctity of marriage. The wives suffered the abduction of children, public humiliations, renunciation and exile, attempts at murder—and they suffered amiably, without the least protest and in silent obedience (to which, in Griselde's case, the wife was explicitly enjoined by her husband). The reward for their steadfastness and loyalty: reconciliation with their husbands. Christine duly enrolls these clerical *exempla* in her *Cité*, but even as she does so, she makes a remark to *Droitture* that calls into question, if only indirectly, the exact virtue which the loving wives serve to illustrate: "I am surprised that so many valiant ladies ["vaillans dames," 924], who were both extremely wise and literate . . . suffered so long without protesting against the horrors ["ont souffert si longuement sans contredire tant de horreurs"] charged by different men when they knew that these men were greatly mistaken" (184–185). Christine seizes this opportunity, the moment at which the silence of women has been praised, to wonder why articulate women have been silent for so long, why they have not written in defense of women (in defense of women who were silent) to protest the *horreurs* charged against them by men (the *horreurs* perpetrated against them by husbands); she wonders why women writers have been so loyal to *clercs*. Her meditation on women's silence finds a faint echo at a distance, through the halls and streets of the City, in a remark made earlier by *dame Raison*: "And the simple, noble ladies ["simples debonnaires dames," 629], following the example of suffering ["pacience"] which God commands, have cheerfully suffered the great attacks which, both in the spoken and the written word, have been wrongfully and sinfully perpetrated against women by men who all the while appealed to God for the right to do so" (10). *Raison* all but says what she cannot say: that the virtue of *patience* (constancy, love, silence), which women (too *simple*) have internalized as God's commandment, is a mystification of the power that men, as a class, exercise over women, as a class, through such institutions as marriage.

Closely related to the stories of patient wives is a set of *exempla* concerning virtuous women who were constant in love outside of marriage and who thereby became—the only possible fate—martyrs to love: Dido, Medea, Thisbe, Hero, as well as Boccaccio's Ghismonda and Lisabetta from the *Decameron*. Once again, Christine draws the conclusion required by her urban master plan—"Thus there is no doubt that the love of a constant woman in which she commits herself totally is very great" (202)—but she immediately appends a brief footnote that unsettles the prescribed conclusion: "But these pitiful examples . . . should in no way move women's hearts to set themselves adrift in the dangerous and damnable sea of foolish love ["folle amour," 952] for its end is always detrimental and harmful to their bodies, their property, their honor . . ." (202). In this aside to women, Christine offers practical advice for living: these female love martyrs, whom male authors loquaciously celebrate, are perilous examples for women to take as their own and emulate. Women should remain chaste at all costs, and not only for the sake of their souls.[38] The last words of the book caution women not to heed the smiles of men, for "under these smiles are hidden deadly and painful poisons": "Oh my ladies, flee, flee the foolish love ["folle amour," 1035] they urge on you" (256–257). It is deadly for the woman to internalize this smile as self-esteem, to *believe in* the image of herself it seductively presents to her. The smile is a "lure" in the service of masculine desire, a "trap" governed by an *ars amatoria*, which the *magister* Ovid has taught to generations of men. At the very culmination of her project, then, Christine engages in a critical reconstruction of the masculine erotic smile—a capstone that is impertinent to the City's architecture but of crucial importance to real women.

After finishing the *Cité*, Christine is immediately driven, though exhausted from her labors, to undertake the composition of a sequel, as if to make up for some failure, or supplement some lack, in her original defense of women. This text is *Le Trésor de la Cité des Dames*. Indeed, we might consider the *Trésor* to be a revision of the *Cité* (just as the *Cité* is a revision of clerical scripture), wherein the marginal notes of the earlier text are greatly amplified and moved to the center as the primary discourse of the later; we might consider the *Cité* as a preface to the *Trésor* rather than the *Trésor* as a pendant to the *Cité* (the relationship usually supposed). As before, the narrative begins with Christine sitting alone in her *celle*. She is again sunk in a state of depression, or lassitude ["en oyseuse," 122], and again the trinity of allegorical *dames* approaches her to delegate a project: "Prens ta plume et escripts" (124). What she is called upon to write/make is a "feminine college" ["colliege femmenin," 125], in which *all* women, not only the exceptional and famous (and not excluding the despised), will be equally welcome:

> First of all to the queens, princesses and great ladies, and then on down the social scale ["de degre en degre," 125] we will chant our doctrine to the other ladies and maidens and all

classes of women ["tous les estas des femmes"], so that the syllabus of our school ["discipline de notre escole"] may be valuable to all ["a tous valable"].[39]

This is a school for women teaching women. Christine first addresses herself to noblewomen, and then to other women *de degre en degre*, instructing each of them in the doctrine specific to her own *estat*; and, at the same time, the women of each estate teach by example precepts of a more general nature to women who occupy a lower *degre*. Christine begs literate women to read appropriate passages to those who are unable to read for themselves (180). It goes without saying that these lessons concern "virtue," but they also, and often more directly, concern what is *valable* to women in a practical sense. Although the text is in the genre of the "conduct book," and there are occasional (marginal) references to the Bible, its program and material do not derive from books written by *clercs* (from the Library), and its style is hardly beautiful or erudite; it is not a scholarly work of translation and compilation suitable for the Field of Letters. Instead, it is a plain account of women's *experience commune* and the individual experiences peculiar to each of their many and varied estates. Christine describes the estates of fifteenth-century French women in factual detail, their social place and quotidian activities: princesses, ladies of the court, baronesses and others who live on their manors, nuns, merchants' wives, young and elderly widows, virgins, artisans' wives, servant women and chambermaids, prostitutes, laborers' wives, indigent women. And she gives advice on how each estate should best be fulfilled, "chanting" her lessons in colloquial prose, in a familiar tone of voice.[40] The *Trésor* does not pretend to the grave dignity of the scholarly Book. It is a kind of *vade mecum*, a text of utilitarian purpose and wide circulation in the world. Unusual for Christine de Pizan's works, it exists in large number of paper copies, which would have been accessible even to women below the ranks of the aristocracy.[41]

The *Trésor* carries further the feminist practice initiated in the *Cité*. In the *Trésor*, the *dames Raison, Droitture,* and *Justice* relinquish control of the discourse, before they have spoken for long, to a new allegorical figure bearing a different sort of name, *Prudence Mondaine*: "We have sufficiently described the teachings and admonitions that the love and fear of God give the good princess or high-born lady. From now on we must speak of the lessons Wordly Prudence gives her" (55). They allege that the new course of teachings will be based upon and consistent with divine law, but the event proves otherwise, for *Prudence*

Mondaine, sensible of the masculine (clerical) interest invested in moral doctrine, advises women to cultivate the *appearance* of virtue only ["dissimuler sagement," 187]—and thus to be, in fact, doubly unvirtuous. Through discreet dissimulation of virtue ["discrete dissimulacion," 201] women can achieve some measure of control over those external circumstances in which they are obliged to behave virtuously. *Prudence* teaches princesses, and other estates of women in turn, how to look to their own advantage while living under the power of someone else, under "la poissance de [lor] seigneur[s]" (129). For example, a wife should try to convince her husband that she loves and honors him, whatever she may actually feel, because by this calculated show of patience and good grace she will "gain more in the long run" (71), and when he dies, he will be inclined to "leave [her] in possession of [his] whole fortune" (146). Let us admit that the imagination of *Prudence* is limited (a limitation of the Middle Ages):[42] she is incapable of imagining radical or substantive social change; for her, the patriarchal organization of society, the hegemony of masculine power, is simply an irremediable fact and the determining condition of women's existence. What *Prudence* teaches is not revolution but, in Michel de Certeau's words, the "countless ways" by which those who have no proper thing/space of their own can "*poach* . . . on the property of others."[43] What is *valable* to a woman in everyday life is a tactic of "hypocrisy" (72), which must be wisely deployed in all social relations: with her husband and with his family and friends, with her own children, with her enemies and rivals, with churchmen, statesmen, merchants, and neighbors. These are the seven cardinal lessons of *Prudence* (55–79). Hypocrisy is necessary, and it is just ["juste hypocrisie," 205]; it is a means of gaining self-possession.

We find that the *Trésor* is the most innovative, and hypocritical, of texts: a subversive conduct book. Christine exploits the opportunity (or "cover") afforded by the conduct-book genre to map out for all estates of women the tactics of resistance to their oppression—a plan of battle. Her text teaches, and is itself the first example of, a political practice. This is a practice based upon *dissimulation*, upon the rhetorical (sophistical) alteration of patriarchal Truth; it operates in particular situations, watching for the "propitious moment" when it can "turn to [its] own ends the forces alien to [it]."[44] Christine pays due respect to the virtues traditionally required of women (patience, silence), but she herself engages in, and she authorizes for other women, a militant, if discreet, contest of language and power. She prepares the way for local victories (which, however, cannot yet be consolidated) of the weak over the strong.

Notes

1. Quotations of the *Cité* in the original French are from Maureen Cheney Curnow, "The *Livre de la Cité des Dames* of Christine de Pisan: A Critical Edition" (Ph.D. diss., Vanderbilt University, 1975); quotations in English are from Earl Jeffrey Richards, trans., *The Book of the City of Ladies* (New York: Persea, 1982). For the sake of readability, I have generally quoted only from the translation, but in certain cases it seemed important to have the exact language of the text. For example, here neither Richards's "opinions of various authors" (3) nor any other brief and simple English phrase adequately covers the semantic fields of the medieval French words *sentence* and *aucteur*, which are still suggestive of the Latin roots *sententia* and *auctor* respectively.

2. For the life and works of Christine de Pizan, see Charity Cannon Willard, *Christine de Pizan* (New York: Persea, 1984). A chronology of major works is provided by Richards, pp. xxii–xxvi. In *L'Avision Christine*, Christine de Pizan herself says that she had written "fifteen principal volumes" by the year 1405; see *Christine's Vision*, trans. Glenda K. McLeod (New York: Garland, 1993), pp. 119–120.

3. Curious evidence of the canonicity of these texts: it was rumored that they were forged by men. In *L'Avision*, Dame Opinion says to Christine: "For some say that students or monks forged them for you" (McLeod, 87). Also, in a fifteenth-century Flemish translation of the *Cité*, a rumor is cited that her work was written by a cleric who, wishing to avoid fame for himself, used the pseudonym Christine (Curnow, 313–314). Her work was sometimes attributed to her son or, later, to her grandson, who was a poet and Benedictine monk (Curnow, 314n23). Several of her books "passed," so to speak, as clerical writing after superficial alteration. Her name was deleted from the English translation of *Othea*, and the preface to one manuscript has it that "Dame Cristine" was a "gentyl-woman of Frawnce" at whose "instavnce & praer" the work was written by the "famous doctours of the most excellent in clerge the nobyl Vniuersyte off Paris"; see Curt F. Bühler, ed., *Epistle of Othea* by Stephen Scrope (Oxford: Oxford University Press, 1970), p. 122. There are copies of *Le Livre des fais d'armes et de chevalerie* (1410) "where no author is mentioned . . . and where even masculine pronouns replace the feminine forms in the original text" (Willard, 186).

4. Willard, *Christine de Pizan*, p. 100. The phrase "fille d'estude" is also used in the first chapter of *Le Trésor de la Cité des Dames*; see Lore Loftfield DeBower, "*Le Livre des Trois Vertus* of Christine de Pisan" (Ph.D. diss., University of Massachusetts, 1979), p. 122. (The book has two alternative titles.) All subsequent quotations of the *Trésor* in the original French are from this edition.

5. McLeod, *Christine's Vision*, p. 117.

6. McLeod, *Christine's Vision*, p. 118.

7. Curnow, *Cité*, pp. 24–25, citing the *Mutacion*.

8. McLeod, *Christine's Vision*, p. 118.

9. See Curnow, *Cité*, p. 25. The quoted English words paraphrase the French in lines 426 and 464 of the following passage from the *Mutacion*:

Je perdi, par faute d'apprendre,	425
A ce tres riche tresor prendre,	
. . .	
Et combien qu'en aye petit,	457
. . .	
Ancor me fait grant avantage	462
Ce que j'en ay et trop de bien,	
Aultre avoir n'est droitement mien.	

Curnow summarizes the passage: "although she was not able to take all of this rich treasure of knowledge, the small amount that she gained is the only thing that she rightly owns, and it will remain with her throughout all of her life."

10. McLeod, *Christine's Vision*, p. 120.

11. Adrienne Rich, "When We Dead Awaken: Writing as Re-Vision," in *On Lies, Secrets, and Silence: Selected Prose 1966–1978* (New York: Norton, 1979), pp. 38–39.

12. Rich, "The Anti-Feminist Woman," in *Lies*, p. 82.

13. Rich, "Anti-Feminist," p. 82.

14. Rich, "Awaken," p. 38.

15. For a brief history of the *débat*, see Joseph L. Baird and John R. Kane, Introduction to *La Querelle de la Rose: Letters and Documents*, ed. Baird and Kane (Chapel Hill: North Carolina Studies in the Romance Languages and Literatures, 1978), pp. 11–33.

16. "Christine de Pisan to Jean de Montreuil" in Baird and Kane, *Querelle*, pp. 48–49, 54–55.

17. "Christine de Pisan to Pierre Col" in Baird and Kane, *Querelle*, p. 136.

18. "Gontier Col to Christine de Pisan" in Baird and Kane, *Querelle*, pp. 60–61.

19. "Jean de Montreuil *ut sunt mores*" in Baird and Kane, *Querelle*, p. 153.

20. "Christine de Pisan to Gontier Col" in Baird and Kane, *Querelle*, p. 63.

21. The following paragraph paraphrases Richards, *City*, pp. 3–5.

22. I have referred to Christine de Pizan's narrative persona by first name alone, as she does with the frequent locution: "Je, Christine."

23. Rich, "Awaken," p. 39.

24. This accident of birth is corrected in the *Mutacion*, where Christine de Pizan undergoes a metamorphosis into a "vray homme." See Diane Bornstein, "Self-Consciousness and Self Concepts in the Works of Christine de Pizan" in *Ideals for Women in the Works of Christine de Pizan*, ed. Diane Bornstein (Detroit: Michigan Consortium for Medieval and Early Modern Studies, 1981), pp. 12–13.

25. Boccaccio's attitude toward his subject is made plain enough by the following sentence from the Preface: "If men should be praised whenever they perform great deeds (with strength which Nature has given them), how much more should women be extolled (almost all of whom are endowed with tenderness, frail bodies, and sluggish minds by Nature), if they have acquired a manly spirit." (*Concerning Famous Women*, trans. Guido A. Guarino [New Brunswick: Rutgers University Press, 1963], p. xxxvii). Boccaccio's praise of famous women assumes and perpetuates the misogyny of the clerical tradition.

26. See, for example, Patricia A. Phillippy, "Establishing Authority: Boccaccio's *De Claris Mulieribus* and Christine de Pizan's *Le Livre de la Cité des Dames*," *Romanic Review* 77 (1986): 167–194; and Maureen Quilligan, *The Allegory of Female Authority: Christine de Pizan's* Cité des Dames (Ithaca: Cornell University Press, 1991). Also Kevin Brownlee, "Martyrdom and the Female Voice: Saint Christine in the *Cité des dames*," in *Images of Sainthood in Medieval Europe*, ed. Renate Blumenfeld-Kosinski and Timea Szell (Ithaca: Cornell University Press, 1991), pp. 115–135; and Susan Schibanoff, "Taking the Gold Out of Egypt: The Art of Reading as a Woman," in *Gender and Reading*, ed. Elizabeth A. Flynn and Patrocinio P. Schweickart (Baltimore: Johns Hopkins University Press, 1986), pp. 83–106.

27. Boccaccio, *Famous Women*, p. 6. On Christine's revision of Boccaccio, see Phillippy, "Establishing Authority," p. 184, and Quilligan, *Female Authority*, pp. 69–85.

28. For further discussion, see Quilligan, *Female Authority*, pp. 214–227, and Brownlee, "Martyrdom." I am indebted to Quilligan's observation that the "most significant difference between Christine's and Vincent's versions of St. Christine's story is the *Cité*'s treatment of her parents" (214).

29. Quilligan's translation of Jean de Vignay's French version of Vincent de Beauvais, p. 226.

30. On manuscripts, see Curnow, *Cité*, pp. 289–299.

31. Rich, "Awaken," p. 39. The passage reads: ". . . she meets the image of Woman in books written by men. She finds a terror and a dream, she finds a beautiful pale face, she finds La Belle Dame Sans Merci, she finds Juliet or Tess or Salomé."

32. See, for example, R. Howard Bloch, *Medieval Misogyny* (Chicago: University of Chicago Press, 1991). Bloch observes (quoting Claude Lévi-Strauss) that schoolmen "used the category of woman as a 'tool to think with' " (90).

33. My argument here is somewhat at odds with the critical mainstream, of which Phillippy, "Establishing Authority," is a fair representative: "Thus while she uses Boccaccio as a source, and invokes him by name as a witness in support of her claims, she is equally involved in a revision and correction of his views on women and their capabilities. . . . These interests inform her handling of *De Claris Mulieribus* and result in a reappropriation of Boccaccio's text which reflects this two-sided relationship of textual dependence and ideological independence" (168). I should emphasize, however, that the limitations I am referring to are not a result of some personal and individual failure, as Sheila Delany argues in her dissenting opinion on Christine de Pizan, but those of the cultural context in which the medieval woman writer lived and wrote. See Delany, " 'Mothers to Think Back Through': Who are They? The Ambiguous Example of Christine de Pizan" in *Medieval Texts & Contemporary Readers*, ed. Laurie A. Finke and Martin B. Shichtman (Ithaca: Cornell University Press, 1987), pp. 177–197. For a rejoinder to Delany, see Quilligan, *Female Authority*, pp. 7–10, 260–274.

34. Catharine A. MacKinnon, *Toward a Feminist Theory of the State* (Cambridge: Harvard University Press, 1989), pp. 83–84.

35. MacKinnon, *Feminist Theory*, p. 8.

36. Curnow, *Cité*, pp. 156–160.

37. Curnow, *Cité*, pp. 193–196.

38. On the political dimension of chastity, see Christine Reno, "Virginity as an Ideal in Christine de Pizan's *Cité Des Dames*," in Bornstein, *Ideals for Women*, pp. 69–90. Reno's thesis is that "[v]irginity implies, in addition to sexual purity, the freedom from any sort of involvement with men that might hamper woman's pursuit of her particular goals. Moreover, Christine's focus in the *Cité* is not the spiritual reward of a more perfect state of eternal bliss that the Church held out to the celibate, but rather a triumph that could be measured primarily in terms of the standards of this world" (70).

39. Sarah Lawson, trans., *The Treasure of the City of Ladies* (Harmondsworth: Penguin, 1985), p. 32. All quotations in English are from this edition.

40. See DeBower's discussion of the work's style, *Trois Vertus*, pp. 89–105.

41. DeBower, *Trois Vertus*, pp. 76, 107.

42. Consider the analogy of medieval peasant movements. Rodney Hilton argues that rebellious peasants did not usually view themselves as acting to

bring about change but, quite the contrary, as defending custom and the old laws, which they felt the lords had been guilty of violating; see *Bond Men Made Free: Medieval Peasant Movements and the English Rising of 1381* (London: Metheun, 1977), p. 114.

43. Michel de Certeau, *The Practice of Everyday Life*, trans. Steven Rendall (Berkeley: University of California Press, 1984), p. xii. The tactic is the "polemology of the 'weak,' " which is "determined by the *absence of power.*" It is deployed "in the space of the other," that is, "within the order established by the 'strong.' " The tactic "must vigilantly make use of the cracks that particular conjunctions open in the surveillance of the proprietary powers. It poaches in them. It creates surprises in them. . . . It is a guileful ruse." (See 37–40.) The tactic is an invention of prudence.

44. De Certeau, *Practice*, p. xix. This paragraph is cast in de Certeau's language; see especially pp. xviii–xx and pp. 29–42.

Anne Boleyn [artist unknown].
By permission of the National Portrait Gallery, London.

Conflicting Rhetoric About Tudor Women: The Example of Queen Anne Boleyn

Retha Warnicke

Writings about English people in the late medieval and early Renaissance period tended to follow a few basic conventions: chivalric types like the Chandos Herald's account of Edward, the Black Prince; saintly or eulogistic ones that fall within the great metaphor of the human pilgrimage toward spirituality, like John Blacman's study of Henry VI, and anti-heroic or demonic types, like John Rous's portrayal of Richard III.[1] Since women participated in chivalric exercises mainly as spectators and as inspirations for male triumphs, studies of them were usually limited to the latter two types, as, for example, Bishop John Fisher's commemorative and eulogistic sermon for Margaret, countess of Richmond, and Nicholas Sander's hostile study of Anne Boleyn. All three conventions were often presented within a rise and fall structure.[2]

These writers had a common method, for none set out to compose a comprehensive study of their subjects, to present a full record of their personalities or to examine their psychologies, as modern biographers usually do. Nor were they concerned with absolute accuracy or balance, for they drew upon facts from the individual's life that best fit the requirements of the specific convention they adopted. Few attempts were made, for example, in the saintly version to come to terms with negative traits unless they formed a significant part of the subject's search for spirituality. References to worldly achievements, such as the publication of a book, like Thomas More's *Utopia*, which were unrelated to the pilgrimage, might well be omitted entirely.[3]

This essay will examine Tudor works about Anne Boleyn with the goal of better understanding why these authors chose to write about

39

her as well as why they adopted the conventions that were utilized. As a final step in this analysis, a brief review will be made of their impact upon the interpretations of late twentieth-century historians, who have researched public and private records that were largely inaccessible in the sixteenth century, and who live at a time in which gender relations are markedly different from those that prevailed in her society. She was, of course, the second consort of Henry VIII; in 1533 he wed her and divorced Catherine of Aragon, whose male infants sired by him had died. These momentous events formed the familial backdrop to the English Reformation. Three years after Anne became queen, in May of 1536, Henry had her executed for adultery and incest with five men, including George, Lord Rochford, her brother.[4]

Information about her will remain somewhat sketchy not only because of the constraints of the conventions the authors, all of whom were male, adopted but also because of contemporary religious and social beliefs, including gender attitudes, that were necessarily utilized in the studies of her life. Sixteenth-century men, who attempted to "fashion women out of a masculine cloth," believed that women, whose honor was defined by how successfully they were able to restrain their lustful impulses, were sexual aggressors.[5] One of Anne's greatest critics was Sander, a priest, who noted, for example: "Experience shows that women . . . are more eager and more dangerous than men. . . . and that men always are more easily and more fatally ensnared by "them." This rhetoric seems to have reflected a fear that women might "break from their nature and theologically determined role of subordination" and create social disorder and disharmony.[6]

Protestant as well as Catholic priests warned men against succumbing to feminine wiles and against being lured into engaging in lustful intercourse with them, even with their wives, for God, it was believed, would visit the sins of parents, particularly their sexual disobedience, upon their children.[7] Sexual innuendoes also permeated Reformation politics because Christians had long associated heresy with lechery.[8]

A further bias is that the rhetoric about Anne was intended basically to serve as religious and dynastic propaganda. That authors were willing to use their compositions to manipulate public opinion in favor of or in opposition to royal figures was far from novel. Earlier writers had, for example, attempted to obtain the canonization of both Edward II and Richard II.[9] Reformers, like John Foxe, who set out to defend Protestantism and therefore the succession of Elizabeth, crafted her mother within the eulogistic convention. In response to his and other reform propaganda, writers, such as Sander, vilified Anne's character, which because of her execution for sexual crimes in 1536, had long been maligned in Catholic circles.

Extant government documents indicate Henry and his ministers seemed to have believed his consort had committed the illicit sexual acts for which she died.[10] Her guilt was accepted by most resident ambassadors in London,[11] including members of the hostile French embassy headed by Anthony Castelnau, bishop of Tarbes, who first arrived in England in mid-1535. Her previous friendly exchanges with these agents of Francis I, in whose court she had lived between 1514 and 1521, had clearly deteriorated after her marriage. The heightened nature of this hostility is symbolized by a poem of Tarbes's secretary, Lancelot de Carles, later bishop of Riez. Written in French and probably finished in June 1536, just after her execution, it is the first extant account of her life.[12]

In 1533, the French had supported both Henry's divorce from Catherine of Aragon and his marriage to Anne Boleyn, but the direction of French foreign policy was to change and, in 1534, Francis began negotiations with Henry to have Anne's stepdaughter Mary wed one of his sons. In his poem about her life, it is, consequently, no surprise that de Carles lingered over praise of Mary and perpetuated the official line about Anne's death; he spoke of her indiscretion and disregard for her honor. That his poem was first published in 1545, after his installation as bishop of Riez and during Anglo-French hostilities, heralds its lack of sympathy for Henry as well as for Anne. It was a public reminder to loyal Catholics that this schismatic king, this enemy of France, had been dishonored because he had been cuckolded not by one man, but by five, and because his wife had been executed for incest and adultery. This was an ominous reminder since adulteresses were equated with witches, whose lustful impulses were condemned in theological treatises. Anne's fate could also be viewed as an example of God's denunciation of the English Reformation that her marriage to Henry had ushered in.[13]

Until the reign of Elizabeth, the attitude that Anne was guilty as charged, despite some private reservations, dominated in printed and official accounts. But for her daughter Elizabeth's accession in 1558, Anne might well have escaped public attacks that were to charge her with lurid adventures with several men besides the five who were executed in 1536.[14] The propaganda of two Protestants, John Ponet and John Foxe, seems to have helped shape and to elicit these later attacks on Anne's morals. Ironically, Ponet's tract made no reference to her, but his demonic description of Stephen Gardiner, the late bishop of Winchester, could well have been a factor in the decision of Sander to compose a witchlike description of her. A long literary tradition identified beauty with perfect love and mystical, divine unions. The opposite side of this coin was that inner evil was associated with monstrous appearances, for, as Ponet said, nature "shaped the outwarde partes, to declare what was within." Perhaps the first and certainly the most famous English victim of this convention was Richard III, who probably had no physical deformity despite More's famous description.[15]

In England the Protestants may have been the first authors after More to utilize this convention. In 1556, Ponet, who had recently been deprived of the bishopric of Winchester and who surely knew about More's history, which was available in print, published a piece against the Marian Catholics in which he included a monstrous description of the late Stephen Gardiner, who had both preceded and succeeded him at Winchester:

> This doctour hade a swart colour, an hanging loke, frowning browes, eies an ynche within the heade, a nose hooked like a bussarde, wyde nostrilles like a horse, ever snuffing in to the wynde, all sparowe mouthe, great pawes like the devil, talauntes on his fete like a grype, two ynches longer than the naturall toes, and so tyed to with sinowes, that he could not be touched, nor scare suffre them to touche the stones. And nature having thus shaped the forme of an outwarde monstre, it gave him a vengeable witte.[16]

John Foxe's "Book of Martyrs" was as sympathetic toward Anne as Ponet's was hostile to Winchester. A tutor in the household of Mary, duchess of Richmond, who appointed him in the late 1540s to instruct her Howard nieces and nephews, Foxe must have been able to glean some information from his patron about her first-cousin Queen Anne in whose court she had resided.[17] In 1563, he first published in English his study of the martyrs, and among those whom he eulogized was this queen. He related that she had loved to read the scriptures and that she had been deeply involved in charitable activities:

> she ever gave three or four pound at a time to the poor people. . . . and sent her subalmoner to the towns about where she lay that the parishioners should make a bill of all the poor householders in their parish. . . . her grace carried ever about

her a certain little purse, out of which she was wont daily to scatter abroad some alms.[18]

Foxe claimed some impenetrable mystery had obscured the reasons for her fall and argued that God had confirmed her innocence by raising her daughter to the queenship. Protestants, who preached that the sins of parents were visited on their children, could not believe God would have permitted the child of an adulterous woman to succeed to the throne. In 1558, as all knew, it was Catherine's Catholic line that had ended with the death of Mary, whose treatment of the heretics Foxe was so effectively attacking.[19] To counter the impact of Mary's failure to bear children, Catholics, such as William Allen, were later to claim that Elizabeth's virginity, which ultimately caused the end of her dynasty, was one of the "signs of God's wrath against England."[20]

Apart from the scriptures, Foxe's "Book of Martyrs" was one of the most popular works in Elizabethan England.[21] Protestant publications like his clearly angered the Catholic refugees, who were settled principally at Louvain, Douai (later Rheims), Paris, and Rome, and they responded in kind. Initially, the queen's ministers had some success in suppressing their books, but after 1570 they appeared in such numbers that the government was overwhelmed. Between 1559 and 1603, more than 200 pieces of Catholic propaganda against her succession and rule appeared.[22]

In the first decade or so of her reign, most Catholic tracts called for her to recognize Mary, queen of Scots, as her heir, a position taken by John Leslie, bishop of Ross, a confidante of Mary's, who was headquartered at Paris and who in 1569 printed a treatise about her dynastic rights, placing her life within the saintly pilgrimage type. By 1571, when the second edition of this book had appeared, just after Elizabeth's excommunication, a different approach was emerging. Dynastic politics took a threatening twist; henceforth Mary's supporters were to hail her as Elizabeth's replacement. A major point of their propaganda, in both 1569 and 1571, was to demonstrate how the Scots queen was worthy of the English crown by denying some of the rumors about her, including the allegation that she was an accessory to the murder of her husband, Henry, Lord Darnley.[23]

During the interval between Anne's death and the accession of her daughter, whose rule Leslie and others were challenging, Reformation politics had given rise to a tangle of accusations about Anne's sexual activities that had remained in manuscript form. These rumors, circulating among English refugees on the continent, focused in part on her relationship to Thomas Wyatt, the Tudor poet, who had been arrested at the time of her fall but who was subsequently freed. In his poem in 1536, de Carles referred only to Wyatt's incarceration and included no other information about him, not even his release from prison. Some twenty years later, Nicholas Harpsfield, a Catholic cleric who had fled to Louvain during the reign of Edward VI when the kingdom became Protestant, gave a more culpable version of Wyatt's involvement. In his account, which was not published until the nineteenth century, Harpsfield asserted that Wyatt had been Anne's lover.[24]

Given Harpsfield's belief and that of other English emigrees that she had indulged in sexual rendezvous with the five executed men, the mere fact of Wyatt's arrest provided sufficient proof that she had also had intimate relations with him. It was generally believed, as Castiglione pointed out, that once a woman's "reputation for purity has been sullied" it could never be "restored."[25] This belief still does not adequately explain why Harpsfield was willing to validate the rumors about Wyatt, already a married man when Henry's romance with Anne began. Even though a double standard did exist, the reputations of men could also be damaged by charges of lechery. It was not a hedonistic age in which they could, like modern playboy types, win public admiration for their sexual conquests, for they were either viewed as having succumbed to the wiles of aggressive women or of being male witches. Alleged lechers might well find themselves charged with crimes, especially heresy. One famous example of this practice was the publication of the Catholic tract in 1584, later entitled *Leicester's Commonwealth*, in which the authors attempted to defame the honor of Robert, Earl of Leicester, by accusing him of sexual crimes.[26] Catholics, such as Harpsfield, were likely to credit any story about Wyatt, the poet, that by implication defamed his namesake son, who rebelled against the government of Queen Mary in response to her decision in 1554 to marry Prince Philip, the Habsburg heir to the throne of Spain. Charges of sexual misconduct went in tandem with dynastic claims.

For religious and dynastic reasons, Nicholas Sander, who was a leader of the Catholic refugees at Louvain between 1564 and 1572, wrote works in Latin that contained even more devastating rumors about Anne than those of Harpsfield's. Born in Surrey about 1530, Sander had fled abroad early in Elizabeth's reign, was ordained as a priest at Rome, and ultimately became Regius Professor of Theology at Louvain. By 1579 he had joined the Irish resistance against Elizabeth, whose succession he equated with the "hour of Satan and the power of darkness." His intention was to secure the crown of England for Mary, queen of Scots.[27]

Before his departure for Ireland, where he was to die in 1581, Sander composed several pieces. The most significant for this essay are: *De Visibili Monarchia Ecclesiae*, one of many responses to Foxe's "Book of Martyrs," and *The Rise and Growth of the Anglican Schism*, also originally written in Latin. The purpose of the *Monarchia*, which included a full defense of Mary Stuart as an exemplary Catholic monarch, was to attack the English royal supremacy, especially as it was exercised by a woman. The work was published in 1571, the same year as Leslie's second edition, and was soon circulating in England.[28] Because it emphasized Elizabeth's illegitimacy, it was viewed as a slur on the honor of her and her parents. After 1571, Catholic tracts, following the example of this work in which Mary was promoted as the rightful queen of England, were frequently produced.[29]

Sander's more important book for a study of Anne Boleyn is his history of the schism. Left incomplete at his death, it was entrusted to Edward Rishton, a priest, who ironically had been sentenced to death in England but had been banished from the kingdom in January of 1585 instead of being executed. Rewriting parts of it, particularly the section on Elizabeth's reign, Rishton embellished Sander's tales of "the sufferings" endured by loyal English Catholics, among them Mary Stuart. He had the work published at Cologne near the end of 1585 and died the following year. David Lewis, the modern translator of the work, was convinced that both Sander and Rishton believed the rumors about Anne's birth and sexual behavior that were included in the book.[30]

Sander had drawn together all of the gossip concerning her family. Even during her lifetime, the king had been forced to deny having had sexual relations with her mother, and thus of having been his consort's father as well as her husband. The story about the liaison with Lady Boleyn actually appeared in print at Paris in 1536. Sander further related that Anne had been sent to France to complete her education after she had engaged in sexual relations with two of her supposed father's servants, a chaplain and a valet. He also elaborated upon the Wyatt episode, claiming the poet had informed the council of his carnal affair with Anne.[31] Adopting the tradition that evil beings ought to be clothed in an outward, ugly form,[32] Sander provided her with the now-famous features of a witchlike creature. She was, he said:

rather tall of stature, with black hair, and an oval face of a sallow complexion, as if troubled with jaundice. She had a projecting tooth under the upper lip, and on her right hand six fingers. There was a large wen under her chin, and therefore to hide its ugliness she wore a high dress covering her throat.

In seeming contradiction to the above portrait, he added:

She was handsome to look at, with a pretty mouth, amusing in her ways, playing well on the lute, and was a good dancer. She was the model and the mirror of those who were at court. . . . But as to the disposition of her mind, she was full of pride, ambition, envy, and impurity.[33]

As unpleasant as this description was, it did fall short of the venomous tone of Ponet's characterization of Gardiner.[34]

Sander's work proved to be extremely popular. Versions were printed at Rome by Father Robert Persons in 1586 and 1588; ultimately, it appeared in at least six languages and a century after it was first printed, it remained the "foremost Catholic indictment of the English Reformation."[35] Sander's popular attack was part of the Catholic strategy to discredit Anne's daughter, "a child," as he charged, who was "born in adultery and worse, and therefore unworthy of the crown" and to validate a replacement for her. These themes were even more explicitly intertwined in the work of Adam Blackwood, the Scottish biographer of Mary Stuart, whose education at the University of Paris she had partially financed. In his book, which was anonymously published in 1587, the year of her execution, and which had appeared in at least five editions before the end of 1589, he adopted Sander's description of Anne and called her daughter a "bastard" and a "usurper."[36]

Blackwood also drew upon *De Jezabelis*, a collection of poems, which he seems to have arranged to be published in 1587 and 1588. In these poems, composed by various authors, Elizabeth was condemned because of her parents' alleged sexual misbehavior. Cardinal du Perron, for example, said about her: "this monster conceived in adultery and incest, her fangs bared to murder, who befouls and despoils the sacred right of scepters, and vomits her choler and gall at heaven." It would be difficult to "overestimate" the importance of Blackwood's propaganda in the history of the literature about Mary Stuart,[37] for through his endeavors, the charges against Anne and her daughter passed into French and Scottish national histories. Sander's work ensured that they were included in all Catholic studies of the Reformation.[38]

The Tudor period ended with two parallel traditions about Anne Boleyn. Foxe's "Book of Martyrs," which retained its popularity in the seventeenth century, was clearly somewhat defensive, for he could not explain to his readers why if she were innocent of the crimes for which she had died, her husband, the father of Queen Elizabeth, had agreed to sign her death warrant. Foxe could only refer to mysterious circumstances and emphasize her charitable activities. Skillfully drawing upon contemporary prejudice toward women, Sander, as well as other Catholic propagandists, used the demonic convention to paint the queen as a witchlike character. Despite some Protestant rebuttals, Sander's tales generally were so compelling they filtered into the intellectual framework of writers, who drew upon them for anecdotes. In 1677, William Lloyd complained that some of the authors who cited them were unaware the priest was actually their author:

> ... one must not take all for true that *Sanders* says; though having the luck to be contemned at the first by them that should have confuted him, he has carried the World before him ever since, being not only transcribed by the Writers of his side, but also followed by many others that seem not to know whence they have their Stories. We that live in a more inquisitive Age have seen *many things* of which he is the author, acknowledged by his (a) Friends to be *very improbable* and by (b) others to have been altogether impossible.[39]

In the second half of the twentieth century, a new interest in court politics and in the fall of Anne Boleyn has developed; historians utilizing primary sources have had to contend with the conflicting writings of the Tudor period, finding it impossible to reconcile them. Moreover, three occurrences have combined together to evoke more complicated modern views of Anne Boleyn than these earlier ones. The first was the publication in the early-nineteenth century of the largely unknown Elizabethan manuscript of George Wyatt, the son of the Marian rebel and the grandson of the poet. Greatly disturbed by Sander's work, George, who appears to have been naive concerning literary conventions, wrote a rebuttal to it in English, reducing the most outrageous of the claims. Born after both Anne's and his grandfather's deaths and thus without personal knowledge of them, George maintained that the relationship between them must have been a mere lighthearted flirtation and admitted for her features only clear skin, some moles, and an extra fingernail, which, he said, was kept hidden; he ignored the other disfigurements. His is the sole apologetic description of her from the Tudor period that concedes this version of the flaws, which none of the people who actually observed her, hostile or friendly, ever mentioned.[40]

His work was printed at a time when perceptions about gender relations were fluctuating and, indeed, undergoing a reversal. The following brief comments will attempt to explain this change but cannot do justice to the diverse and complicated histories of women and of sexuality. From the early-eighteenth century, the English courts had refused to try women for witchcraft and, in the early-nineteenth century, women of property and high social standing began apparently to be placed on pedestals; increasingly, they were lauded as having greater moral fiber than men and were protected from sexual innuendoes and even language that named intimate body parts. The concept of marriage was also changing with a shifting emphasis from wife as helpmate and mother to wife as lover and companion, a development often attributed to the influence of the romantic movement which promoted a union of opposites: she was passive and emotional, he aggressive and rational. The adherence of the romantics to the love relationship between spouses was based in part upon a revived interest in medieval chivalric epics. Even as these notions were gaining ground, feminist calls for equality that often focused on the issues of suffrage and married women's property rights were by the late-nineteenth and early-twentieth centuries successfully challenging some gender stereotypes. Subsequent women's movements, especially from the 1960s, promoted equality in gender relations at the workplace and in the home.[41]

The early-nineteenth century shifts in gender relations and the appearance of Wyatt's manuscript, in addition to the late-nineteenth-century publication of the letters of Eustace Chapuys, the Imperial ambassador, form the backdrop to the first of three scholarly works on Anne that appeared in the 1980s and 1990s. In his letters written in 1536, Chapuys reported that Cromwell, the king's secretary, had revealed that the queen was innocent and that her fall was the result of a factional conspiracy he had devised. Accepting Chapuys' statements at face value, Eric Ives, in his 1986 biography of her, claimed that the king and his minister had known Anne was not guilty of the crimes for which she died. He failed to explain, however, why Cromwell so readily revealed such damaging matters, if they were true, to the agent of a foreign country whose activities had only recently led the secretary to have him secretly observed. It is likely that the revelations were part of a plot to deceive the Imperial embassy about her death. Ives also utilized a misguided version of Tudor love relations, called courtly love, which seems to be an amalgam of chivalric ideals and later romantic notions, for he maintained that the seemingly artificial practice met the needs of the participants "for warm emotional ties." Thus, according to Ives, Anne had made herself vulnerable to the charges because of her lighthearted, courtly love flirting with the young members of her husband's privy chamber. In short, she manipulated these gentlemen with methods similar to those of Chrétien de Troyes's Queen Guenevere. Ives, furthermore, generally validated the Wyatt version of Sander's description of her.[42]

Before Ives's biography was published, I had begun a study of Anne Boleyn, which was to appear in 1989. Influenced by my long-held interest in the history of women and of sexuality, I was committed to analyzing her life within the framework of Tudor beliefs about the nature of women's sexuality. Cognizant of the implications of the demonic convention, I denied that she was disfigured and also claimed that the king believed that she was guilty of the sexual crimes for which she died. The evidence for this view can be found in many documents, including a letter of a courtier, John Russell, who referred to the "cursedness and unhappiness" of Henry in his marriage to her.[43]

The indictments charged her with witch like activities, and it seemed obvious that something had occurred that caused some of her contemporaries, who believed in her guilt, to utilize this rhetoric. I speculated that she had miscarried a deformed fetus, a tragedy that would have led her husband to assume that she was guilty of gross sexual behavior. An amateur theologian, he viewed even uncomplicated miscarriages as evil omens and possible signs of demonic interference in natural events. That he considered her a witch who with kisses and touches lured men into illicit sexual behavior may explain the reason why, when his government charged her and her alleged lovers of sexual crimes in May of 1536, no attempt was made to ensure she was at the rendezvous on the days and the places mentioned. For example, her brother Rochford was charged with having had relations with her at Winchester on 5 November 1535, when as was well known she was actually with the king at Windsor.[44]

Further, I doubted that she had impugned her reputation by courtly flirtations with his servants. Relying upon the comments of Foxe and other clerics, at the time and later, and upon the advice in well-known courtesy books detailing the proper behavior of women, it seemed to me that the extant evidence actually supported the conclusion that she had attempted to lead the pious and charitable life expected of a well-educated, married queen, whose greatest hope and need was for a divine gift in the guise of a healthy male child.[45]

In a 1991 article in *English Historical Review*, George Bernard reversed this modern trend and claimed she was guilty of adultery. He denied that she could have miscarried a deformed fetus because no one actually said she/he had seen it and disputed the suggestion that the charges against her referred to witch-like behavior. He also dismissed the notion that she was a victim of court politics. Instead, like Sander, seeing that many dignitaries thought that she was promiscuous, he concluded that the charges against her were true, although he did not also claim that she had had relations with any men besides those executed. Relying upon the poem of de Carles, which versified the official position, Bernard asserted that because she had been made "jealous" by Henry's affairs, she had chosen to exercise the same sexual freedom he enjoyed. Bernard justified this view with the following comment that reveals more about his reaction to modern women's movements than about gender relations in the Tudor period:

> To the charge that the general interpretation advanced here is just the surmise of a man lacking in understanding of female psychology, just a "wicked woman" view of history which sees nymphomaniacs everywhere, it could be counted that Anne's behavior had been presented as defiant rather than passive.[46]

At the end of the Tudor period, despite Protestant refutations of the Catholic attacks, Anne's reputation was more deeply damaged than it had been at her death in 1536. The lurid tales made for more compelling reading than the pious strictures. Modern historical methods, the printing of relevant Tudor manuscripts, and changes in the perception and reality of gender relations have all failed to resolve and, indeed, may have further confused, the controversial issues about her. As in Foxe's day, a mystery continues to obscure the events of 1536, and the conflicting rhetoric about her appearance, her sexuality, and her death seems destined to continue. Still, the most valid approach to her life surely must be one that is willing seriously to consider Tudor gender relationships.

Notes

1. The Herald of Sir John Chandos, *Life of the Black Prince*, trans. M. K. Pope, and E. C. Lodge (Oxford: Clarendon Press, 1910); John Blacman, *Henry the Sixth*, trans. M. R. James (Cambridge: Cambridge University Press, 1919);

for Rous see Alison Hanham, *Richard III and His Early Historians* (Oxford: Clarendon Press, 1975), pp. 153–90. See also John W. McKenna, "Piety and Propaganda: The Cult of Henry VI" in *Chaucer and Middle English Studies in Honor of Rossell Hope Robbins*, ed. B. Rowland (Kent, Ohio: Kent State University Press, 1974), pp. 72–88; Richard Wendorf, *The Elements of Life: Biography and Portrait Painting in Stuart and Georgian England* (Oxford: Clarendon Press, 1990), p. 29.

2. *The English Works of John Fisher, Bishop of Rochester*, Extra Series, 27 (London: Early English Text Society, 1876), pp. 289–310; Nicholas Sander, *The Rise and Growth of the Anglican Schism*, ed. D. Lewis (London: Burns & Oates, 1877), p. 240; see also Patricia Ann Lee, "Reflections of Power: Margaret of Anjou and the Dark Side of Queenship," *Renaissance Quarterly*, 39 (1986): 210.

3. *Two Early Tudor Lives*, ed. R. Sylvester and D. Harding (New Haven, Ct.: Yale University Press, 1962).

4. Retha M. Warnicke, *The Rise and Fall of Anne Boleyn: Family Politics at the Court of Henry VIII* (Cambridge: Cambridge University Press, 1989).

5. Deborah Greenhunt, *Feminine Rhetorical Culture: Tudor Adaptations of Ovid's Heroides* (New York: Peter Lang, 1988), pp. viii–ix; for a modern scholar's difficulty in taking Tudor gender attitudes seriously, see D. R. Woolf, *The Idea of History in Early Stuart England: Erudition, Ideology and 'The Light of Truth' From the Accession of James I to the Civil War* (Toronto: University of Toronto, 1990), p. 38.

6. Sander, *Anglican Schism*, p. 240; Lee, "Margaret of Anjou and the Dark Side of Queenship," p. 210.

7. Nicholas Harpsfield, *A Treatise on the Pretended Divorce Between Henry VIII and Catherine of Aragon*, ed. Nicholas Pocock, Camden Society, N.S. 21 (London: Royal Historical Society, 1878), pp. 250–51; William Perkins, *Christian oeconomie: or, a short survey of the right manner of ordering a familie, according to the scriptures* (London: F. Kingston and F. K. Weaver, 1609), 98–114

8. Joseph Klaits, *Servants of Satan: The Age of Witchhunts* (Bloomington, Ind.: Indiana University Press, 1985), p. 26.

9. McKenna, "Piety and Propaganda," pp. 72–88.

10. *Letters and Papers, Foreign and Domestic of the Reign of Henry VIII*, ed. J. S. Brewer, J. Gairdner, and R. H. Brodie, 21 vols., (London: Her Majesty's Stationery Office, 1862–1932), vol. 10, pp. 873, 876, vol. 11, p. 29; Samuel S. Singer, *The Life of Cardinal Wolsey by George Cavendish*, 2d ed. (London: Harding & Lepard, 1827), pp. 460–61; Edward Hall, *Henry VIII*, ed. C. Whibley, 2 vols. (London: T. C. & E. C. Jack, 1904), pp. 268–69.

11. For the exception, see *Calendar of Letters, Despatches, and State Papers, Relating to the Negotiations Between England and Spain*, ed. G. A. Bergenroth, P. de Gayangos, G. Mattingly, M. A. S. Hume, and R. Taylor, 13 vols., 2 supplements, (London: Kraus Reprint, 1969), especially vol. 5, p. 29.

12. *Espistre contenant le procès criminel faict à L'encontre de la royne Anne Boullant d' Angleterre* (Lyon: pres nostre Dame de Confort, 1545), printed in Georges Ascoli, *La Grande-Bretagne Devant L'Opinion Française* (Paris: Librairie Universitaire J. Gamber, 1927), from which references are taken. See especially lines 239–50, 679–1038.

13. Warnicke, *Anne Boleyn*, pp. 191–233.

14. For example of a printed negative comment, see *The Anglica Historia of Polydore Vergil, A.D. 1485–1537*, Camden Society, 74 (London: Royal Historical Society, 1950), p. 336. Positive comments remained largely in manuscript until modern times. See for example, M. Dowling, ed., "William Latymer's 'Chronickille of Anne Bulleyne,' "in *Camden Miscellany XXX*, Camden Fourth Series, 39 (London: Royal Historical Society, 1990), pp. 46–65.

15. For demons, see Rosemary Woolf, *The English Mystery Plays* (Los Angeles: University of California Press, 1972), p. 110; John Ponet, *A Short Treatise of Politic Power*, 1556 (Menton, Eng.: Scolar Press, 1970), Sig. I4, K4. See also, Warnicke, "Richard III and the Mystery Plays," *Historical Journal*, 35 (1992): 761–78, and Warnicke, "The Physical Deformities of Anne Boleyn and Richard III: Myth and Reality," *Parergon*, N. S. V (1986): 135–53.

16. Ponet, *Short Treatise*, Sig. I4–5.

17. Ponet was a patron of Bale, who met John Foxe in the household of the duchess of Richmond. See Leslie Fairfield, *John Bale: Mythmaker for the English Reformation* (West Lafayette, Ind.: Purdue Univ. Press, 1976), p. 90.

18. *The Acts and Monuments of John Foxe*, ed. George Townsend (New York: AMS Reprint, 1965), V, pp. 60, 135–37.

19. *The Acts and Monuments of John Foxe*, V, pp. 60, 135–37.

20. Allen cited by James Phillips, *Images of a Queen: Mary Stuart in Sixteenth-Century Literature* (Los Angeles: University of California Press, 1964), p. 114.

21. G. R. Elton, "Persecution and Toleration in the English Reformation," *Studies in Chruch History*, 21 (Oxford: Basil Blackwell, 1984), pp. 172–78; Warren W. Wooden, *John Foxe* (Boston: G. K. Hall, 1983), pp. 30–76.

22. A. C. Southern, *Elizabethan Recusant Prose, 1559–1582* (London: Sands & Co., 1950), pp. 3, 129. In 1561, Gabriel de Saconay, an ecclesiastical censor at Lyons, defamed the parentage of Elizabeth. His book was withdrawn and the pages were rewritten at her insistence. See Phillips, *Images of a Queen*, pp. 23–24.

23. Thomas H. Clancy, *Papist Pamphleteers: The Allen-Persons Party and the Political Thought of the Counter-Reformation in England, 1572–1615* (Chicago: Loyola Univ. Press, 1964), pp. 3–6; John Leslie, bishop of Ross, as M. Philippes, pseud., *A defence of the honour of Marie Quene of Scotlande* (London: G. Diaeophile, 1569 on the title page but actually printed abroad, probably in Paris), and *A treatise concerning the defence of the honor of Marie Queen of Scotland* (Leodii: ap. G. Morberium, 1571).

24. Harpsfield, *A Treatise on the Pretended Divorce*, p. 253; Southern, *Elizabethan Recusant Prose*, pp. 25–27.

25. Baldesar Castiglione, *The Book of the Courtier*, trans. G. Bull (New York: Penguin, 1967), p. 57.

26. *Leicester's Commonwealth: The Copy of a Letter Written by a Master of Art of Cambridge (1584) and Related Documents*, ed. D. C. Peck (Athens, Ohio: University of Ohio Press, 1985), pp. 80–88; Wyatt the poet was also accused of lechery. See John Bruce, "Recovery of the Lost Accusation of Sir Thomas Wyatt the Poet by Bishop Bonner," *Gentleman's Magazine*, 33 (1850): 563–70.

27. Thomas M. Veech, *Nicholas Sander and the English Reformation, 1530–1581* (Louvain: Bureau du Recueil, 1935), pp. 5, 23; Southern, *Elizabethan Recusant Prose*, pp. 26, 126–27, 205–07, 219; Sander, *Anglican Schism*, p. 233.

28. Sander, *De Visibili Monarchia Ecclesiae* (Louvain: Joannes Fourleri, 1571), pp. 686, 708.

29. T. J. Reynolds, "Queen Elizabeth in the Writings of the Recusants," Ph.D. diss., Harvard University, 1956, p. 219; Phillips, *Images of a Queen*, pp. 109–15.

30. Veech, *Nicholas Sander*, p. 234; for Rishton, see *Dictionary of National Biography*; Sander, *Anglican Schism*, pp. xiii–xiv; Phillips, *Images of a Queen*, p. 110.

31. Sander, *Anglican Schism*, pp. 25, 132. For the incestuous reference in Henry's reign, see *LP*, pp. XII–ii, 1537 and for its appearance in print, see Joseph Code, *Queen Elizabeth and the English Catholic Historians* (Louvain: Bureaux du Recueil Bibliothèque L'Université, 1935), p. 18.

32. Sander, *Anglican Schism*, pp. 25–30, 132–33. Although he claimed she had miscarried an undifferentiated mass, he blamed her fall on her sexual behavior, particularly her alleged attempt to have a child with her brother.

33. Sander, *Anglican Schism*, pp. 25–30, 132–33.

34. The association of spiritual evil with distorted physical features seems to have continued to modern times. See Hammond Innes, *The Conquistadors* (New York: Knopf, 1969), p. 33. My thanks to Helen Maurer, History Deprtment, University of California, Irvine, for this reference.

35. J. E. Drabble, "Gilbert Burnet and the History of the English Reformation: The Historian and his Milieu," *Journal of Religious History*, 121–4 (1983): 351–63; Veech, *Nicholas Sander*, p. 235; J. H. Pollen, "Dr. Nicholas Sander," *English Historical Review* 6 (1899): 35–46; Clancy, *Papist Pamphleteers*, p. 16.

36. Sander, *Anglican Schism*, p. 231; Adam Blackwood, *Martyre de la royne d'Éscosse* (Edinburgh: Jean Nafeild, 1587, but probably published in Paris), p. 8.

37. Phillips, *Images of a Queen*, pp. 146, 162–64, 172–77, 180.

38. J. Brodeau, *La vie de Maistre du Molin advocat au Parlement de Paris* (Paris: J. Guignard, 1654), pp. 4–5, cited both Sander and Blackwood; Gregoire Leti, *La vie d'Elizabeth Reine d'Angleterre*, trans. Louis a Le Peleteur, 2 vols. (Amsterdam: Henri Desbordes, 1694), pp. I, 116.

39. W. Lloyd, *Considerations touching the true way to suppress popery in this kingdom* (London: H. Brome, 1677), p. 91; see also Thomas Browne, *The Story of the Ordination of Our First Bishops in Queen Elizabeth's Reign At the Nag's Head Taverne in Cheapside, Thoroughly Examined* (London: Wiliam Innys, 1731), pp. 51–52.

40. Singer, *The Life of Cardinal Wolsey*, pp. 424–33; Warnicke, *Parergon*, pp. 142–43.

41. It is impossible to do justice to the complexity of the changes in these world views toward women and the movements that promoted them. See, for example, Vern L. Bullough, *The Subordinate Sex: A History of Attitudes Toward Women* (Baltimore, MD.: Penguin Books, 1974), pp. 288–294.

42. Eric Ives, *Anne Boleyn* (Oxford: Blackwell, 1986) pp. 49–52, 87, 358–82; Peter S. Noble, *Love and Marriage in Chrétien de Troyes* (Cardiff: University of Wales Press, 1982).

43. Warnicke, *Anne Boleyn*, pp. 191–233.

44. Warnicke, *Anne Boleyn*, pp. 3, 58–9, 65, 191–233; see also my article, "The Fall of Anne Boleyn Revisited," *English Historical Review* (July, 1993): 108–428, 653–665.

45. Warnicke, *Anne Boleyn*, pp. 3, 58–9, 65, 191–233.

46. George Bernard, "The Fall of Anne Boleyn," *English Historical Review*, 106 (July, 1991): 609; see also Warnicke, *English Historical Review* 653–65.

An Allegory of the Tudor Succession: The Family of Henry VIII.
By permission of the Yale Center for British Art.

Elizabeth I—
Always Her Own Free Woman

Ilona Bell

> The more I think over this business, the more certain I am that everything depends upon the husband this woman may take.
> —*Count de Feria to King Philip of Spain*

i. Camden's Virgin Queen

In 1630 when Camden's *Historie of the princesse Elizabeth* first appeared in English, the powerful religious and economic forces which threatened Elizabethan England all seemed subordinate to the trauma of female power which shook and then somehow miraculously preserved the social order, leaving the very foundation of society still in tremors: "A woman, and (if that be not enough) an vnmarried Virgin, destitute of all helpe of Parents, Brethren, Husband, beset with diuers Nations her mortall enemies; (while the Pope fretted, the *Spaniard* threatened, and all her Neighbour Princes . . . as had sworne to Popery, raged round about her) held the most stout and warlike Nation of the English foure and forty yeares and vpwards, not onely in awe and duty, but even in *Peace* also . . . "[1] According to Camden, Elizabeth's most remarkable achievement is not defeating the Spanish Armada (which is only noted parenthetically) but keeping her own unruly male subjects, the "stout and warlike" English, from rebelling against her female rule.

Camden's history is at once a tribute to a woman who successfully wields power in a man's world and a forceful reminder that it *is* a man's world. No one marvels that King Henry VIII is always his own free man, or that King James I is subject to no one, but it does seem remarkable that Elizabeth "tempered, and restrained [her male coun-

57

selors] in such sort, that they were to her most deuoted, and she was alwayes her owne free woman, and obnoxious [meaning, subject to the *rule, power or authority of no one*] to no one" (Camden 1:13). Despite the encomiastic glorification of death, the voice of a patriarchal culture persists, amazed and, if truth be told, a mite disturbed, to discover that a woman can govern the country so successfully—alone. Even as Camden attempts to contain Elizabeth's independence within the familiar and reassuring rhetoric of Petrarchan love poetry ("they were to her most deuoted"), he recognizes that Elizabeth is not the traditional sonnet lady, the idealized object of male desire, but something new, "always her owne free woman, and [subject] to no one," neither father nor husband.

Many of the difficulties facing Elizabeth as a woman acting in the public sphere are still with us today, remarkable as that may seem. The media's obsessive fascination with Hillary Clinton's role during the campaign, the public outcry whenever she deigns to say anything which makes it seem as if she might have an opinion or will of her own, gives us an inkling of the much greater problems facing Elizabeth I when she ascends the throne, a twenty-five-year-old orphan with considerable personal experience of political intrigue but no training in English government or international relations, trying to assert her will and establish her power in a world where women are not supposed to have either will or power. Entire segments of the American public are in an uproar whenever Hillary refers to herself as Hillary Rodham Clinton. The mere mention of her maiden name suggests that she is not the submissive wife, content to stay at home baking cookies, but still, despite her marriage, determined to remain always her own free woman, and subject to no one.

Not surprisingly, one of Elizabeth's first confrontations with parliament is over the sensitive and highly symbolic question of what she is to be called, and specifically whether she can be called "head" of the church, for that would make her male subjects the feet, or if they are lucky the hands. Negotiations eventually reach a stalemate: "left open for consideration is the clause where she is to take the title of head of the Church and for the present only assumes the style of 'Governor.' This is said to have been done on the ground that she may marry and her husband might then take the title" (*CSP Sp* 1: 68–69). Elizabeth hopes that parliament will relent; parliament expects marriage to solve this problem along with all the other problems posed by Elizabeth's sex and marital status.

Because Elizabeth I, like Hillary Clinton, occupies an unprecedented political position, she becomes a symbolic figure, the locus for larger social controversies about male authority and female subordination. When analyzing the role she plays, we need to consider, on the one hand, the ways in which her words and actions are colored by her female sex and by her culture's construction of femininity. On the other hand, we also need to consider the ways in which her "entirely novel and unprecedented" speech and actions call into question the very notion of what it means to be a woman.[2] If feminism can be defined "as a political instance, not merely a sexual politics but a politics of experience, of everyday life, which later then in turn enters the public sphere of expression and creative practice, displacing aesthetic hierarchies and generic categories, and which thus establishes the semiotic ground for a different production of reference and meaning . . . an original 'cultural creation' . . . a new aesthetic, a rewriting of culture," then, as I hope to show, Elizabeth's politics of courtship should be defined as a form, howsoever primitive or inadvertent, of feminism.[3]

By placing a woman in the role of hero, when the culture's myths cast her as the savior's mother or the patriarch's wife, history produces political, social, and representational confusion.[4] In a world where "All [women] are to be understood either married, or to be married, and their desires are subject to their husbands," Elizabeth's conjugal status, "A woman, and (if that be not enough) an vnmarried Virgin," poses the most disturbing ideological problem of all.[5] From the early years of Elizabeth's reign up to almost the present day, there seems to have been a powerful need to believe that Elizabeth is sworn to virginity. To some extent, she encourages this assumption by insisting on her right to remain single, if she so desires, it "being unfitting and altogether unmeet for you," as she warns her first Parliament, "to take upon you to draw my love to your liking or frame my will to your fantasies," and to rule the country herself, regardless of whether or not she chooses to marry.[6] At the same time, however, she makes a point of informing the 1559 Parliament that she *will* consider the prospect of marriage "whensoever it may please God to incline my heart to another kind of life."

Moreover, when the second Elizabethan Parliament convenes in 1563, Elizabeth specifically denies any mistaken assumptions that she is in any way sworn to remain a virgin: "if any here doubt that I am as it were by vow or determination bent never to trade that kind of life [i.e. a single life], put out that heresy, for your belief is therein awry" (Neale 1: 127). Heresy! Elizabeth could not have chosen a more emotionally or politically sensitive term, given the burgeoning fears of invasion by the Catholic powers in Europe and treason by Catholic sympathizers in England. Then, in a tone which is at once politically reassuring and boldly self-assertive, Elizabeth rejects the Catholic rhetoric of celibacy (the English Reformation has closed the nunneries, removed the comforting statues of the Virgin Mary from the parish church, permitted priests to marry, and transferred the ideal of chastity to marriage): "And if I can bend my liking to your need, I will not resist such a mind" (Neale 1: 127).[7] Petrarchism defines subjectivity and desire as inherently male, but Elizabeth's rhetoric—like the language of "love," "liking," "will" [meaning primarily *intention* or *determination to act* but also *carnal desire*], "fantasies," "incline," and "heart" from her 1559 speech—claims both female subjectivity and female desire.

For the first half of her reign, until the Alençon courtship finally fizzles, Elizabeth represents herself, in her speeches, letters, audiences, and actions, not as a virgin forever married to God and country, "Chaunting faint hymns to the cold fruitless moon," but as a marriageable virgin, willing to consider any appropriate suitor who acknowledges her sovereign power.[8] Camden rewrites Elizabeth's first Parliamentary speech to make it seem as if she is committed from the very start of her reign to living and dying as a holy virgin.[9] In fact, Camden probably constructed the parts of the 1559 speech that are most frequently cited by modern scholars and critics. Elizabethan versions of the speech do not contain either the description of marriage as "a point of inconsiderate Folly" or the oft-cited reference to the queen's symbolic marriage to England—"I haue already ioyned my selfe in marriage to an husband, namely, the Kingdome of *England*. And behold (said she, which I marvaile ye haue forgotten,) the pledge of this my wedlocke and marriage with my Kingdome, (and therewith, she drew the Ring from her finger and shewed it)."[10] To cinch matters, Camden revises the ending to make Elizabeth's willingness to remain single ("this shall be for me sufficient") into an unqualified glorification of virginity ("And to me it shall be a full satisfaction"). By marrying Elizabeth to England, Camden solves the moral threat of a masterless woman. By comparing her to the Virgin Mary, he canonizes her beatific chastity.[11] Yet, despite the power of Camden's history, disturbing differences between these two famous virgins persist. Elizabeth, unlike Mary, does not have a husband to whom her desires are subject, nor does she give birth to the son and savior England so desperately desires. Moreover, Elizabeth neither talks nor acts like a saint, sublimely free from carnal desires.

Without Camden's interpolations and revisions, all confirming his overarching vision of the virgin queen, Elizabeth's views about courtship and marriage remain difficult to ascertain, especially in the early years of her reign, when both her political power and her marital status are wide open questions. Throughout her life, whenever it is to her political advantage, Elizabeth is a master of intricately enigmatic prose.[12] She knows the value of enigma from her painfully insecure younger years, when, powerless and accused of treason, she writes the epigram, "Written with a Diamond on her Window at Woodstock": "Much suspected by me, / Nothing proved can be, / Quoth Elizabeth prisoner."[13] Still relatively powerless at the time of her first and second parliamentary speeches, Elizabeth veils her intentions behind the cryptic, contradictory rhetoric which is to become one of her most successful diplomatic strategies.[14] Variously reiterating her personal preference for the single life and affirming her willingness to marry, she squelches the idea that she has taken a vow of chastity, even as she asserts her readiness to live alone, if she so desires, and her determination to rule the country in her own right, whether or not she chooses to marry.

Passing into myth, Camden's tale of the virgin queen, married to God and country, has been repeated so often that it still shapes our assumptions about Elizabeth I in ways that we may not even realize. To counter Camden's power over our critical inheritance, it seems all the more important, at this particular juncture, to reexamine the marriage negotiations afresh, in their original historical context.[15] Since Elizabeth's marriage speeches have been analyzed by John King and by myself in another context, this essay juxtaposes Camden's retrospective vision of the virgin queen with another extremely rich source of information from the early years of Elizabeth's reign: Count de Feria's and the Bishop de Quadra's accounts of their negotiations with Elizabeth on behalf of the Spanish King and the Austrian Emperor, published in the *Calendar of Letters and State Papers Relating to English Affairs, Preserved Principally in the Archives of Simancas*, volume 1.

These letters are frequently cited by historians and biographers because they contain some of the juiciest gossip of the reign. The ambassadors' letters quote Elizabeth's words and describe her actions in great detail, and I quote generously from them, so that my readers can judge the queen's words and the ambassadors' explanations for themselves. I want to reconsider the letters dealing with the marriage negotiations because they tell a fascinating story very different from Camden's myth of the virgin queen, married to God and country. Of course, the information Feria and de Quadra provide is not pure, unadulterated historical data (if there is such a thing), but a text—a text which, like Camden's history, may be a more or less accurate record of what actually occurred. Yet it is a particularly useful text for it enables us to see how Elizabeth's private, thought still official, speech is subject to and distorted by gender stereotypes.

Elizabeth's relationship with the ambassadors is extremely cordial and at times remarkably intimate. Yet again and again their conversations end with a serious break down of communication, for the ambassadors seem unable to distinguish what Elizabeth says from what they think she ought to say, both as a woman and as a queen. And to make matters worse, what they expect from her as a woman often conflicts with what they expect of her as a monarch. Nonetheless, they frequently quote Elizabeth saying something which explicitly contradicts their own interpretation of the situation, so it seems safe to infer that they are not systematically altering the record to justify their own views. In letter after letter, one factor recurs and confounds interpretation above all others: Elizabeth does take a vow in 1559, but not to live and die a virgin.

ii. "The Queen says the most extraordinary things"

In the early months of her reign following the delivery of Elizabeth's first marriage speech in February, the capital is alive with balls and festivities. All the major powers of Europe are vying for Elizabeth's hand. The prospect of a royal marriage continues to dominate international relations and disrupt domestic politics, and Feria, the Spanish ambassador, writes King Philip that "[t]he most discreet people fear she will marry for caprice" (*CSP Sp* I: 8). To Feria and Philip, all personal considerations seem capricious. Kings and Queens are supposed to marry for the kind of military, dynastic, and political reasons Philip himself enumerates when he calculates the credits and debits of a potential alliance with Elizabeth (*CSP Sp* I: 22–28). On 19 March 1559, Elizabeth tells Feria, as he reports to Philip, that she "could not marry your Majesty as she was a heretic" (*CSP Sp* I: 37). Feria assumes that the "heretics" advising Elizabeth have convinced her that Philip only desires the marriage to secure England as a Catholic ally. If so, their intelligence is accurate, as Philip's letter to Feria proves.

On April 4 Elizabeth tells Feria "that your Majesty could not have been so much in love with her as I had said, as you had not had patience to wait four months for her; and many things of the same sort, as if she was not at all pleased at the decision adopted by your

Majesty" (*CSP Sp* I: 49). To justify her decision to end their already fizzled courtship, Elizabeth produces a list of impediments. The complex blend of personal and political considerations begins with the premise that "she had no desire to marry, as she had intimated from the first day," and ends with the problem "that the people did not wish her to marry a foreigner. And, finally, that several persons had told her that your Majesty would come here and then go off to Spain directly" (*CSP Sp* I: 35). Whenever it becomes politically expedient or personally desirable to dampen a particular courtship, Elizabeth reiterates her preference for the single life. What cannot be sufficiently explained by a theory of political Petrarchism is that even as Elizabeth veils her intentions like a conventional Petrarchan lady, she asserts her desires like a man or, some say, a strumpet.

"The Queen says that she has taken a vow to marry no man whom she has not seen, and will not trust portrait painters" (*CSP Sp* I: 70), reports de Quadra (the Bishop of Aquila and King Philip's man in London) who is commissioned, once Philip's own suit falls by the wayside, to arrange a Catholic marriage between Elizabeth and the Archduke Charles, the Emperor's younger son and Philip's cousin. De Quadra begins his negotiations with the premise that Elizabeth's personal preferences will determine the outcome. When he arrives on the scene, the negotiations are stalled because "the Queen had been informed that the Archduke had a head larger than that of the earl of Bedford" (*CSP Sp* I: 72). Asking her pardon, de Quadra "begged her to consider that in a matter of this gravity touching the welfare and tranquillity of their kingdoms and those of their neighbours kings and queens could not always follow their own desires to the prejudice of those of their subjects without doing great wrong and grievous sin, and therefore she should not consult her own inclination about her marriage but should look at the ruin that would come to her country by her doing so" (*CSP Sp* I: 72).[16]

Having argued that she should agree to a marriage regardless of her own inclinations, de Quadra then informs Elizabeth that the emperor is not proposing Ferdinand of the large head but his younger brother Charles: he "possessed extremely good and fitting qualities which I recounted at length. She was a long while demurring and doubting [but] when she was quite satisfied about this by your Majesty's letter (wherat, as I thought, she was pleased) she went back again to her nonsense and said she would rather be a nun than marry without knowing with whom and on the faith of portrait painters" (*CSP Sp* I: 72). To Camden, Elizabeth's commitment to virginity is all but grounds for canonization. To de Quadra it is sheer "nonsense." But to Elizabeth, a vow of virginity is much worse than "nonsense," it is "heresy," as she tells the 1563 Parliament.

In telling de Quadra that she "would rather be a nun than marry without knowing with whom," Elizabeth expresses not a divine commitment to chastity, but a personal aversion to arranged marriage. Her position is less like Shakespeare's Isabella, who says, "I speak not as desiring more, / But rather wishing a more strict restraint / Upon the sisterhood" than like Hermia, who prefers to live and die "in single blessedness," rather than "yield my virgin patent up" unto Demetrius "whose unwished yoke, / My soul consents not to give sovereignty."[17]

Elizabeth has no use for idealized royal portraits. She wants to gaze at her lover like a male love poet, and to decide for herself whether he is someone she wises to marry. And that is just the beginning of her demands: "We continued at this for some time wasting words and at last she said she was resolved not to marry except to a man of worth whom she had seen and spoken to, and she asked me whether I thought the archduke Charles would come to this country that she might see him. . . . I do not know whether she is jesting which is quite possible, but I really believe she would like to arrange for this visit in disguise" (*CSP Sp* I: 73). The Duke's arrival would surely have been known at court, as is the Duke of Alençon's when he arrives incognito in 1579. Still, the pretense of secrecy heightens the drama, while easing the political pressure. If the courtship should fail, Charles could return home quietly without having to face the humiliation of a public rejection.[18]

By representing herself as a monarch who is pleased to remain single, though willing to consider suitors who might please her, Elizabeth forces the world to recognize her will, meaning both her determination to act and carnal desire.[19] "[D]etermined to see and know the man who was to be her husband" (*CSP Sp* I: 73), willing to consider only "a man of worth whom she had seen and spoken to" (*CSP Sp* I: 73), she wants to judge her suitor's physical attractiveness *and* his verbal wit. In fact, the epigram written in her French Psalter—"No crooked leg, no bleared eye, / No part deformed out of kind, / Nor yet so ugly half can be / As is the inward suspicious mind"—suggests that she is less concerned with outer than inner deformity. Elizabeth would probably have agreed with Milton that "a meet and happy conversation [is] the chiefest and the noblest end of marriage."[20] Perhaps she wants the conversation without the marriage. Perhaps she realizes she can gain power from others' desire for conversation with her.

De Quadra could no more read Milton on marriage and divorce, than he could read Elizabeth on marriage and the single life. His interpretation of the situation ranges from the qualified optimism of May 30, 1559, based on his own conviction that Elizabeth's marriage is a political necessity—"yet I cannot help thinking that, so clearly is the need for her to marry being daily more understood by herself and her advisers, notwithstanding her disinclination to say yes, I need not despair of her listening to the proposal" (*CSP Sp* I: 75)—to the gloomy cynicism of June 19, based on his belief that Elizabeth is personally disinclined and politically duplicitous: "She makes her intimates think that she is favourable to the archduke's affair, and her women all believe such to be the case, as do the people at large, but there is really no more in it than there was the first day, and I believe for my part that she is astutely taking advantage of the general opinion to reassure somewhat the Catholics who desire the match and to satisfy others who want to see her married and are scandalized at her doings. She has told the ambassador how earnestly your Majesty has endeavoured to bring about this marriage with the archduke. She has just given 12,0000 £ to Lord Robert as an aid towards his expenses" (*CSP Sp* I: 77). In the gap between those "others" who are "scandalised at her doings" and de Quadra's ever so circumspect addendum, "12,0000 £ given to Lord Robert," lies our first clue to the larger social context in which these negotiations are taking place, the vast arena of gossip, either so false or so shocking as to be unspeakable, even under the cover of diplomatic correspondence.

Far from acting like the unmarried virgin, vowed to celibacy and forever married to God and country, Elizabeth exhibits little interest in the Petrarchan lady's pose. Instead, she publicly flouts conventional standards of chaste female behavior by openly demonstrating her physical attraction to Robert Dudley. The two are constantly in each other's company. Elizabeth appoints him Master of the Horse, and they gallop through the countryside alone together. "It was no small part of the scandal that she fondled Dudley like a lover in public. Then, too, she may have taken him as her lover out of sheer exultant rebelliousness. For in the first year of her reign—and beyond—Elizabeth was stridently, aggressively self-willed."[21] "The slander proceeds from many persons," the Emperor writes his son the Archduke Maximilian in June, "the harm done is great, and even though it be granted that it very often happens that a woman of good repute is spoken ill of, I do not wish to waste words on such, but when the outcry is so great, and comes from so many sides and always has the same tenor, it is indeed an awkward matter, and very dangerous" (Klarwill 99).[22] When Kat Ashley, Elizabeth's former governess and trusted confidante, expresses her growing concern that the rumors about Dudley could tarnish her Majesty's honor irreparably, Elizabeth says it is all nonsense for she and Dudley are never left alone. Having said that, however, she proceeds to defend her freedom to pursue her own sexual pleasure, if she should so desire: "if she had ever had the will or had found pleasure in such a dishonorable life, from which God preserve her, she did not know of anyone who could forbid her" (Klarwill 114). Feria reports that she is in Dudley's chamber day and night (*CSP Sp* I: 57). The ladies-in-waiting are in hers!

The rumors about Dudley continue, and in October, 1559, Elizabeth tells de Quadra "she did not dare to summon [the Archduke] as she feared he might not be satisfied with her" (*CSP Sp* I: 104), though clearly she is at least as concerned that she might not be satisfied with him. De Quadra reassures her, and "she replied that he might not be dissatisfied with what he saw but with what he heard about her, as I knew there were people in the country who took pleasure in saying anything that came into their heads about her. This she said with some signs of shame" (*CSP Sp* I: 104). At this point de Quadra still seems to think the tales are unfounded, for he replies: "if there were anything which the Archduke should not hear or learn, the idea of his coming would not have been entertained by us. . . . I saw she was pleased as she no doubt thought that if the Archduke heard any of the idle tales they tell about her (and they tell many) he might take advantage of them to the detriment of her honour if the match were broken off, and, although from this point of view I was not sorry, as the fear may not be without advantage to us" (*CSP Sp* I: 104). Everything, even malicious gossip, can be turned to political advantage, as de Quadra recognizes.

The negotiations drag on for months until two events suddenly make the prospect of marriage seem imminent. On September 7, 1559, de Quadra reports that the plot to kill Dudley and poison the Queen, combined with "the French war preparation for Scotland, seems to have decided the Queen to marry" (*CSP Sp* I: 95). At this juncture Mary Sidney, sister to Dudley, mother to Mary and Philip, and the Queen's trusted lady-in-waiting, pays her famous visit to de Quadra, saying "the Queen wished the Archduke to come at once, and I ought to write to the Emperor to send him" (*CSP Sp* I: 95). Soon afterward de Quadra speaks to Dudley and he, too, says that "the marriage had now become necessary" (*CSP Sp* I: 96). When de Quadra tries to discuss these conversations with Elizabeth, however, she brushes the matter aside without allowing him to make his point. On a subsequent occasion, she insists that Mary Sidney is acting completely on her own initiative (*CSP Sp* I: 113), though that seems highly unlikely, for, as Mary Sidney parries, such insubordination "might cost her her life" (*CSP Sp* I: 95).

On one central point, however, Elizabeth's position is explicit and consistent. From the start and throughout the negotiations she remains absolutely faithful to her original "vow to marry no man whom she had not seen." When de Quadra persists, saying Philip needs "to know whether [Elizabeth] would marry the Archduke . . . her answer was that she did not want to marry him or anybody else, and if she married at all it would only be to a man whom she knew" (*CSP Sp* I: 98–99). Is Elizabeth indeed determined to remain single? Or is she losing interest in the archduke because she has begun to think about marrying Dudley? I don't know. Perhaps she doesn't either. Regardless, her language seems calculated to perplex the ambassador and thus to prolong the negotiations as long as possible. To him, Elizabeth seems completely fickle and unreasonable: "she said that she did not wish the Archduke to come, by any means, as she did not wish to bind herself even indirectly to marry him. . . . We were at this for a long time wasting words, and at last she said . . . 'Shall I speak plainly and tell you the truth? I think that if the Emperor so desires me for a daughter he would not be doing too much by sending his son here without so many safeguards. I do not hold myself of so small account that the Emperor need sacrifice any dignity in doing it' " (*CSP Sp* I: 98–99).

Throughout this interview, or at least throughout this unusually rich and lengthy letter, Elizabeth never budges from this main point: "she reminded me that we were to agree that she was not to be bound to marry the Archduke if he came" (*CSP Sp* I: 100). Not wanting to create even the appearance of encouraging the Archduke, lest she seem to bind herself in advance, Elizabeth will not bid him to come to her— "She says it is not fit for a queen and a maiden to summon anyone to marry her for her pleasure" (*CSP Sp* I: 99). Of course, Elizabeth admits by her very formulation that she would never have considered summoning him in the first place if it were not a question of her "pleasure." She clearly would like him to come, if he can do so without any assurances from her, for as de Quadra reports two weeks later, "the Queen is very pleased and gay, as she thinks the Archduke is coming, but otherwise as fickle as ever, and as determined to see him before deciding" (*CSP Sp* I: 107).

Despite Elizabeth's attempt to state her position as plainly as possible, de Quadra is unwilling or unable to hear what she says. As a result, this letter contains some of the most blatant and fascinating discrepancies between her assertions and his interpretations: "Sometimes again, she said it might be so, but she was not decided one way or the other: in short, if I were to tell your Majesty that I considered the business otherwise than certain, I should be going against my conscience" (*CSP Sp* I: 103). It would only make sense to conclude that the matter is anything *but* certain, since Elizabeth's comments insist upon the ambiguity of her situation and the uncertainty of her feelings. But de Quadra is incapable of considering the business otherwise than certain: "she reminded me that we were to agree that she was not to be bound to marry the Archduke if he came, and knowing that this was only dissimulation and that she really means to marry him, as I think, for otherwise she would never consent to his coming which she has always refused hitherto, I agreed to this condition, and said all should be as she wished" (*CSP Sp* I: 100).

De Quadra simply refuses to heed Elizabeth's expressly stated position. She will not budge either. When she says maybe, she means it, but the words go right over his head. In context, de Quadra's confidence seems positively baffling: "It can hardly be believed, moreover, that if she did not mean to marry she would condescend to such vanity as to bring a son of your Majesty here to no purpose" (*CSP Sp* I: 101). Of course, there is a purpose in bringing the Archduke to England, but de Quadra just doesn't get it. In one sense, however, he is absolutely right: he *is* incapable of believing that Elizabeth would bring the Emperor's son all the way to England in order to decide whether she wants to marry him—or even whether she wants to marry at all.

Realizing what she is up against, Elizabeth threatens to write down the terms upon which the archduke is welcome to visit, and to send them directly to the Emperor herself: "when I pressed her much she seemed frightened and protested again and again that she was not to be bound, and that she was not resolved yet whether she should marry; but this was after we had agreed about the Archduke's visit. At length, she gave me to understand that she was serious in her demand, she repeated what we had agreed upon in order that I should put it in writing, and when I took this as a joke she said she would not trust me as she knew I was deceiving her, and she would write to the King herself" (*CSP Sp* I: 100–01). No matter that Elizabeth insists she is not eager to marry. No matter that she has already told him of her vow to say nothing about her marital intentions until she can see and know her suitor. No matter that de Quadra has previously agreed to this condition. He is ideologically incapable of believing that she can possibly mean what she says—or that what she says can possibly mean anything that unprecedented.

Here, as in the 1559 marriage speech, Elizabeth takes considerable care to provide reassurances that she will never accept a marriage proposal that is "prejudicial to the realm . . . put that clean out of your heads" (Neale 1: 49). Having offered the necessary reassurances, however, she admits that her personal inclinations supersede, or at least complicate, the clear-cut diplomatic alternatives de Quadra poses. What kind of a woman would speak this way? Elizabeth is acting neither like a proper lady, chaste, silent, and obedient, nor like a conventional queen. De Quadra concludes, she must be a bad woman, a woman who deserves the anti-feminist accusations which continue to crop up amidst his most serious political calculations. Even if Elizabeth's institutional position commands respect, her sex still provokes suspicion and contempt. Frustrated by his own failure to cinch the negotiations and annoyed that Elizabeth is not acting according to decorum, de Quadra can only assume that she is driven by more powerful female failings. "With her all is falsehood and vanity" (CSP Sp I: 89), he concludes.[23]

Just below the surface of these marriage negotiations lies misogyny, and its handmaiden, the negative stereotype, "a complex, ambivalent, contradictory mode of representation, as anxious as it is assertive" (Bhabha 22).[24] Feria thinks Elizabeth "a very strange sort of woman" (CSP Sp I: 12). De Quadra thinks she is "in short, only a passionate ill-advised woman" (CSP Sp I: 102). Feria and de Quadra both express their anti-feminism unabashedly when, free from the constraints of official diplomacy, they exchange letters with each other. Making no attempt to disguise his derision, Feria writes: "I should be glad if that woman [Elizabeth] were to quite lose her head and bring matters to a point, although when I think what a baggage she is and what a crew she is surrounded by, there is probability enough of my wish coming true. It seems the Emperor up to the present refuses leave for his son to go, and, to tell the truth, I cannot persuade myself that he is wrong, nor do I believe that she will either marry him, or refuse to marry him, whilst the matter at issue is only his visit. Real necessity, however, may make her open her eyes and marry" (CSP Sp I: 106). Does Feria think Elizabeth would be crazy to accept the archduke? Or does he think she would be crazy to reject him? Probably the latter, although given the political and religious complications, it is hard to tell which would, in fact, be crazier. What does seem clear, however, is that Feria thinks Elizabeth has all but lost her head already. To his way of thinking, any woman who thinks she can escape the powerful cultural psychomachia that divides woman into marriageable virgins and "baggage," or whores, must be crazy.

De Quadra, feeling even more thwarted by Elizabeth's unconventional female behavior, agrees that she is quite without moral compunctions. But instead of assuming that she is about to go mad, he concludes that she is just plain dumb: "Your Lordship's opinion with regard to the Queen's marriage would hold good in the case of a woman of brains and conscience with which this one is not troubled, but as it is, I think she either will not marry, or, if she does, it will only be because she had brought the Archduke here and likes him. . . . [T]he Queen says the most extraordinary things" (*CSP Sp* I: 108). De Quadra seems to recognize that women with "brains and conscience" exist in theory, but his conception of conscience leaves so little leeway for brains that he obviously cannot recognize "one" when he sees her.[25]

These men would have been willing to forgive Elizabeth's female sex, if she had been willing to act like a proper female, that is, if she had concealed her sexual desire along with her powerful intelligence; but in their political world of rumor, gossip, and factionalism, female sexuality is all but synonymous with immorality and irrationality.[26] When sustained reiteration finally forces the ambassadors to consider the possibility that Elizabeth is serious about making no predetermination one way or the other *until* she has seen and talked to her suitor for herself, they respond with a conventional moral condemnation born of misogynist prejudice.

Shortly thereafter, Dudley's wife falls down the stairs of their country house and dies under what can at best be described as suspicious circumstances.[27] The world is abuzz with nasty rumors that Elizabeth and Dudley conspired to kill his wife so that he will be free to remarry. The charge has been discredited by most modern biographers, but De Quadra joins the chorus: "I had heard from a certain person who is accustomed to give me veracious news that Lord Robert has sent to poison his wife. Certainly all the Queen has done with us and with the Swede, and will do with the rest in the matter of her marriage, is only keeping Lord Robert's enemies and the country engaged with words until this wicked deed of killing his wife is consummated." A fine choice of words! "The same person told me some extraordinary things about this intimacy, which I would never have believed, only that now I find Lord Robert's enemies in the Council making no secret of their evil opinion of it" (*CSP Sp* I: 112).[28]

Before long, Elizabeth's provocative behavior spawns widespread rumors of illegitimate children. In 1560, Mother Anne Dowd is imprisoned for "openly asserting that the Queen was with child by Robt. Duddeley."[29] Dionisia Deryck says the Queen "hath already had as many children as I, and that two of them were yet alive, one a man child and the other a maiden child, and the others were burned . . . my Lord of Leicester [Dudley] was the father and wrapped them up in the embers in the chimney which was in the chamber where they were born."[30] Edmund Baxter says "that Lord Robert kept her Majesty, and that she was a naughty woman, and could not rule her realm, and that justice was not being administered." Baxter's wife says Elizabeth "looked like one lately come out of childbed."[31]

One could argue that the spreading scandal shows Elizabethan society mustering its forces to condemn Elizabeth's license, but it seems equally reasonable to conclude that the uncontainable vitality of the rumors shows just how subversive Elizabeth's wanton disregard for social decorum seems. As Natalie Davis writes, "the image of the disorderly woman did not always function to keep women in their place. On the contrary, it was a multivalent image that could operate, first, to widen behavioral options for women within and even outside marriage, and second, to sanction riot and political disobedience for both men and women in a society that allowed the lower orders few formal means of protest. Play with the unruly woman is partly a chance for temporary release from the traditional and stable hierarchy; but it is also part of the conflict over efforts to change the basic distribution of power within society."[32] Although a queen is a highly unlikely "image of a disorderly woman," many of Elizabeth's contemporaries see her in just those terms. And if the unruly acts of powerless, marginal women contribute to changing the basic distribution of power, wouldn't a queen's unruly behavior shake the distribution of power even more profoundly?

De Quadra's alarmist rhetoric shows that he and many others indeed fear what Davis describes, that Elizabeth's scandalous behavior will sanction riot and encourage political disobedience: "I have again told her how undesirable it is for her to remain unmarried, and how great is the danger which results to the tranquillity of her country. I then showed her the advantage that might be expected from a match with the Archduke, seeing how much your Majesty desires it. She replied that she had very good reasons by which she could prove to me that it was not desirable that she should marry at present" (*CSP Sp* I: 122). In bringing up this decisive political argument which she says she could but then does not make, Elizabeth's defense performs her claim that she will not defer to the traditional social and political hierarchy: "the reason why she did not marry was really only because she could not incline herself to change her state, and she did not know how long this condition of mind would last, but she was quite certain she would never desire to marry until she had seen the person who was to be her husband, and so we are brought back again to the old position" (*CSP Sp* I: 122). The record is stuck replaying the same old worn out tune, but the sound is getting harsher. As de Quadra grows more irate, Elizabeth becomes more tenacious.

For de Quadra, the only legitimate construction of desire is political, as in "kings and queens could not always follow their own desires to the prejudice of those of their subjects without doing great wrong," or "I again told her how undesirable it is for her to remain unmarried." In de Quadra's economy, desire hungers for and feeds political power. Yet Elizabeth's struggle to rule as a woman in a male world places her in constant danger of having her female desire subjected by her male government which is all too willing to rule for her, until it can find a man to rule over her. Hence, the assertion and recognition of her desire are the quintessential proof of her political consequence. As she has already told de Quadra, "I think that if the Emperor so desires me for a daughter he would not be doing too much by sending his son here without so many safeguards" (*CSP Sp* I: 99).

At this point, in what amounts to a climactic showdown with de Quadra, Elizabeth restates her position more unguardedly than ever: "nothing would suffice to make her think of marrying, or even treating of marriage; but the person she was to marry pleasing her so much as to cause her to desire what at present she has no wish for, and if this was not the case it was no good thinking that she would ever marry at all. If the Emperor thought it did not suit him to send his son until she had expressed her desire, she, for her part, did not choose to declare it until she had seen the person she was expected to love" (*CSP Sp* I: 123). Adopting an uncharacteristically confessional mode ("the reason why she did not marry was really only because"), Elizabeth invokes her original vow, using the discourse of desire more boldly than ever. On this note of Elizabethan pique, of mutual irony born of ideological incompatibility, the marriage negotiations reach an impasse.

At times, Elizabeth is thoroughly inscrutable. At other times, she is bluntly insistent. Feria and de Quadra seem equally inept at analyzing her language in either case. When she is straightforward, they assume she is lying. When she is elusive, they assume she is concealing a secret plan. The more assertive she is, the more confounding they find her words and actions: "her language (learnt from Italian heretic friars who brought her up) is so shifty that it is the most difficult thing in the world to negotiate with her" (*CSP Sp* I: 89). If her uncertainty looks politically irresponsible and dangerously self-indulgent to de Quadra (as it does to many in her own government), their rigidity looks politically obtuse and personally threatening to her. As Elizabeth's confidence in the validity of her own will and the acumen of her political judgments grows stronger, so does her impatience with the constraints of arranged marriage. Yet however ready Feria and de Quadra are to dismiss Elizabeth's views as "falsehood and vanity" (*CSP Sp* I: 89), they do not silence her, either when conversing with her or when reporting on her. Throughout the negotiations, Elizabeth remains faithful to her original "vow to marry no man whom she had not seen," until she finally feels bold enough to tell de Quadra that she will not marry unless she meets a man who arouses her desire.

Whatever her ulterior motives, whatever may have been going on between her and Dudley in private, whatever fears she may have about losing power by accepting a husband in a patriarchal society, Elizabeth remains indecisive about the Archduke for the straightforward reason that she reiterates repeatedly. She has never met him, so how can she possibly know whether she wants to marry him? De Quadra is unable to fulfill his mission because their conversations keep returning to this point of misunderstanding. Elizabeth says that she wants to reserve the right to say no if she decides, after the meeting, that she does not like the archduke, or his conception of marriage, or the very idea of marriage in any form whatsoever.

This motive, so commonplace now as to be barely worth noting, is so radical at the time, so contrary to what tradition dictates and good sense seems to require, that it takes months and months before the ambassadors are willing to consider that Elizabeth means what she says. Perhaps she only says it and doesn't mean it. Perhaps she realizes her vow will prolong the negotiations and protect her alliance with King Philip and the Emperor (as Feria and de Quadra continue to suspect).

Regardless of her motives, her vow proves a highly successful strategy for a female monarch. Elizabeth's politics of courtship increase her power by keeping opportunity calling, encouraging negotiations without committing her to a marriage that might displease or disempower her. At the same time, her "vow to marry no man whom she has not seen" is a bold and radically difficult position for a woman in early modern Europe to maintain, even if she is a queen. Indeed, for her male opponents, it looks all the more dangerous, and is all the more threatening, precisely because she *is* the queen.

iii. A Phenomenon

> From the moment of her accession until the time of her death Elizabeth I was a phenomenon—it is not too strong a word—in European history. She was at once a crowned monarch and an unmarried woman. To such an unconventional conjunction some of the stiffest problems of the reign must be attributed. The Queen's methods of dealing with them often bewildered her contemporaries. They have not been any clearer to the historians.
>
> Williams, "In Search of the Queen"[33]

To this day, historians, unaccustomed to considering gender an important category for historical analysis, continue to find the unconventional conjunction of crowned monarch and unmarried woman baffling and bewildering.[34] MacCaffrey concludes, ever so cautiously, "And perhaps underlying this jealousy for her power was the suspicion that her masculine courtiers never quite believed in the royal capacities of a mere woman. This deeply buried sense of insecurity added another stratum to a complex character."[35] But exactly whose insecurities are we talking about? By slipping almost imperceptibly ("This deeply buried sense . . . ") from the male courtiers' doubts about Elizabeth's ability to govern, to Elizabeth's own psychic turmoil, MacCaffrey, like the Elizabethan courtiers he invokes, essentially denies Elizabeth's subjectivity.

When we reexamine the shaping of the Elizabethan regime from a feminist point of view, beginning with the premise that gender is a useful and important category of historical analysis, we find the insecurity about Elizabeth's sex, always right under the surface throughout her reign, splattered all over Elizabethan political life whenever events raise the least concern about national security. When Elizabeth gets sick, when there is a plot to assassinate her, everyone immediately begins to think "the marriage had now become necessary" (*CSP Sp* I: 96). When Elizabeth manages to solve the problem politically, people simply wait for what Neale at one point calls "the inherent weakness" of "the regiment of a woman" (Neale 1: 142) to show itself. "Real necessity" will, they are sure, "make her open her eyes and marry" (*CSP Sp* I: 106). Continual pressures to marry, couched in the most alarming (or alarmist, depending on your point of view) rhetoric about her inability to rule the country alone, come from all quarters, from Protestant subjects, Catholic subjects, Parliament, Privy Council, foreign allies, and potential enemies. Elizabeth bravely withstands them all.

Whatever Elizabeth's actual relationship with Dudley may have been, her visible expression of sexual desire is widely noted and discussed by Elizabethan men and women. The historical and ideological reasons for idealizing, Petrarchizing, bowdlerizing, muting Elizabeth's life are self-evident. In fact, the virgin Queen's courtly admirers continue to find the lingering hints of scandal disturbing well into this century. Neale does his best to play down the more shocking episodes, or to pretend they don't exist. Chamberlin writes *The Private Character of Queen Elizabeth* to demonstrate that the only passion Elizabeth ever experienced was love for England.[36] As proof, he cites the medical axiom that "the great majority of women, unlike men, never feel any sexual inclination before marriage" (151)! Chamberlin might have been more savvy about Elizabeth if he had read some of the Elizabethan antifeminist tracts which excoriate licentiousness as a principle female failing. Yet Chamberlin's painstaking defense of Elizabeth's honor against charge after charge yields unforeseen results: not only do his outmoded premises demonstrate that gender and sexuality are historical constructs, but his text makes the offending rumors all the more easily accessible to subsequent readers, readers who seem increasingly less scandalized than heartened by the possibility that Elizabeth had an active love life.

At this point in history, rather than trying to solve the mystery of a regal hymen long since turned to dust and food for worms, it seems more important to confront the fact that Elizabeth's extraordinary and unprecedented behavior challenges long-standing assumptions about both monarchs and women. After six years of negotiations, the proposed marriage between Elizabeth and Archduke Charles is still stuck for the very reasons that stymied the negotiators in the first place. In the intervening years, Charles' brother, Maximilian, has become the Emperor and in 1565, he sends his envoy Zwetkovich to England to "make diligent inquiries concerning the maiden honour and integrity of the Queen" (Klarwill 231). Zwetkovich provides the requisite reassurances: "the Queen becomes fonder of His Princely Highness and her impatience to see him grows daily. Her marriage is, I take it, certain and resolved upon" (Klarwill 237).

The Emperor disagrees. He thinks the matter is "still very dubious and questionable, for the illustrious Queen, who had formerly declared that she did not desire to marry, still abides by her former resolve to marry no one whom she has not previously seen. Among Kings and Queens this is entirely novel and unprecedented, and we cannot approve of it. If, therefore, no greater and surer certitude can be given that our beloved brother will not return with his object unaccomplished we cannot express ourselves content with the reasons advanced in your letters" (Klarwill 239). Once again, the sticking point is Elizabeth's vow to marry no man she has not seen.

Maximilian proceeds to analyze the terms of the proposed marriage agreement, arguing that the differences between the two countries must be worked out before a visit can even be considered. The Archduke must be guaranteed the freedom to practice his Catholic religion in private, the Queen's request for a dowry must be dropped, the King's expenses must be provided out of the English treasury, and Elizabeth must accept the "King's share in the governance of the country, whether he by virtue of this marriage will be placed on an equality with the Queen as regards honour and the royal title, and will assist her in ruling over this realm and its dominions" (Klarwill 241). Precisely what Elizabeth refuses to concede.

"We do reject women, as those whom nature hath made to keep home and to nourish their family and children, and not to meddle with matters abroad, not to bear office."[37] This could well have been written by a member of the moral majority, denouncing Hillary Clinton in the 1992 presidential campaign, but it is, in fact, written by Thomas Smith in *De Republica Anglorum* in 1565 as the debate about Elizabeth's failure to marry is reaching a climax. Although Elizabeth faced continual pressure to marry during the first half of her reign, she valiantly resists the patriarchal assumption that she is a weak, frail woman who needs a husband to bear office for her. Instead, she insists upon her authority to rule the country alone, despite threats of invasion from abroad and treason at home, and to live alone unless, or until, she finds someone so much to her "liking," "pleasing her so much," without reducing her power or the country's security, "as to cause her to desire what at present she ha[d] no wish for."

As the political obstacles to negotiating a major international alliance combine with the personal stress of negotiating a major crisis in gender redefinition, Elizabeth's rhetorical and ideological challenge is to maintain the mutual dignity of both choices, neither allowing her satisfaction with the single life and political sovereignty to preclude the possibility of marriage, nor allowing her expression of female desire to tarnish her capacity to rule as a single woman.

When we recuperate Elizabeth's side of the conversations with the foreign ambassadors, what emerges is a distinctly un-Petrarchan tale of female will. Successful beyond all expectations as a monarch, Elizabeth fails the culture's primary expectation of her as a woman, to marry and give birth to a male heir—though I would rather say that her life symbolically violates and subverts the very expectations that transform sex into gender. Her highly unconventional politics of courtship redefines marriage and power from the woman's point of view, not as a foregone conclusion requiring dutiful female subjection, but as a political debate which can only escape its own enigmatic uncertainties if or when a suitor appears capable of matching Elizabeth's personal charisma and verbal daring: "pleasing her so much as to cause her to desire what at present she has no wish for."

Within the first year of her reign Elizabeth develops a rhetoric of courtship which establishes the grounds for a different production of reference and meaning. During the first decade, gathering increasing courage to speak against the grain of Renaissance prescriptive literature which enjoins women to silence, obedience, and domesticity, she begins to represent herself, both in public and in private, less as the embodiment of the king's eternal male soul than as both a woman and a monarch. Establishing an ongoing dialogue with the male voices of Parliament, Privy Council, foreign heads of state and their male ambassadors, she unsettles society's expectations of appropriate female behavior and beings to forge "an original 'cultural creation' "[38] By insisting that her fate as an unmarried woman is a matter for her rather than the Privy Council or the parliament to decide, Elizabeth brings a woman's experience of courtship into the public sphere.

The prolonged marriage negotiations between Elizabeth and parliament, and between Elizabeth and the foreign ambassadors, place a vocal female voice at the center of political debate, giving relations between the sexes an unprecedented public visibility and import, "displacing aesthetic hierarchies and generic categories," precipitating a passionate social controversy about courtship which is enacted in the popular controversy over women and poetry, in Shakespearean drama, and in the Elizabethan love lyric.[39] When Elizabeth's politics of courtship merges with a broader social and political debate about courtship, it produces "a new aesthetic, a rewriting of culture" (de Lauretis 10)—in sum, Elizabeth becomes a symbolic figure, who represents an early modern form of feminism.

Notes

The epigraph is quoted from *Calendar of Letters and State Papers Relating to English Affairs, Preserved Principally in the Archives of Simancas*, vol. 1, Elizabeth. 1558–1567, ed. Martin A. S. Hume (London, 1892; Nendeln/ Liechtenstein: Kraus, 1971), p. 3. All further references will be cited in the text as *CSP Sp*.

1. William Camden, *The Historie of the . . . princesse Elizabeth*, trans. R. N[orton] (London: 1630), sig. A3.

2. Quoted from *Queen Elizabeth and Some Foreigners*, ed. Victor Von Klarwill (New York: Brentano, 1928), p. 239. All further references appear in the text.

3. Quoted from Teresa de Lauretis, "Feminist Studies/Critical Studies: Issues, Terms, and Contexts," in *Feminist Studies/Critical Studies*, ed. de Lauretis (Bloomington: Indiana University Press, 1986), p. 10. See also Susan Bassnett, *Elizabeth I: A Feminist Perspective* (Oxford: St. Martin's Press, 1988); Moira Ferguson, ed., *First Feminists: British Women Writers*: 1578–1799 (Bloomington: Indiana University Press; Old Westbury, NY: Feminist Press, 1985); Hilda Smith, *Reason's Disciples: Seventeenth-Century English Feminists* (Urbana: University of Illinois Press, 1982). For a more critical view of Elizabeth, see Allison Heisch, "Queen Elizabeth I and the Persistence of Patriarchy," *Feminist Review* 4 (1980): 45–56, and "Queen Elizabeth I: Parliamentary Rhetoric and the Exercise of Power," *Signs* 1 (1975): 31–55.

4. See Margaret Ezell, *The Patriarch's Wife: Literary Evidence and the History of the Family* (Chapel Hill: University of North Carolina Press, 1987). Dayton Haskin, "Milton's Portrait of Mary as a Bearer of the Word," in *Milton and the Idea of Woman*, ed. Julia Walker (Urbana: University of Illinois Press, 1988), pp. 169–84, offers a rich collection of Protestant iconography of the Virgin Mary, and a lucid analysis of the ways in which English Protestants altered the conventional image.

5. Quoted from *The Lawes Resolvtions of Womens Rights* (London, 1632), p. 126, and Camden, sig. A3.

6. J. E. Neale, *Elizabeth I and Her Parliaments* (1953; London: Jonathan Cape, 1957), I: 49. All further references to Neale appear in the text.

7. See Maurice Ashley, "Love and Marriage in Seventeenth-Century England," *History Today* 8 (1958): 667–75; William and Malleville Haller, "The Puritan Art of Love," *Huntington Library Quarterly* 5 (1942): 235–72; Roland Mushat Frye, "The Teachings of Classical Puritanism on Conjugal Love," *Studies in the Renaissance* 2 (1955): 148–59; Kathleen M. Davies, "Continuity and Change in Literary Advice on Marriage," in *Marriage and Society: Studies*

in the Social History of Marriage, ed. R. B. Outhwaite (London: Europa, 1981), pp. 58–79.

8. Quoted from *A Midsummer Night's Dream*, in *The Riverside Shakespeare*, ed. G. Blakemore Evans, et al (Boston: Houghton Mifflin, 1974), 1.1.73.

9. See John N. King's ground breaking essay, "Queen Elizabeth I: Representations of the Virgin Queen," *Renaissance Quarterly* 43 (1990): 30–74.

10. Camden, *The Historie*, 1: 26.

11. Camden celebrates Elizabeth as a type of the Virgin Mary at the very historical moment when the Protestant Reformation is discrediting the cult of the Virgin, closing the nunneries, smashing beloved images of holy mother and child, and most importantly, sanctioning marriage for the clergy, thereby ending the medieval exaltation of chastity over marriage. On the connections between Elizabeth and the Virgin Mary, see Frances Amelia Yates, *Astraea: the Imperial Theme in the Sixteenth Century* (1975; London: Ark, 1985), pp. 76–80; Philippa Berry, *Of Chastity and Power: Elizabethan Literature and the Unmarried Queen* (London: Routledge, 1989).

12. Elaine Showalter, "Feminist Criticism in the Wilderness," in *The New Feminist Criticism: Essays on Women, Literature, and Theory*, ed. Showalter (New York: Pantheon Books, 1985), p. 193, writes, "the problem is not that language is insufficient to express women's consciousness but that women have been denied the full resources of language and have been forced into silence, euphemism, or circumlocution."

13. Quoted from *The Poems of Elizabeth I*, ed. Leicester Bradner (Providence: Brown University Press, 1964).

14. For a useful account of the problems facing Elizabeth when she is first crowned, see Norman L. Jones, "Elizabeth's First Year: the Conception and Birth of the Elizabethan Political World," in *The Reign of Elizabeth I*, ed. Christopher Haigh (Athens: University of Georgia Press, 1985), pp. 27–53. On the question of her succession, see J. E. Neale, "Parliament and the Succession Question in 1562/3 and 1566," *English Historical Review* 36 (1921): 497–519.

15. Camden's version of Elizabeth's 1559 speech is cited not only by classic studies such as Forster's "The Political Petrarchism of the Virgin Queen," in *The Icy Fire: Five Studies in European Petrarchism* (London: Cambridge University Press, 1969), but also by more recent studies such as Montrose's "Elizabethan Subject and the Spenserian Text," in *Literary Theory/Renaissance Texts*, ed. Patricia Parker and David Quint (Baltimore: Johns Hopkins University Press, 1986), and Valerie Wayne's introduction to *The Flower of Friendship*, ed. Wayne (Ithaca: Cornell University Press, 1992).

16. Clearly, this particular argument was formulated to advance de Quadra's bargaining position, but he makes even more dire predictions when

writing directly to his compatriots: "This woman's troubles are growing apace, and her house will be in a blaze before she knows it" (*CSP Sp* I: 107).

17. Quoted from *Measure for Measure*, 1.4.3-5, and *A Midsummer Night's Dream*, 1.1.78–82.

18. The Emperor's ambassador, Baron von Breuner, supports the plan enthusiastically: "I thereupon again told her that if she wished to remain unpledged, and also would not marry His Highness without seeing him, it was in my opinion better if His Highness came here incognito; that if he then found favour in her eyes, Your Imperial Majesty might let him stay here, and then at a favourable opportunity proclaim him to be her consort" (Klarwill 148); "I had often written before, beseeching His Imperial Majesty not to make any difficulties, but to send the Archduke here in all secrecy as this would be done with the Queen's consent" (Klarwill 156).

19. During this period, Elizabeth invites von Breuner, the Emperor's ambassador, to her barge. He reports, "she conversed with nobody else, and often of her own accord began to talk about the Archduke Charles . . . she frequently said that she was certainly not willing to marry before she had seen the wooer in person. I endeavored to argue her out of this, and begged her to resolve to give a favourable and final answer. Hereupon she asked what she should say, as she had not yet made up her mind to marry" (Klarwill 96).

20. Quoted from *The Complete Prose Works of John Milton*, ed. Ernest Sirluck, vol. 2 (New Haven: Yale University Press, 1959), 246.

21. Carolly Erickson, *The First Elizabeth* (New York: Summit, 1983), 181.

22. Von Breuner "made most diligent inquiries into the calumnies that are current not only abroad but also here in England." He hires a certain François Borth who is very friendly with the ladies of the bedchamber, who "all swear by all that is holy that her Majesty has most certainly never been forgetful of her honour." The ladies admit, however, that "Mylord Robert, is preferred by the Queen above all others, and that Her Majesty shows her liking for him more markedly than is consistent with her reputation and dignity" (Klarwill 113). In December, von Breuner reports that he has "made diligent inquiries, but concerning the person of the Queen has heard nothing definite" (Klarwill 157).

23. For a review of these anti-feminist stereotypes as represented in the controversy over women, see Katherine Usher Henderson and Barbara F. McManus's introduction to *Half Humankind: Contexts and Texts of the Controversy about Women in England* 1540–1640 (Urbana: University of Illinois Press, 1985), pp. 47–63.

24. Homi K. Bhabha, "The Other Question: Homi K. Bhabha Reconsiders the Stereotype and Colonial Discourse," *Screen* 24 (1983): 18, explains that the

sterotype is a "form of knowledge and identification that vacillates between what is always 'in place,' already known, and something that must be anxiously repeated," something "that needs no proof, can never really, in discourse, be proved." Thus, a process of *ambivalence* is central to the stereotype which "must always be in excess of what can be empirically proved or logically construed."

25. Cynthia Griffin Wolff, "A Mirror For Men: Stereotypes of Women in Literature," in *Woman: An Issue*, ed. Lee R. Edwards, Mary Heath, and Lisa Baskin (Boston: Little Brown, 1972), p. 218, writes, "The ultimate truth of these [stereotypical] images of women does not rest in their ability to capture feminine experience or women's life-problems; it inheres, ironically, in their capacity for revealing masculine dilemmas and postulating fantasied solutions to them."

26. Von Breuner reports that she is "puffed up with pride, and imagines . . . she may therefore marry whomever she pleases. But herein she errs, for if she marry the said Mylord Robert, she will incur so much enmity that she may one evening lay herself down as Queen of England and rise the next morning as plain Mistress Elizabeth" (Klarwill 157). During the Alençon courtship, Fénélon, in an attempt to reassure Catherine de Medici, makes the same argument in reverse: "In her own court, she is very greatly honored . . . all ranks of her subjects fear and revere her, and she rules them with full authority, which I conceive could scarcely proceed from a person of ill-fame and where there was a want of virtue" (quoted by Elizabeth Jenkins, *Elizabeth the Great* (1958; London: Victor Gollancz, 1985), p. 175.

27. The situation seems all the more suspicious because even before her death there had been rumors that Robert was trying to poison his wife, as both von Breuner (Klarwill 157) and de Quadra (*CSP Sp* I: 58) report.

28. Carole Levin, "Queens and Claimants: Political Insecurity in Sixteenth-Century England," in *Gender, Ideology, and Action: Historical Perspectives on Women's Public Lives*, ed. Janet Sharistanian (Westport, Conn.: Greenwood Press, 1986), pp. 41–66, argues that these rumors reveal the country's anxiety about the legitimacy of a female ruler.

ʹ 29. Quoted in *Calendar of State Papers, Domestic series, of the reigns of Elizabeth and James I*, ed. Mary Anne Everett Green (London: Longmans, 1872), 12: 13.

30. F. G. Emmison, *Elizabethan Life: Disorder* (Chelmsford: Essex County Council, 1970), p. 42.

31. *CSP Dom Eliz*, 12: 534. For a more detailed political analysis of these documents, see Levin, "Queens and Claimants."

32. Natalie Zemon Davis, *Society and Culture in Early Modern France, Eight Essays* (Stanford: Stanford University Press, 1965), p. 131. For a superb

analysis of the "figure of the female transgressor as public spectacle" and the "relationship between symbology and social change," see Mary Russo, "Female Grotesques: Carnival and Theory," in *Feminist Studies/Critical Studies*, pp. 213–29.

33. C. H. Williams, "In Search of the Queen," in *Elizabethan Government and Society: Essays Presented to Sir John Neale*, eds. S. T. Bindoff, J. Hurstfield, and C. H. Williams (London: University of London, Athlone Press, 1961), p. 2.

34. See Joan Scott's compelling essay, "Gender: A Useful Category of Historical Analysis," *American Historical Review* 91 (1986): 1053–75.

35. Wallace T. MacCaffrey, *The Shaping of the Elizabethan Regime* (1968; London: Jonathan Cape, 1969), p. 300.

36. Frederick Chamberlin, *The Private Character of Queen Elizabeth*, 2nd ed. (New York: Dodd Mead, 1922).

37. Thomas Smith, *De Republica Anglorum* (London, 1584).

38. The particular factors cited in this paragraph parallel the definition of feminism by de Lauretis, 10, cited at the beginning of this essay.

39. This is the subject of the book I am currently completing, *Passion Lends them Power: the Poetry, Politics, and Practice of Elizabethan Courtship.*

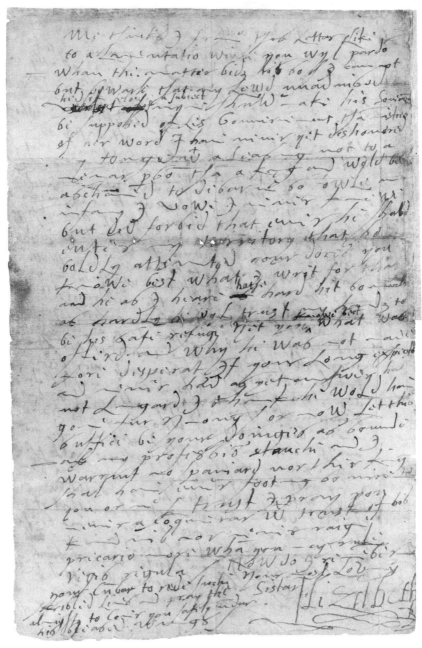

Letter from Elizabeth I to King James of Scotland. This autograph letter of
March 1593 from Elizabeth to James concludes, "Now do I remember Cumbar
[care] to read such scribbled lines and pray the almighty to Cover you safely
under his blessed wings. Your most Loving Sister, Elizabeth R."
By permission of the Folger Shakespeare Library.

The Fictional Families of Elizabeth I

Lena Cowen Orlin

Elizabeth I inherited the crown of England as the only remaining member of her immediate family. She would not have succeeded to the throne otherwise, given that family's particular history, her birth order, and her gender. After her death, Francis Bacon recalled that she had had "no helps to lean upon in her government, except such as she had herself provided; no own brother, no uncle, no kinsman of the royal family, to share her cares and support her authority." Her soli tary survival and her sex, in other words, seemed natural hazards to effective rule. This was a situation that her refusal to marry perpetu-ated and that her political practice compounded. For the latter, as Bacon continued, "even those whom she herself raised to honour she so kept in hand and mingled one with another, that while she infused into each the greatest solicitude to please her she was herself ever her own mistress."[1]

With this, Bacon approached the heart of the matter and of this essay: Elizabeth as "ever her own mistress." In effecting her mistressship, I argue, Elizabeth transformed natural hazards into a source of political strength. She exploited her very loss of parental and sibling relations rhetorically, by insinuating and manipulating fictional familial relationships. She remained the daughter of Henry VIII, but she also became wife to her kingdom, mother to her people, cousin to England's nobility, and sister to foreign princes. Most of these fictions were conventional; the meanings with which she freighted them often were not. Her tropic consanguinities adopted the characteristics of their familiar models, especially in their uneasy yoking of affect and hierarchy. Thus, Elizabeth used her familial tropes not only to express and exhort intimate emotion but also to evoke and impose the structures and obligations of the family, and, in turning both to her own political purposes, to remake patriarchal theory. In a final irony, I conclude, Elizabeth's familial rhetoric exposes a political conviction regarding what were in fact the transrelational responsibilities of royal office and the disassociations required by divine election to it.[2]

Underlying the argument is an essential and by no means unfamiliar recognition of the conceptual difficulties raised in the patriarchal society of sixteenth-century England by Elizabeth's coincident and seemingly oxymoronic sovereignty and gender. Elizabeth's legend is rich with complaints of her sex that were also challenges to her authority. Many anxieties predated her accession, like John Knox's insistence that "it is more than a monster in nature that a woman shall reign and have empire above man." But there were, further, the Bishop of Aquila's 1559 report to the Emperor Ferdinand that "Her Highness is after all a woman, influenced by insidious advice and very susceptible to passions"; Francis Knollys' 1568 protest against Elizabeth's desire to be herself "the ruler or half-ruler," overly independent of counsel; and laborer John Feltwell's seditious avowal of 1591 that "The Queen is but a woman and ruled by noblemen."[3] Aquila, Knollys, and Feltwell shared Bacon's implicit conviction of a woman ruler's incompleteness, her need for masculine "support" of her authority. (They differed, of course, on the extent to which Elizabeth observed that need.)

For her part, Elizabeth seems to have been content to exploit ambiguity. If the 1588 report from Tilbury is true, she stated then that, "I know I have the body but of a weak and feeble woman; but I have the heart and stomach of a king, and of a king of England too." Hers was an unusual variation on the medieval theory of the king's two bodies, a conspicuous subtext for the Tilbury formulation.[4] In her case the body natural, the weak and mortal body, was specifically female, but the body political was—or she would have it be, or the conventions of sovereignty would require her to have it be—male.

In fact, the uneasy concurrence of her gender and her sovereignty provoked a species of category confusion, for which a report of the Venetian ambassador to France may serve as a representative example. In 1582, Lorenzo Priuli wrote the Doge that Elizabeth had given a ring to the French Duke of Alençon, as if in pledge of marriage. As it became clear that the third of her sons would be disappointed in suit to the English queen, Queen Mother Catherine de Medici told Priuli that Elizabeth "may possibly excuse herself by saying that the ring meant nothing, for the engagement ring is given by the man to the woman, not by the woman to the man." Priuli then added his own editorial comment to the Doge: "Your Serenity sees in what a state of ambiguity their Majesties are."[5] The challenge hereby posed to gender boundaries was also a challenge to established ritual and traditional political meanings.

In the words of Christopher Haigh, the new queen "had to find an image of monarchy which was appropriate for a woman yet which invited obedience."[6] Available queenly precedent, the short tenure of Elizabeth's (married) sister, had provided an insufficient model for resolving the difficulties of "unsupported" female rule and for fixing female authority. In the present context, one which is concerned less with tracking the immediate political success of Elizabeth's strategies for sovereignty than with decoding the conceptual underpinnings of those strategies, Haigh's emphasis on the importance of an *image* for monarchy is particularly apt. In her search to create a female sovereignty, Elizabeth found many. She was Astrea, the English Deborah, Diana, Cynthia, Gloriana. The familial tropes—Elizabeth as daughter, wife, mother, cousin, and sister—were but one subset of her image-making arsenal.

Among the familial relations that Elizabeth evoked, only those regarding her paternity were not fictional. Still, some discussion of them is useful here to establish a baseline for the afterlife of domestic images, for how Elizabeth could deploy them, for how they took hold in the popular imagination, and for how the familial achieved political resonance. During her coronation procession, for example, the new queen smiled so pointedly as to be "demanded the cause." The cause, she replied, was a cry from the crowd: "Remember old King Henry the eighth." The incident was recorded for immediate national dissemination in the pamphlet report of *The Queen's Majesty's Passage*, where it was further commented that the smile showed Elizabeth to be "A natural child, which at the very remembrance of her father's name took so great a joy that all men may well think that as she rejoiced at his name whom this realm doth hold of so worthy memory: so in her doings she will resemble the same."[7]

She certainly exploited her physical resemblance to her father. Receiving visitors in the Privy Chamber at Whitehall, she stood under Henry VIII's portrait in Holbein's painting of the Tudors. And she maintained as a personal emblem, even when artificial means were required, the red hair that had come to seem a token of her ancestry. But Elizabeth was to proclaim resemblance in her "doings" as well as in appearance. Immediately in 1559, Elizabeth told Parliament that "we hope to rule, govern and keep this our realm in as good justice, peace and rest, in like wise as the king my father held you in." And she returned to the subject in 1566, again in a speech to Parliament: "though I be a woman I have as good a courage answerable to my place as ever my father had." This was the claim of blood that lent authority to the assertion that immediately followed: "I am your anointed Queen."[8]

She was widely acknowledged to be true heir to her father. In 1588, as the defeat of the Spanish Armada seemed to demonstrate that Elizabeth's courage was indeed answerable to the place she had inherited from Henry, James Aske wrote in *Elizabetha Triumphans* that "Although she be by Nature weak, / Because her sex no otherwise can be: / Yet wants she not the courage of her Sire, / Whose valor won this Island great renown." Far more remarkable than this propaganda piece, though, were the early patrilinear testimony of Philip II's envoy the Count of Feria and the later account of her own godson, John Harington. Feria reported that the English queen "seems to me incomparably more feared than her sister, and gives her orders and has her way as absolutely as her father did." Harington, striking a similar note, wrote after Elizabeth's death that "she could put forth such alterations, when obedience was lacking, as left no doubtings whose daughter she was."[9] It is yet another testimony to the gender "ambiguities" of Elizabeth's rule that Harington, who had no personal experience of Henry VIII, nonetheless like Feria constructed Elizabeth's ability to command in terms of her paternity, and thus maintained it as a masculine talent even while crediting it to this female ruler.

Meanwhile, in the first of her fictional relations, Elizabeth turned her maidenhood to political advantage. It is recorded that in a speech to Parliament on 10 February 1558, the new queen declared:

> ". . . now that the public care of governing the Kingdom is laid upon me, to draw upon me also the cares of marriage may seem a point of inconsiderate folly: yea, to satisfy you, I have already joined my self in marriage to an husband, namely, to the Kingdom of England. And behold," said she, "which I marvel ye have forgotten, the pledge of this my wedlock and marriage with my Kingdom," and therewith she drew the Ring from off her finger and showed it, wherewith at her Coronation she had in a set form of words solemnly given herself in marriage to her Kingdom.

Because record of the speech dates from the 1630s, Haigh cautions that this tale, like that of Tilbury, may be apocryphal. In fact, however, there survives independent confirmation that the marital association was made during Elizabeth's life, and in such similar terms that the posthumous record may be substantially accurate. In his 1584 pamphlet *A Watchword to England*, Anthony Munday called the queen "the husband of the commonweal, married to the Realm, and the same by ceremony of Ring as solemnly signified, as any other marriage." In a complaint to the lord mayor and sheriffs of London, he argued that "breach of this bond of sacred wedlock" could not be tolerated without great harm.[10]

Elizabeth's early use of the spousal trope is unsurprising and signifies as a local, mainly rhetorical strategy for dealing with parliamentary pressure to marry; her later inventions were more innovative. In 1596, notably, she declaimed that "Between Princes and their Subjects there is a most straight tie of affections. As chaste women ought not to cast their eye upon any other than their husbands, so neither ought subjects to cast their eyes upon any other Prince, than him whom God hath given them." Leah Marcus has pointed out that Elizabeth here positions herself as husband to her kingdom, not wife, in a characteristic exploitation of the ambiguities of her situation. It was one that *A Watchword to England*, perhaps among others, had anticipated.[11]

A further remembrance from John Harington, finally, both demonstrates the doubleness of Elizabeth's thinking with respect to her gender and sovereignty and links the issue, once again, to her authority:

> The Queen did once ask my wife in merry sort, "how she kept my good will and love, which I did always maintain to be truly good towards her and my children?" My Mall, in wise and discreet manner, told her Highness "she had confidence in her husband's understanding and courage, well founded on her own steadfastness not to offend or thwart, but to cherish and obey; hereby did she persuade her husband of her own affection, and in so doing did command his."—"Go to, go to, mistress," sayeth the Queen, "you are wisely bent I find: after such sort do I keep the good will of all my husbands, my good people; for if they did not rest assured of some special love toward them, they would not readily yield me such good obedience."[12]

While Harington's wife says that she as a good wife cherishes and obeys her husband and while Elizabeth claims a parallel, the sovereign in fact reorders the terms and redirects responses: as a wife she loves her people, but as good husbands her people obey her. The old commonplace that "love goeth downward; duty cometh upward" had implicitly borne a different gendering before Elizabeth adopted and adapted it.[13]

From the time of the parliamentary speech in which Elizabeth reportedly affirmed her marriage of the kingdom, she also constructed her fictional motherhood of its people. The maternal metaphor circulated widely among encomiasts and polemicists. In 1575, Edward Hake rhapsodized that the English people lived with "a loving Queen / who like a Mother reigns"; George Whetstone in 1587 referred to the "kind affection and motherly love" that she expressed toward London; William Averell in 1588 praised the queen who "hath till this time been a mother in England"; a public prayer of 1601 gave thanks for the "deliverance" of Elizabeth from traitors who "like unnatural children have rebelled against the Mother of their own times, that took them up from their cradles, and cherished them in her own bosom"; an "Epitaph upon the Renowned Queen Elizabeth" referred to her as "Women's glory, England's Mother."[14]

Elizabeth's own use of the maternal metaphor was daringly literal. While her sister had preceded her in deploying her gender to this strategic end, Mary spoke in analogies and conditionals: "Certainly," Henry's first daughter had said, "if a prince and governor may as naturally and earnestly love her subjects as the mother doth love the child, then assure yourselves that I, being your lady and mistress, do as earnestly and tenderly love and favour you." In sharp distinction, Elizabeth flatly told Parliament in 1558 that "every one of you, and every Englishman besides, are my children and relations." She added in 1563 that "I assure you all that though after my death you may have many stepdames, yet shall you never have any, a more natural mother, than I mean to be unto you all."[15]

The word "natural" is so depreciated in our modern vocabulary that the force of its reference to divine constitution may be obscured to us. To recover it, compare the Biblical foundation for patriarchal philosophy: "kings shall be thy foster fathers, and Queens they nursing mothers."[16] That is, political patriarchalism originated in an analogy nuanced by the implications of surrogacy conveyed by "foster" and "nursing." Elizabeth, in stark contrast, claimed authenticity. The mark that she left upon tradition can be tracked through many texts.

In 1581, Thomas Bentley referred to her as "natural mother and noble nurse" of the Church of England; seven years later Aske lamented the Babington plotters, "unnatural sons / Who seek to ruin her their mother dear" as well as to "slay their careful Nurse"; Averell called Elizabeth not only "a diligent nurse" but also "a loving mother." In an urgent plea that she name a successor, Peter Wentworth flattered Elizabeth by integrating her distinction of choice: while by marrying a foreigner Mary Tudor would "have had this Island to have become a dwelling for strangers: much like unto an unnatural nurse," he said, Elizabeth had maintained England "in peace and prosperity, most like unto a natural nursing mother, for the use of the ancient inhabitants thereof." Again, the most direct testimony was that of Harington, who wrote his wife late in 1602 that "Our dear Queen, my royal godmother, and this state's natural mother, doth now bear show of human infirmity."[17] His reference to the queen as suffering the effects of her age once again puts in play the unmistakable antipodes of the sovereign's two bodies, the royal (or politic) and the human. The further associations are casual but conspicuous: Harington suggestively identifies Elizabeth's body politic (as distinct from her infirm body human) with a national motherhood.

Elizabeth was rewriting political theory. The full flowering of patriarchalism is usually associated with her Stuart successor. In the sixteenth century, the patriarchal metaphor for kingship had been used either by the king, to profess his fatherly care for his people, or to the king, to remind him of the care incumbent upon him. Wentworth offered an example of the latter sort, as he turned tradition to a familiar purpose in declaring that the "names and titles" of foster fathers and nursing mothers "are given you, to teach you your duties, and what you ought to be towards the people committed unto your charge." With James, however, the metaphor was adapted to the new end of demanding from the people the obedience owed by a child to its father. In other words, the seventeenth century developed a patriarchal theory of comprehensive political obligation.[18] That which has gone unnoticed in histories of political theory, though, is that early intimations of the parental metaphor as a resource for monarchic authority are very much present in Elizabeth's rhetoric. She professes her parental care for her people, true, but she also uses the maternal metaphor to make demands of her people—even if only, as in her first use of the analogy, to ask that the people not make demands of marriage and childbirth upon her. By 1569, however, she made the terms more explicit:

> First, we [desire] all persons to understand, that of our own natural disposition, through God's goodness, we have been always desirous to have the obedience of all our subjects of all sorts, both high and low, by love and not by compulsion, by their own yielding and not by our exacting, allowing that which was well said by a wise prince of the Greeks: "That king to be in most surety that so ruled over his subjects as a father over the children."

This was from a speech summarizing "the Queen's Proceedings since her Reign," which Elizabeth ordered to be read in parish churches throughout the nation.[19]

It will not have gone unnoticed that in the passage last cited, just as she had earlier become husband rather than wife, Elizabeth here became father rather than mother. These were rhetorical strategies that capitalized upon the ambiguities of her position but that would not have obscured her essential gender. Nor would she have wanted them to; she relied upon her sex in order, as Marcus has put it, "[to tap] into the emotional power behind the images of wife and mother."[20] An ecclesiastical petition of 1588 affords a glimpse of the contemporary sense of the gender distinctions: it describes "a Father, to beget us with the immortal seed of the word" and "a Mother, to nourish us up in the same." The primary associations with the maternal were with mercy, care, and nurture. Elizabeth herself stated in a letter to her ambassador in France that "it is a natural virtue incident to our sex to be pitiful of those that are afflicted."[21] She imported these feminine attributes into the masculine roles mandated by sovereignty and by this means advanced a patriarchal theory of obligation cloaked in the traditional gentleness of her gender.

In other words, emotive power was far from an end in itself; the end was Elizabeth's authority. More direct in its appeal to simple emotion than either her figuration as wife or mother (but in a sense an extension of both) was her self-representation as her people's beloved. Even in this relation, however, affect was linked to obedience. J. E. Neale describes *The Queen's Majesty's Passage* as a "picture of Queen and citizens courting one another," and the pamphlet reports that "The people again were wonderfully ravished with the loving answers and the gestures of their princess." But it also concludes that Elizabeth's London welcome "argue[d] a wonderful earnest love of *most obedient subjects* toward their sovereign" [emphasis added]. Harington, to whom I once again turn for a last word, may have exaggerated their effect but nonetheless saw clearly the aim toward which these sentiments were directed:

> Her speech did win all affections, and her subjects did try to show all love to her commands; for she would say, "her state did require her to command, what she knew her people would willingly do from their own love to her." Herein did she show her wisdom fully: for who did choose to lose her confidence, or who would withhold a show of love and obedience, when their Sovereign said it was their own choice, and not her compulsion? Surely she did play well her tables to gain obedience thus without constraint.[22]

Love and obedience are conjoined—and enjoined—with peculiar intensity in the family, and the family was manifestly the model for Elizabeth's relational politics with her people.

The affect that Elizabeth fostered in her nobility, meanwhile, was anchored in yet another familial fiction, the aim of which was not to engender obedience, per se, but rather a supra-familial loyalty. The fiction was again a conventional one, that her lords were her "dear cousins" (as she saluted them in correspondence) or "Cousin mine" (as she varied the formula for the first earl of Essex). In a letter to George Talbot, Earl of Shrewsbury, and his wife, Bess of Hardwick, we see how the trope could be extended—"Being given to understand from our cousin, the Earl of Leicester how honourably he was lately received and used by you, our cousin the Countess at Chatsworth . . ."—until all was spun into a single great consanguine circle centered on the sovereign. Elizabeth observed the rituals of kinship: she provided her courtiers with London residences, received them into the Privy Chamber for games and dancing, gave and accepted New Year's gifts, attended their weddings, negotiated some nuptials, served as godmother to noble children.[23]

But her understanding of her kinships went beyond convention and imitated, even challenged natural affiliation, as her unusual kindnesses to her "cousins" demonstrated. Shortly before his death, Burghley marvelled to his son that "Though [the queen] will not be a mother, yet she showeth herself by feeding me with her own princely hand, as a careful nurse." Harington wrote feelingly to his wife in December 1602 of Elizabeth's "goodness" to him even before his birth (through her "affection" to his mother, a waiting woman, and her generosity to his father) and thereafter of her "watchings over my youth, her liking to my free speech, and admiration of my little learning and poesy, which I did so much cultivate on her command." She had news of the death of the earl of Huntingdon suppressed so that she could deliver it to his wife personally; she did the same for Margaret Ratcliffe at the loss of her brother.[24]

The language in which Elizabeth phrased her care for her courtiers was marked by the very emotive extremity through which she had converted her conventional nursing motherhood of the people of England into a radical natural motherhood. Learning that her ambassador to France, Sir Henry Unton, was sick with an ague, she wrote him "wishing you to have care of your own health, which we desire as much to hear of as any friend you have, excepting your own wife." When Sir John Norris died in the queen's service in Ireland, Elizabeth wrote to his mother that "nature can have stirred no more dolorous affection in you as a mother for a dear son, than gratefulness and memory of his services past hath wrought in us, his Sovereign, apprehension of our miss of so worthy a servant."[25] She claimed preeminence in emotion as in rule, and in this way emotion was a tool of her rule.

It was characteristic, then, that Elizabeth also turned to political purpose her membership in the figurative family of European sovereigns. This was a conventional fiction, too. By means of a sibling trope Elizabeth was initiated into the ancient fellowship of monarchs, and she readily adopted the reciprocal custom of terming herself "sister" to foreign princes: to successive Roman Emperors Ferdinand and Maximilian; to a series of rulers in France, including Catherine de Medici, Charles IX, Henry III, and Henry IV; to Mary of Scotland, her son James VI, and his wife Anna of Denmark. By tradition Elizabeth addressed James, Henry III, and Henry IV in letters as "Right dear Brother," "dearest Brother," or "my beloved Brother" and signed herself "Your very affectionate sister" or "Your most affectionate sister and cousin." In public proclamations James was "the King of Scots, her good brother" or "our good brother the King of Scots," and Henry IV was "her good brother and confederate." Just how formulaic the usage could be is revealed in an autograph draft of a letter from James to Elizabeth: he closes, "oblige me to be, as of before I was, your most lov . . ."; the copy sent to the queen was completed by a scribe, "your most loving and dearest brother."[26]

While she was often content to address her state correspondence with similar inattention, on other occasions Elizabeth willed ritual designations to signify afresh. In the business of princes, diplomatic details were often left to ambassadors and royal representatives to negotiate. Direct correspondence could thus be a matter of large reassurances, of professions of noble intent, of expressions of good will, and of reminders of the bond of sovereignty (whether disingenuous or not). The rhetoric of kinship inscribed and reinscribed the message that sovereigns shared certain self-legitimating interests that superceded local and parochial concerns, and Elizabeth recognized its utility for immediate political purposes. Early on, in 1567, she wrote Maximilian as "from the heart of a woman who esteems Your Majesty as a brother, honours you as her best friend, is imbued with the greatest reverence for the House of Austria, and entertains supreme respect for Your Majesty's person," signing herself "Your Majesty's most affectionate sister and cousin."[27] In the same year, Elizabeth extended the fiction of kinship to Mary Stuart, protesting that she was Mary's "good neighbour, a dear sister and a faithful friend, and so shall you undoubtedly always find and prove us to be indeed." A year later, she wrote Mary as "one Prince and near cousin regarding another" and "in terms of friendship require[d] and charge[d her] not to forbear from answering."[28]

For Elizabeth, the trope of royal kinship carried the burden of exhorting affect; when dissatisfied, however, she threatened to disown custom. Thus, on the one hand, in 1594 she addressed James: "Dear Brother, use such a friend, therefore, as she is worthy, and give her ever cause to remain such a one as her affection hath ever merited." Similarly, in a letter scribed by her secretary to Anna of Denmark in 1596, she added emotive urgency with a note in her own hand: "Sister, I beseech you let a few of your own lines satisfy me." But then again, on the other hand, in 1584 she signed herself the "loving sister and cousin" of James only "*if* so well your merits shall require" (emphasis added). In 1598, when James's remarks to his Parliament had offended her, she termed herself "Your more readier Sister than yourself hath done, for that is fit."[29]

In fact, Elizabeth's occasional purposive neglect of the sibling trope indicates most persuasively of all the principle with which she employed it. By 1563, Elizabeth had initiated a correspondence with Catherine de Medici, Queen Mother and regent of France, in which she called Catherine her "good Sister"; by 1570, though, while Catherine continued her "good Sister," Catherine's son Charles became simultaneously Elizabeth's "good Brother"; by 1572, in letters to her French ambassadors, even as Charles continued the "good Brother," Catherine became merely "the king's mother," deprived of the sisterly affectation. Francis Bacon's *Memoriam* places the practice in the context of

Elizabeth's world view and of her own self-identification as one in the small family of late-sixteenth-century monarchs:

> And speaking of her morality, I remember a circumstance in point. Having ordered a letter to be written to her ambassador concerning a message which was to be given separately to the Queen Mother of the Valois, and finding that her secretary had inserted a clause directing the ambassador to say to the Queen Mother by way of compliment, that they were two Queens from whom though women no less was expected in administration of affairs and in the virtue and arts of government than from the greatest men,—she would not endure the comparison, but ordered it to be struck out; saying that the arts and principles which she employed in governing were of a far other sort than those of the Queen Mother.[30]

The St. Bartholomew's Day massacre was undoubtedly responsible for the heat of Elizabeth's response, but at the heart of it was also her recognition that Catherine's de facto rule—and thus her sisterhood—had ceased with the majority, marriage, and regnal determination of her son. The force of the sibling trope was its implication of parity in sovereignty.

For all this, Elizabeth could return to the trope when it suited her own purposes of rhetorical expediency—as it did on July 1584, when Charles IX had been succeeded by Henry III. In a letter to Catherine then, written at the news of Anjou's death, Elizabeth as was now customary referred to Henry as her "good brother," assured Catherine and Henry that they would find Elizabeth "the faithfullest daughter and sister that ever Princes had," concluded that to Catherine she would be as faithful "as if I were your natural daughter," and finally and immediately thereafter signed herself "Your very affectionate sister and cousin"—letting pass, in other words, no graceful (if biologically perplexing) protest of kinship.[31]

This flexibility of the sibling trope, its susceptibility to the pressure of topical political intent, had been similarly demonstrated with respect to Mary Stuart. Some three years after Mary's abdication, already styling herself James's "sister," Elizabeth had nonetheless persisted in protesting (although, admittedly, in the muted form of metaphor rather than simile and in past tense rather than present) "my natural inclination towards you, with whom I desired to live as a neighbour and a good sister." Later, however, publicly denying a petition for Mary's execution, Elizabeth argued that Mary "[first] dif-fers not from me in sex, [second, is] one of like quality and degree, [and, third, is] one of the same race and stock and so nearly related to me in blood"; she did not, in this instance (fourth), insist that Mary was a fellow prince, nor did she even imply the fact by naming Mary a sister.[32] This was a telling divergence from her regular practice, and it suggests that she mooted her public defense of Mary in some rec-ognition of its long-term futility.

The outcome for Mary provoked one of the most exaggerated examples of Elizabeth's many claims to emotional precedence. Her letter to James on the subject addressed her grief for the death of his mother, not his grief: "My dear Brother, I would you knew (though not felt) the extreme dolor that overwhelms my mind, for that miser-able accident"—that is, Mary's execution at English hands—"which (far contrary to my meaning) hath befallen. . . . for your part, think you have not in the world a more loving kinswoman, nor a more dear friend than myself. . . . [Signed] Your most assured loving sister and cousin." Elizabeth pled the intimacy of the fictional connection of a fellow sovereign as superceding even his natural connection with his birth mother. (And she seems to have known her audience. James wrote to Leicester: "How fond and inconstant I were if I should prefer my mother to the title."[33])

Elizabeth's willingness to exploit the rhetoric of conventional royal relations, to manipulate and reconfigure it to her own political ends, can seem cynical to our eyes. But, as her abandonment of that rhetoric with regard to Catherine de Medici and Mary Stuart suggests, she honored its moral imperative, as well. Certainly, Elizabeth's long resis-tance to the execution of Mary confirms her to have been a subscriber to the mystical fiction of royal kinship, and her familial stylings were never so formulaic that they lost the deeper significances of a divine-right political philosophy. A letter of 1593 to Henry IV reveals how easily the two instincts to reinvent and to respect the familial fiction could coexist. There, Elizabeth responded to the news of Henry's con-version to Catholicism:

> And where you promise me all friendship and faith, I confess that I have dearly merited it, and of that I shall not repent, provided that you will not change your father: otherwise I shall be to you but a bastard sister, or at least not of the same father. For I shall prefer always the natural to the adopted, as God best knows, Who guides you to the right way of the best

feeling. [Signed,] Your very assured sister, if it be after the old manner; with the new, I have nothing to do.[34]

With this, as had been the case with her declaration that she was England's "anointed queen," Elizabeth offered a glimpse of her own conviction of the proximity of divinity and monarchy.

If we remain tempted to dismiss Elizabeth's familial fictions as rhetorical affectations or—perhaps more invidiously—as psychological strategies for negotiating her peculiar isolation, the particular case of her correspondence with James VI of Scotland is a corrective. Her battle with him for control of the familial tropes makes clear how heavily they were invested with political meaning. Mary's son was by convention Elizabeth's "brother." But others of Elizabeth's familial roles were implicated in her complex exchanges with him, too, including the natural one of blood (by which he was a cousin at some removes), and also a variation on the fictional one of her maternity (because he was to be her successor). In this instance, in an extended struggle between the two of them for dominance, the familial tropes were an arena of contestation.

In June 1585, James wrote to thank Elizabeth extravagantly for the present of some horses and for her own epistolary protests of affection and allegiance. He adopted the language of Ciceronian friendship: the gifts seemed rather "to have proceeded from some *alter ego* than from any strange and foreign prince." And he imagined offering in requital "my person, and all that is mine, to be used and employed by you as a loving mother would use her natural and devoted child." The letter had opened as was customary, to "Madame and dearest sister," but the heightened rhetoric inspired him to revise the address near the letter's end, to "madame and dearest mother." He signed himself "Your most loving and devoted brother and son." From the correspondence with Catherine de Medici we know how Elizabeth felt about queen mothers. She returned a letter in which, unmoved, she addressed him as "Right dear brother" and "*mon bon frère le roi d'Écosse*"; she signed herself "Your very assured loving sister and cousin."[35]

She continued to resist his maternalizing advances throughout the summer, as he inscribed her "madame and mother" and termed himself "Your most loving and devoted brother and son." Then, in August, James went so far as to "pray" her "to continue still" with a title she had never accepted, that of "my loving mother," adding that he would "be your devoted son." With this, Elizabeth lost patience. In her own hand she addressed her "Right dear brother," signed herself "Your true assured cousin and sister," and then added a postscript on the subject of Scotland's treacherous Catholic earls: "Fear not, for your life must be theirs, or else they shall smart well, every mother's son of them." A modern editor calls this an "especially curious" postscript, and so it seems when detached from its context. In effect, however, Elizabeth restored the language of motherhood to the literal, removed it from figurative circulation, and refused to be implicated herself in James's tropic trespasses. Her message was sufficiently sharp that in December James wrote to "madam and dearest sister" and called himself "Your truest and assured brother and cousin," and he did not vary the salutation again.[36]

As long as the line of direct address was properly and formally maintained at the open and close of each epistle, as the unfixed foundation for their relational politics, Elizabeth was thereafter willing to engage in speculative analogy in the body of her letters. In March of 1586, she danced closer to the maternal metaphor herself. "Only natural affection *ab incunabulis*"—from the cradle—"stirred me to save you from the murderers of your father," she wrote. James was himself willing to dance to Elizabeth's tune. After the death of his natural mother, he observed the preferred formula by greeting Elizabeth as his sister and calling himself her brother, and when he tried to embellish his address of her he took care to add the stutter-step of metaphor: "I promise to behave myself, not as a stranger and foreign prince, but as your natural son and compatriot of your country." Thereafter, Elizabeth set the pace. In 1592, she proclaimed "The dear care, my dear brother, that ever I carried, from your infancy of your prosperous estate and quiet." In 1593, still insisting on their sibling parity as sovereigns, she nonetheless grew more explicit in maternal allusion: "You know, my dear brother, that since you first breathed, I regarded always to conserve it as my womb it had been you bare." That same year, James thanked Elizabeth for her "motherly care in all my ados," and in 1594, when Elizabeth stood godmother (by proxy) to James's son Henry, he wrote that "as it hath been your fortune to be godmother both to me and my son, so ye will be a good mother to us both."[37]

Elizabeth may have insisted that her overriding relationship with James was that of brother and sister, but she unequivocally saw herself as the older sister, and she aggressively adopted the related roles of tutor and mentor. She felt free to write the Scottish monarch that "The weight of a kingly state is of more poise than the shallowness of a rash young man's head can weigh." In fact, James may have initiated his ill-fated maternal designations as much in thinly disguised resentment of her continual "advice" as in half-playful quest of recognition as her heir. He did not suffer gladly such remarks as the following from late 1593 or early 1594: "But be you persuaded by sisters. I will advise you, void of all guile, and will not stick to tell you, that if you tread the path you choose, I will pray for you, but leave you to your harms." And she erupted, "Lord! what wonder grew in me, that you should correct [the Catholic earls] with benefits, who deserve much severer correction. . . . For your own sake play the king, and let your subjects see you respect yourself, and neither to hide or to suffer danger and dishonour."[38]

Elizabeth's chastisements may also explain the edge with which, about half a year later, James made pointed reference to the inferior gender that never ceased to threaten her command: "I ever bear that reverence to all virtuous ladies, but above all to you." In 1598 he was patronizing: "it becomes me not to strive with a lady." True, in 1602 he came to call the aged Elizabeth his "only oracle," saying that "upon [her] advice only" would he "ground [his] behavior," but by then it is clear that he considered her no longer a worthy epistolary adversary. For the first time he lavished upon her such transparently sycophantic addresses as "so wise a prince and trusty a friend," "so noble, so wise, and so faithful a friend," and a "right excellent right high and mighty princess."[39] Time was on his side.

There remains one last observation to gather from Elizabeth's tutelage of James, and it has to do with the event that first snapped any pretense of restraint in her counsel. For all her long fretting over his indulgence of the Catholic lords, the flash point was not a public action on his part, notably enough, but a private one. In September 1589, she congratulated James on his upcoming marriage to Anna of Denmark; characteristically, Elizabeth claimed emotional precedence in writing that no one longed more than she "to see the performance of such alliance."[40] But the performance was delayed when Anna encountered rough winds en route from Denmark and was obliged to shelter in a remote harbor in Norway. In a fine show of chivalry, James set sail to intercept her and himself bring her to Scotland.

For Elizabeth, this was an "untimely and, if I dare tell truth, evil-seasoned journey," because he left Scotland in the hands of the treasonous earls: "Accept my hourly care for your broken country, too, too much infected with the malady of strangers' humors. . . . Good Lord! who but yourself would have left such people to be able to do you wrong." She could not resist urging him to "hie your return," even though she well knew that she went further than was diplomatic: "My dear brother, you see how far my entire care draws me out of the limits that another's affairs should pluck me to, but all such error I hope you will impute to affection."[41] Clearly, it was not affection that moved her but a raging impatience with James's inaptness as her pupil, what she saw as his political ineptitude and inattention. As always for Elizabeth, the private had political implications.

In a second letter written during his absence, she expostulated without further apology: "For God's sake and your own surety, look better to your kingdom than you have done." She advised that his "home causes" needed "a king's eye." When James finally returned in May 1590, she wrote that "no one that liveth thanks God more devoutly for all your escapes, nor is more joyful of your sure arrival than myself" but then quickly returned to the business of cautioning him about the state of Scottish affairs. In a patent reference to the likely distractions of his new marriage, she warned that "If any respect whatever make you neglect so expedient a work" as acting against opponents, "I am afraid your careless hide will work your unlooked danger."[42]

It would seem that Elizabeth had long before calculated that the tensions between state interests and domestic pursuits were irreconcilable, for she had strictly sorted her own priorities in such matters. Three days after Mary Tudor died, Elizabeth told Mary's counselors that while "the law of nature moves me to sorrow for my sister," human emotion could not be expected to be her presiding sentiment. She now knew herself to be "God's creature ordained to obey His appointment," and she "desir[ed] from the bottom of my heart that I may have assistance of His grace to be the minister of His heavenly will in this office now committed to me." Similarly, in 1561 she told an envoy of Mary Stuart that "as examples show, princes cannot even love their children who are to succeed them."[43]

In 1564, more to the point of her message for James, she reportedly said to envoy Ahasverus Allinga that "I am too much burdened with cares to turn my attention to marriage; for Love is usually the offspring of leisure, and as I am so beset by duties, I have not been able to think of Love."[44] By her lights, James had behaved appropriately with regard to his mother, but he had betrayed the model she set him by privileging marriage over duty at a critical moment. Allison Heisch, too, has remarked the astonishing consistency of Elizabeth's written record: Elizabeth's speeches, letters, and conversations over the course of her long career testify to the obsession she wished upon James, an unrelenting preoccupation with the responsibilities of office.

As early as 1558, the new queen asked the members of Parliament "to be assistant to me, that I with my Ruling and you with your Service may make a good accompt to Almighty God." This was a statement of sovereign intent that Parliament was incapable of reading, Heisch suggests, because it was "blinded by its own [gender] assumptions." Elizabeth knew this blindness for what it was, for she also told the Commons that she refused "to frame my will to your fantasy."[45] The fact was that by the accident of her gender her will was awarded less regard than was true for male monarchs, and their fantasies were lent more license than was usual. Nonetheless, Elizabeth herself, ever her own mistress, remained convinced that hers was the will, or the access to God's will, while theirs were the fantasies: the gynephobia, the misogyny, and the misapprehensions that were products of these superstitions. Most of the histories and anecdotes by which we now know Elizabeth even today are similarly tinged by the fantastical, by the masculinist perspective that has constructed the reporters and their reports. To redirect this perspective in some degree has been one ambition of this essay.

In a revealing moment, Elizabeth declared that "I have had good experience of this world; I have known what it is to be a subject, and I now know what it is to be a sovereign." She spoke often of the years when she had been a private citizen, when her ascent to the throne seemed uncertain, when she had been imprisoned by her sister. Directed inward, these references were her constant reminders of the lessons of those years; Elizabeth's time as a subject provided her with a set of familial models by which she ordered her experience, established relationships with those around her, and developed a pattern for her own anomalous role.[46] The family lent her a universal language of entitlement, affect, and obligation by which she was able to articulate her demands of her countrymen as well as of herself. Directed outward, however, remembrances of her turbulent private history tended not to humanize her (as is the case with twentieth-century political figures) but to emphasize the great gulf between that private life and the public role she assumed by divine election.

In Elizabethan England there were many fictions of the family. These had to do with ideal household constitutions, with the household as a model for political government, with rigorous internal hierarchies, with the absolute authority of the householder, with the gendered division of domestic duties. Elizabeth's administration necessarily subscribed to these fictions and promulgated them, as ideologies fundamental to the precarious early modern social order. The irony is that for Elizabeth, it would seem, families themselves were fictions. For all her skill in decoding and deploying familial rhetoric, structures, and significances, at base she believed that monarchs had no families in the regular sense of the term—no natural families. Or, more precisely, sovereigns could not permit themselves the luxury of a regular domestic life. Perhaps, in fact, in this apprehension lay the source of her rhetorical ingenuity.

The fictionality of the family, for her, was not merely a function of her own lack of kinsmen. It went deeper than circumstance and was a matter of her conviction that the monarch was required to cast off the natural family and inhabit fully the available metaphoric families. Elizabeth's long practice of claiming emotional precedence with her people and fellow rulers was one symptom of her transcendence of the natural and one mark of her political self-definition. In Oxford in 1592, when she overtly proclaimed that she surpassed relation, Elizabeth told adoring students that "Your love for me is of such a kind as has never been known or heard of in the memory of man. Love of this nature is not possessed by parents, it happens not among friends, no, not even among lovers." It was peculiarly owing to her, and the students' "services," she continued, "are of such kind that I think they would be eternal, if only I were eternal."[47] Her personal life as she and others chose to construct it may have been full of emotional privation—no husband, no own brother, no uncle, no kinsman, no helps—but here, in her public life, we come upon the sign of an occasional ecstasy.

Notes

An earlier version of this paper was presented in a seminar chaired by Richard C. McCoy at the 1991 International Shakespeare Congress in Tokyo and in a 1991 session arranged by Catherine Belsey for the Centre for Critical and Cultural Theory at the University of Wales College of Cardiff. I am grateful to those who read or heard and commented upon it on those occasions. This revision was guided by the very helpful readings of Constance Jordan, Annabel Patterson, Jenny Wormald, and, most especially, Carole Levin.

1. Francis Bacon, "In Felicem Memoriam Elizabethae Angliae Reginae," translated as "On the Fortunate Memory of Elizabeth Queen of England," in

The Works of Francis Bacon, ed. James Spedding, Robert Leslie Ellis, and Douglas Denon Heath, vol. 6 (London: Longman, 1858), p. 310. So many defining perspectives on Elizabeth—even those we call "contemporary"—are belated ones, written after 1603 and serving the political agendas of later years and subsequent reigns. Bacon's tribute is a reminiscence; so are Camden's 1617 *History of the Most Renowned and Victorious Princess Elizabeth* and John Harington's 1606 letter, both of which I cite later. There survives as well a small library of commemorative pamphlets issued at her death. While I consult all of these, my principal sources are Elizabeth's speeches, reported conversations, and especially letters. I follow the revisionist model established by Allison Heisch in her splendid "Queen Elizabeth I: Parliamentary Rhetoric and the Exercise of Power," *Signs,* 1, No. 1 (1975): 31–55.

2. Christopher Haigh, in his useful *Elizabeth I* (Profiles in Power, gen. ed. Keith Robbins [London: Longman, 1988]), has preceded me in itemizing Elizabeth's familial definitions, though to the rather different end of describing her permutations on "typically feminine" roles: "Elizabeth presented herself in female roles which were elevated far above those of other women. She was not just a virgin, but a virgin of Mary-like significance; not just a wife, but the wife of the realm; not just a mother, but the mother of the English people and the English Church" (p. 20). Important work in this area has also been contributed by Leah Marcus. See especially "Shakespeare's Comic Heroines, Elizabeth I, and the Political Uses of Androgyny" in *Women in the Middle Ages and the Renaissance,* ed. Mary Beth Rose (Syracuse: Syracuse University Press, 1986), pp. 135–53; and chapter 2, "Elizabeth," in *Puzzling Shakespeare: Local Reading and its Discontents* (Berkeley: University of California Press, 1988), pp. 51–105.

3. John Knox, *The First Blast of the Trumpet Against the Monstrous Regiment of Women* (1558) in *The Political Writings of John Knox,* ed. Marvin A. Breslow (Washington: Folger Books, 1985), p. 38. Bishop of Aquila to Emperor Ferdinand, 3 October 1559, reprinted in *Queen Elizabeth and Some Foreigners: Being a series of hitherto unpublished letters from the archives of the Hapsburg family,* ed. Victor von Klarwill (London: The Bodley Head, 1928), p. 133. Francis Knollys cited by J. E. Neale, *Queen Elizabeth* (London: Jonathan Cape, 1934), p. 178. John Feltwell cited by F. G. Emmison, *Elizabethan Life: Disorder* (Chelmsford: Essex County Council, 1970), p. 57.

4. *The Public Speaking of Queen Elizabeth: Selections from her Official Addresses,* ed. George P. Rice, Jr. (New York: Columbia University Press, 1951), p. 96 (hereafter cited *Public Speaking*). See also Ernst H. Kantorowicz, *The King's Two Bodies: A Study in Medieval Political Theology* (Princeton: Princeton University Press, 1957), and Marie Axton, *The Queen's Two Bodies: Drama and the Elizabethan Succession* (London: Royal Historical Society, 1977).

5. *Calendar of State Papers, Venetian 1581–91,* ed. Horatio F. Brown, No. 63 (11 January 1582), p. 27.

6. Haigh, *Elizabeth I*, p. 172.

7. *The Quenes Maiesties Passage through the Citie of London to Westminster the Day before her Coronacion* (1558), ed. James M. Osborn, with intro. by J. E. Neale (New Haven: Yale University Press, 1960), sig. E3^r. Here as throughout I have modernized spelling and punctuation.

8. For the Holbein in the Privy Chamber and the speech in 1559, see Haigh, *Elizabeth I*, p. 21. For the speech of 1566, see Rice, *Public Speaking*, p. 81. Elizabeth also used her descent to establish a relationship with foreign princes. To the Emperor Ferdinand, for example, she wrote on 26 November 1558 that "We pledge Our royal word that we shall remain of the same mind and affection as Our well-beloved father"—as also of Edward VI and Mary I (Klarwill, *Queen Elizabeth and Some Foreigners*, p. 26).

9. James Aske, *Elizabetha Triumphans* (London: 1588), sig. B1^v. Haigh notes that Elizabeth also claimed the courage of her father when speaking to an envoy of the Spanish Netherlands in 1576 (*Elizabeth I*, p. 21). Feria cited by Neale, *Queen Elizabeth*, p. 75. John Harington to Robert Markham, 1606, in *The Letters and Epigrams of Sir John Harington*, ed. Norman Egbert McClure (Philadelphia: University of Pennsylvania Press, 1930), p. 122.

10. This story is best known from Camden's 1617 *History*. To demonstrate the wide currency of the story, I've quoted a less familiar version from an anonymous pamphlet of 1639, *The Life and Death of Queen Elizabeth* (sigs. C3^v–C4^r). Haigh, like most of us, does want to believe the story is true (*Elizabeth I*, p. 20). See Anthony Munday, *A Watchword to England to Beware of Traitors* (London: 1584), sig. A3^r. In 1603, Elizabeth's coronation ring had to be sawn off (Neale, *Queen Elizabeth*, pp. 389–90).

11. Elizabeth cited by Marcus, "Shakespeare's Comic Heroines," pp. 141–42.

12. Harington, "Brief Notes and Remembrances," in *Nugae Antiquae: Being a miscellaneous collection of original papers in prose and verse written during the reigns of Henry VIII, Edward VI, Queen Mary, Elizabeth, and King James*, ed. Henry Harington, vol. 1 (London: Vernor and Hood, 1804), pp. 177–78.

13. I cite Thomas Gataker, *Marriage Duties* (London: 1620), sig. B3^r, but see also proverb no. L535 in Morris Palmer Tilley, *A Dictionary of Proverbs in England in the Sixteenth and Seventeenth Centuries* (Ann Arbor: University of Michigan Press, 1950): "Natural love descends but it does not ascend."

14. Edward Hake, *A Commemoration of the Most Prosperous Reign of our Sovereign Elizabeth* (London: 1575), sig. A7^v. George Whetstone, *The Censure of a Loyal Subject, upon those Traitors* (London: 1587), sig. B1^r. William Averell, *A Marvelous Combat of Contrarities* (London: 1588), sig. F2^v. Prayer excerpted by G. B. Harrison in *A Last Elizabethan Journal* (London: Constable, 1933), p. 153, from *Certain Prayers Fit for the Time* (1600). *The Life and Death of Queen Elizabeth*, sig. C8^r.

15. Mary quoted by Anthony Fletcher, *Tudor Rebellions*, Seminar Studies in History, 3d ed. (London: Longman, 1983), p. 74. For Elizabeth in 1558, see "Second Version of the Speech Concerning the Queen's Marriage," reported by Camden and excerpted in translation from the Latin in Rice, *Public Speaking*, p. 117. For her speech of 1563, see Heisch, "Queen Elizabeth I," p. 54. The maternal trope entered Elizabeth's personal prayers, according to a report of 1579: "Preserve then the mother and the children, whom thou hast given to her, so shall we serve thee yet better for the good of thy poor Church" (cited by Haigh, *Elizabeth I*, p. 20).

16. Thomas Bilson cites the Biblical passage prominently in *The True Difference between Christian Subjection and Unchristian Rebellion* (London: 1585), sig. L2^r.

17. Bentley cited by Haigh, *Elizabeth I*, p. 156. Aske, *Elizabetha Triumphans*, sig. C2^v. Averell, *Marvelous Combat*, sig. E3^r. Peter Wentworth, *A Pithy Exhortation to her Majesty for Establishing her Successor* (London: 1598), sigs. F6^{r-v}. Harington to Lady Mary Harington, 27 December 1602, in Harington, *Letters and Epigrams*, p. 96.

18. Wentworth, *A Pithy Exhortation*, sig. B3^v. See also Bilson: "If private men be bound to train up their families in the fear of God and love of virtue, much more are Princes (the public fathers of their countries and exalted to far greater and higher authority by God's ordinance than fathers or masters)" (*True Difference*, sig. S5^r). On patriarchalism and political obligation, see Gordon J. Schochet, *Patriarchalism in Political Thought* (New York: Basic Books, 1975).

19. Rice, *Public Speaking*, p. 127; see also p. 125. Haigh points out that wide distribution of Elizabeth's speeches was common from 1585: "Her carefully rehearsed rhetoric was not to be wasted" (*Elizabeth I*, p. 120).

20. Marcus, *Puzzling Shakespeare*, p. 53. See also p. 57: "The formula 'The Queen our sovereign Lady' lingered on in contexts for which an evocation of her feminine nature was particularly appropriate: during a plague, when the measures she took assumed the aura of maternal concern for her stricken people, or in famine, in connection with feeding the hungry." Elsewhere, however, Marcus repeats the story of a carter whose work for the queen was three times delayed, until he cried, "Now I see that the Queen is a woman as well as my wife." Marcus concludes: "The remark is brief but revealing: like others among her subjects, he had been doubtful whether she was female or not" (p. 59). This seems to me to be overreading a joke about "female" unpunctuality; its sense is not that the carter is surprised that she is a woman but that he jests that she is *but* a woman.

21. *An Humble Petition of the Community to their Most Renowned Soveraign* (London: 1588), sigs. C8^v–D1^r. Elizabeth to Dr. Valentine Dale, 3 February 1574,

in *The Letters of Queen Elizabeth I*, ed. G. B. Harrison, 2d ed. (London: Cassell, 1968), p. 123.

22. Neale, "Introduction" to *Quenes Maiesties Passage*, p. 7; see also sigs. A2ᵛ, A2ʳ. Harington to Robert Markham, 1606, in Harington, *Letters and Epigrams*, p. 122.

23. See Harrison, *Letters of Queen Elizabeth I*, passim, and for the Shrewsburys, 4 June 1577, pp. 125–26. In *Elizabeth I*, Haigh observes the convention of designating the nobility as royal "cousins," p. 47, and notes her gifts and favors, p. 57.

24. Burghley cited by Neale, *Queen Elizabeth*, p. 349. Harington, *Letters and Epigrams*, 27 December 1602, pp. 96–97. On Huntingdon, see Neale, p. 217. For Ratcliffe, see Harrison, *Last Elizabethan Journal*, pp. 34, 49–50, 54. When Ratcliffe, despite Elizabeth's care, grieved to death, the queen honored her memory by burying her as a nobleman's daughter and by dressing all the women of the court in black.

25. Elizabeth to Unton, 22 August 1591, in Harrison, *Letters of Queen Elizabeth I*, pp. 210–11. Elizabeth to Lady Norris, 22 September 1597, in Harrison, p. 250. Lord Henry Norris and Lady Norris lost four sons in Ireland: William in 1579, Sir John in 1597, and Henry and Sir Thomas in 1599, leaving only Edward.

26. For salutations in correspondence, see Harrison, *Letters of Queen Elizabeth I*, passim, for examples to French and Scottish monarchs; see Klarwill, *Queen Elizabeth and Some Foreigners*, for letters to the Holy Roman Emperors. For Ferdinand, even reference to Elizabeth in correspondence with a third party, Baron Breuner, was to "the Queen of England, our beloved sister and cousin" (Klarwill, pp. 67, 150); so, too, for Maximilian writing to Leicester (Klarwill, p. 236). Also noteworthy is that, in writing to James, Elizabeth referred to the King of France as *his* "good brother" (6 January 1603, Harrison, pp. 295–96). For proclamations, see *Tudor Royal Proclamations*, ed. Paul L. Hughes and James F. Larkin, vol. 3 (New Haven: Yale University Press, 1969). I refer specifically to No. 732, "Prohibiting Traffic with Rebels of French King," 14 April 1591 (pp. 77–79); No. 782, "Ordering Peace Kept on Scottish Border," 20 August 1596 (pp. 166–68); and No. 788, "Ordering Peace Kept on Scottish Borders," 13 August 1597 (pp. 181–82). For James's abortive signature, February 1587, see *Letters of King James VI & I*, ed. G. P. V. Akrigg (Berkeley: University of California Press, 1984), p. 85.

27. Elizabeth to Maximilian, 10 December 1567, in Klarwill, *Queen Elizabeth and Some Foreigners*, p. 283. Similarly, Elizabeth wrote James VI on 1 July 1588 that her agent came with "matters which he hath to communicate unto you" and as evidence of "my desire of answering your good friendship and amity in as ample sort as with honor I may, as one that never seeks more of

you than that which shall be best for your self. Assure your self of me, therefore." From *Letters of Queen Elizabeth and King James VI of Scotland*, ed. John
Bruce, Camden Society, 46 (1849), pp. 49–50.

28. Elizabeth to Mary Stuart, 23 June 1567 and 21 December 1568, in
Harrison, *Letters of Queen Elizabeth I*, pp. 51 and 54.

29. Elizabeth to James, May 1594, in Harrison, *Letters of Queen Elizabeth I*,
p. 230. Elizabeth to Anna, 28 January 1596, in Harrison, p. 241. Elizabeth to
James, 18 May 1584, in Bruce, *Letters of Queen Elizabeth and King James*, p. 10.
Elizabeth to James, 4 January 1598, in Harrison, p. 258. Her threat to withdraw
the conventional relationship is not unprecedented. See, for example, the letter of an agent of the Roman Emperor to the English Orator Thomas Danett
on July 1566: "Above all His Imperial Majesty hopes to receive in the near
future the definite answer that he desires, which would enable him at all times
to show his brotherly affection for the Queen and to further the weal and
prestige of her entire realm, in doing which his zeal and goodwill should
never be found wanting" (in Klarwill, *Queen Elizabeth and Some Foreigners*,
p. 264).

30. For Elizabeth to Catherine de Medici, 7 February 1563 and 16 Oc-
tober 1567, see Harrison, *Letters of Queen Elizabeth I*, pp. 42–43 and 51–52.
For Elizabeth on Charles IX, see letter to ambassador Sir Henry Norris, 23
February 1570, in Harrison, pp. 68–82. For Elizabeth to ambassador Sir
Francis Walsingham, December 1572, see Harrison, pp. 115–18 (in letters of
1571 to Walsingham, she referred to the "King and the Queen Mother").
See further Elizabeth to ambassador Dr. Valentine Dale, 3 February 1574,
in Harrison, pp. 121–23. For Bacon, see "On the Fortunate Memory of
Elizabeth," p. 317.

31. Elizabeth to Catherine de Medici, July 1584, in Harrison, *Letters of
Queen Elizabeth I*, pp. 162–63.

32. Elizabeth to Mary Stuart, 20 February 1570, in Harrison, *Letters of
Queen Elizabeth I*, p. 65. Reply to petition, 12 November 1586, in Rice, *Public
Speaking*, p. 88.

33. Elizabeth to James, 14 February 1587, in Harrison, *Letters of Queen
Elizabeth I*, p. 188. In July 1584, meanwhile, Elizabeth had written to Catherine
de Medici on the death of her son: Catherine's regret, she declared, "I assure
myself cannot exceed mine; for, although you were his mother, yet there remain to you several other children. But for myself, I find no consolation if it
be not death, which I hope will make us soon to meet" (Harrison, p. 162).
James cited by Neale, *Queen Elizabeth*, p. 278.

34. Elizabeth to Henry IV, July 1593, in Harrison, *Letters of Queen Elizabeth
I*, p. 225. Haigh has remarked that Elizabeth "would never support any rebellious subject's disobedience to a prince," for she "had a legitimist view of

politics, and saw international affairs in terms of relations between monarchs" *Elizabeth I*, (p. 69).

35. James to Elizabeth, 27 June 1585, in Bruce, *Letters of Queen Elizabeth and King James*, pp. 14–15; Elizabeth to James, June or July 1585, pp. 16–17; see also Elizabeth to James, August 1585, pp. 19–20.

36. James to Elizabeth, 19 July 1585, 3 August 1585, 13 August 1585, and especially 19 August 1585, in Bruce, *Letters of Queen Elizabeth and King James*, pp. 16, 18–19, 20–21, and 21–22 (and see also Akrigg, *Letters of King James*, pp. 64–66). Elizabeth to James, November 1585, in Bruce, pp. 22–24; the comment on the "curious" postscript is Bruce's. James to Elizabeth, 20 December 1585, in Bruce, pp. 24–25.

37. Elizabeth to James, March 1586, in Bruce, *Letters of Queen Elizabeth and King James*, p. 30. James to Elizabeth, 1 August 1588, in Bruce, p. 52. Elizabeth to James, 11 September 1592, in Bruce, p. 75 (and also Harrison, *Letters of Queen Elizabeth I*, p. 221). Elizabeth to James, January 1593, in Bruce, p. 72 (and also Harrison, p. 223). James to Elizabeth, 19 September 1593, in Bruce, p. 90 (and also Akrigg, *Letters of King James*, p. 126). James to Elizabeth, 11 September 1594, in Akrigg, p. 136.

38. Elizabeth to James, October 1594, in Bruce, *Letters of Queen Elizabeth and King James*, pp. 108–10. (She may have referred specifically to the nineteen-year-old earl of Argyll, whom James had advanced, but the applicability of her remarks to James himself was clearly intentional.) Elizabeth to James, 1593–94, in Bruce, p. 98. Neale has termed her correspondence with James "curiously maternal and tutorial" (*Queen Elizabeth*, p. 385). 1593–94, in Bruce, p. 98.

39. James to Elizabeth, 5 June 1594 and February 1598, in Bruce, *Letters of Queen Elizabeth and King James*, pp. 107 and 124. The later, sycophantic correspondence includes the following letters in Bruce: after July 1602, pp. 145–47; 12 October 1602, pp. 147–48; autumn 1602, pp. 151–53; and late 1602, pp. 153–54.

40. Elizabeth to James, September 1589, in Bruce, *Letters of Queen Elizabeth and King James*, p. 56.

41. Elizabeth to James, 1590, in Bruce, *Letters of Queen Elizabeth and King James*, pp. 57–58. According to Bruce, this letter was written during James's absence in Denmark. See also Harrison, *Letters of Queen Elizabeth I*, pp. 200–202.

42. Elizabeth to James, 16 April 1590, in Bruce, *Letters of Queen Elizabeth and King James*, p. 166. Elizabeth to James, May 1590, in Bruce, p. 60.

43. Elizabeth to Mary's counselors cited by Neale, *Queen Elizabeth*, p. 63. Elizabeth to envoy William Maitland cited by Neale, p. 114. Maitland sought to have Mary Stuart established as Elizabeth's heir.

44. Ahasverus Allinga to Emperor Ferdinand, 30 January 1564, in Klarwill, *Queen Elizabeth and Some Foreigners*, p. 193.

45. Elizabeth to the House of Commons, 10 February 1558, in Rice, *Public Speaking*, p. 115. Heisch, "Queen Elizabeth I," p. 33.

46. Elizabeth to Parliament, Novemenber 1586, in Rice, *Public Speaking*, p. 89. She also observed during this speech that "Good neighbors I have had, and I have met with bad, and in trust I have found treason." In the same year, she reminded the French ambassador that "I myself was a prisoner in the days of the Queen, my sister, and am aware of the artifices that prisoners use to win over servants and obtain secret intelligence" (as cited by Neale, *Queen Elizabeth*, p. 271). Heisch has observed another lesson from Elizabeth's years as a subject: "From study and direct observation, Elizabeth knew how she *ought* to be regarded" ("Queen Elizabeth I," p. 34).

47. Cited by Haigh, *Elizabeth I*, p. 154.

Elizabeth I, Egerton MS 944. By Permission of The British Library.

Dutifully Defending Elizabeth: Lord Henry Howard and the Question of Queenship

Dennis Moore

> When they urge us daily to allege some certain proof of women's sufficiency to rule, it were enough to answer by alleging only the renowned name of Queen Elizabeth, as Demosthenes repeated this word "Action" thrice together to a certain person that desired to understand the first, the second, and third part of an orator.
>
> Lord Henry Howard
> *A Dutiful Defense of the Lawful Regiment of Women*

The question of whether a woman might rightfully rule was bound to prove troublesome for Mary I and Elizabeth I—the daughters of Henry VIII who governed England for the second half of the sixteenth century—and for their cousin Mary Queen of Scots. Prevailing conceptions of womanhood made queenship anomalous, and British history offered scant precedent. (Witness the desperation with which Tudor apologists invoke the legendary Queen Cordelia.)[1] Queen Elizabeth had been delivering a practical argument in favor of queenship for more than thirty years when her cousin Lord Henry Howard presented her with *A Dutiful Defense of the Lawful Regiment of Women* (1590), but issues of legal right and moral propriety—of whether a woman *ought* to rule—could not be settled de facto. Nor could one example establish a general law, especially since not everyone would agree to put Elizabeth (or her sister or cousin Mary) on the same side of the ledger.

The most famous entry in the theoretical debate is certainly John Knox's *First Blast of the Trumpet Against the Monstrous Regiment of Women* (1558), to which John Aylmer responded almost immediately with *An Harbor for Faithful and True Subjects Against the Late Blown Blast* (1559), but the debate continued throughout Elizabeth's reign. Then as now, the controversy held interest not only as a forum for issues of sex and gender but also because of its bearing on other topics ranging from the royal succession to ecclesiastical polity to theories of sovereignty. (How valid is a claim to the throne based on female heirs? Can a woman preach and administer sacraments, and if not, how can the queen rule the church? Is a queen regnant by definition a tyrant, and if so, may subjects rightly rebel?) So significant are such matters that Paula Scalingi describes most "participants in the great debate over gynecocracy" as "concerned with the religion, politics, and moral character of the ruler *rather than* with the sex."[2] Yet none of these concerns precludes the others, and we gain more by studying their interrelationships than selecting among them.

Historians of the controversy have usually recorded the mere existence of Howard's *Dutiful Defense* without pretending to have read it.[3] More than anything else, the material fact that the treatise was never printed explains its persistent marginality in their accounts. Admittedly, it is a daunting task to analyze five hundred folio pages written in secretary hand, let alone an unfamiliar work full of Latin and crammed with enough legal, historical, and theological references to lend substance to its formulaic apologies for copiousness. (Of course, a briefer and less learned performance might well have been less effective in displaying the writer's intellectual wares and implying his respect for his elite audience.) Some scholars who have written about the treatise without reading it have no doubt discouraged others by publishing unwarranted surmises concerning its nature and purpose: for instance, by dismissing it as a belated reply to Knox, a description that (as we shall see) does little justice to one of the century's most erudite and wide-ranging attempts to theorize a woman's regal authority. Moreover, the near oblivion into which *A Dutiful Defense* has fallen suggests the uncritical way print publication is sometimes valued. How important can a text be, one may wonder, if it was not even published? But absence from the marketplace and lack of popularity are dubious grounds for presuming insignificance in Elizabethan affairs of state. A work of political argument written expressly for the queen and formally presented to select courtiers may have its own lessons to teach about the queenship debate.

The first part of this chapter uses contemporary documents, including the letter dedicating *A Dutiful Defense* to Elizabeth, to describe the situation in which Howard composed and disseminated the work. Since the contents of this unpublished treatise will be unfamiliar to most readers, the second part sketches the broad outlines of Howard's argument and analyzes its force. Although it may be tempting to find feminism in sixteenth-century defenses of women's rule, Howard will be seen to speak more in the name of conservative tradition than feminist revision, his challenge being to reconcile queenship to patriarchy.

I

The Book and the Letter

Let us begin at the front of *A Dutiful Defense* and turn a few pages. The manuscripts begin with a title page announcing the subject of the book in some detail:

> *A Dutiful Defense of the Lawful Regiment of Women, Divided into Three Books. The First Containeth Reasons and Examples Grounded on the Law of Nature; the Second, Reasons and Examples Grounded on the Civil Laws; the Third, Reasons and Examples Grounded on the Sacred Laws of God. With an Answer to All False and Frivolous Objections Which Have Been Most Unjustly Countenanced with Deceitful Colors Forced Out of These Laws in Disgrace of Thier Approved and Sufficent Authority.*[4]

The echo of Knox's title places Howard's book firmly in the tradition of the long Tudor debate over the "regiment of women," in which the best known texts were *The First Blast* and Aylmer's counterblast. Yet the terms of the title also set Howard apart. Consider his emphasis on civil law. Knox mentions the topic briefly; Aylmer elevates it to the status of a major issue only to maximize the damage inflicted when he declares it irrelevant. By contrast, Lord Henry devotes his entire Second Book to civil law (a subject he taught at Cambridge). Further differences will emerge in part II when we examine his argument, but for now it is enough to note the epigraph at the bottom of the title page: a Biblical verse in which Daniel chastises one of the elders for bearing false witness against the godly, beautiful Susanna. No need to belabor the obvious application of this passage to men of apparent authority who wrongfully oppose a virtuous queen.

In most copies of *Dutiful Defense*, turning the title page reveals the brightly illuminated coat of arms of a privy councilor, along with Latin verses honoring that person. The Harvard manuscript, for example, bears the arms of the royal favorite Robert Devereux, second earl of Essex, another of Lord Henry's eminent cousins and a key patron in the revival of his fortunes. Although Howard's work was never printed, the poems and coats of arms are vivid reminders that he did not leave its circulation to chance but rather promulgated in at court with considerable industry and care. Given its length and the number of individuals likely to have received copies, he must have supervised an extraordinary scriptorial effort, his active participation in the reproduction of his work extending well beyond the composition of liminary verses and the hiring of scribes. His distinctive handwriting can be seen filling gaps left by a puzzled copyist, adding references in the margins, signing the epistle dedicatory. No printed text could have had such cachet for each recipient; no volume produced for the queen alone could have made the case for Lord Henry's worth to so many leading courtiers. As material objects, then, the texts of *A Dutiful Defense* amply testify to a key aspect of its audience, occasion, and purpose: Howard was making an extraordinary bid for patronage.

The next part of the book, the dedicatory epistle to Queen Elizabeth, explains why he needed to do so. This letter is by no means just another commonplace nod to a potential patron but a tour de force exercise in establishing *ethos*, its fifty folio pages earnestly justifying both author and treatise. Some seventeenth-century readers copied out the epistle and circulated it separately, perhaps for its rhetorical virtuosity and certainly for its interest as an autobiographical statement by a prominent Jacobean minister of state.[5] It makes most sense, though, read in context as preface to *A Dutiful Defense*.

A Railing Invective and a Dutiful Defense

The letter opens with an account of how Howard undertook his defense of female rule and why it took so long to complete. He claims that thirteen years earlier (that is, around 1577), "an honorable privy council" had urged him to answer "the copy of a railing invective against the regiment of queens in general, with certain malapert exceptions to matters of state which were at that time in dispute."[6] A government official seeking an effective propagandist might well have turned to the learned Lord Henry. In 1566, two years after matriculating fellow-commoner from King's College, Cambridge, he had commenced MA and migrated to wealthy Trinity Hall, where he lectured on rhetoric and civil law until the end of the decade—an extraordinary pursuit for a man of aristocratic birth. In 1574, he had published a defense of the established church.[7]

What was this "railing invective" that Howard was supposed to answer? The queen (to whom the letter is addressed) probably knew, or if not she could have asked, but Howard's cryptic comment is our only guide. Some commentators take for granted that Howard refers to *The First Blast*—an unlikely identification. For one thing, Knox hardly fits Lord Henry's suggestion that the author of the invective has been "enriched by so many favors by Your Majesty's most happy and prosperous government," a phrase more reminiscent of Howard's repeated complaint that Christopher Goodman "both lived and received benefits by the favor of Her Majesty, yet he refused obstinately to recant his invective" (*A Dutiful Defense* 1.7). Goodman's invective is *How Superior Powers Ought to Be Obeyed of Their Subjects* (1588), its purport better suggested by the running title "How to Obey or Disobey." The book expounds the same doctrines of political resistance that underwrite Knox's call for the deposition of queens, doctrines he promised to treat in the *Second Blast*. Not only were such ideas anathema to Queen Elizabeth, but Goodman goes beyond other Marian exiles (even Knox) by specifically denying Elizabeth's right to rule, as well as her Catholic sister's.[8] Like *The First Blast*, Goodman's book seems a somewhat shaky candidate for the "railing invective," since it was closer to thirty years old than thirteen by the time Howard presented *A Dutiful Defense* to Queen Elizabeth.

Still, the topic of *How Superior Powers Ought to Be Obeyed* was indeed disputed "at that time" (around 1577) because George Buchanan's *De Jure Regni Apud Scotos* was then in vogue with the earl of Leicester's circle. Like Goodman's book, Buchanan's *De Jure Regni*— another candidate for identification as the "railing invective"—justifies tyrannicide in the name of popular sovereignty.[9] Although the alleged misrule of Mary Queen of Scots occasions Buchanan's dialogue, the printed texts do not raise the issue of women's rule per se, so the book opposes "the regiment of queens in general" only insofar as it challenges all monarchs. Lord Henry writes,

> In his book *De Jure Regni apud Scotos*, [Buchanan] takes in hand to prove that not only ladies of great state and dowagers but princes absolute also may be called to account for all their actions by parliament and (according to the quality of their offense) either fined, put to death, or deposed. . . . I touch this point to this end only: that other queens may with greater patience digest his declamations when his own king cannot escape the shafts of his quiver (1.7).

The reference to "his declamations" points to the text on which Howard focuses his most virulent attacks: not *De Jure Regni* but the long speech against women's rule assigned to Archbishop Kennedy in Buchanan's *Rerum Scoticarum Historia* (1582).

If Howard does conflate *De Jure Regni* with Kennedy's diatribe, then he errs in the company of modern historians. Calling the speech "the most famous passage in the whole History," P. Hume Brown describes it as "simply another statement of the doctrines of *De Jure Regni*," a comment W. A. Gatherer cites approvingly to support the idea that "the treatise was considered to be the *thesis proposita* and the History a compendium of 'proofs' illustrating and lending authority to the principles enunciated in the tract."[10] Likewise, historians from Hume Brown to I. D. McFarlane share Howard's view that Buchanan "foisteth in a bitter invective of his own invention in the bishop's name":

> There is no doubt but Buchanan would very gladly have discoursed upon this theme if fear of giving offense to the queen our sovereign (who by her wisdom and most loving care of the young king her cousin saved and preserved Scotland both from civil war and foreign spoil) had not restrained in some sort his poetical invention. Wherefore, not daring to deliver with his mouth what he believed in heart, nor directly to impugn or weaken her authority that was a mother to his country and a strength to all his friends, he rather chose to thunder like old Saturn in a cloud and to walk upon the stage under the vizard of a grave and godly metropolitan (*Dutiful Defense*, 1.7).

Lord Henry singles out Buchanan as "he that seems most bitter in all the brotherhood" (that is, among the men who oppose female rule), and although *De Jure Regni* does not focus on queens, it is obviously part of the same propaganda campaign against Mary Queen of Scots that includes Kennedy's declamation in the *Historia*.

Interpreting *A Dutiful Defense* does not require us to identify the "railing invective," which (if it ever existed) was in any case but one among many texts to which Howard responds. For all we know, the passage in question alludes to a work that no longer survives, a fate the Privy Council did its best to secure for such "malapert" writings. Rhetorically, its identity may be less significant than the implications of Howard's decision not to name it. Candidates have been reviewed here not to close the question but to open it up, since the common assumption that Howard must be alluding to *The First Blast* leads to the reductive conclusion that the whole *Dutiful Defense* answers Knox—simply because Knox happens to be the adversary most familiar to twentieth-century readers.[11]

The Indictment and the Queen of Scots

Whoever wrote the "railing invective," Howard assures the queen that he agreed it was a poisonous work requiring an answer, yet he also admits reluctance to write about current affairs—knowing "by late experience of wiser men how captious the world was grown in censuring all works and writers that refer the drift of their discourse to present time"—and especially about queenship, considering "how far the poison of prejudicate conceit against the question itself had been conveyed by railing pens." Most discouraging is the example of Aylmer, now bishop of London and "sharply slandered and unjustly challenged" for remarks in his loyal answer to Knox.[12]

Despite Lord Henry's misgivings, he says, trust in God and faith in the queen's acceptance of his "loyal purpose in this piece of service" made him undertake the work. Yet events amply confirmed his fears:

> The drift of my discourse was wrongfully indicted at a privy session before it could appear by any outward act. Process was served on my arguments before they could be set in readiness to pass, and I myself—uncited, unexamined, unheard—was adjudged guilty by the voice of many spiteful jurors among the vulgar sort which wanted wisdom to conceive, conscience to weigh, and learning to understand their evidence.

Their ignorant and malicious charges culminated in the most damning of all:

> Another company accused me of sailing with a side wind, of haling to the north point (like a cunning bargeman) when mine eye was in the south; of offering to saints unknown and seeking, under the safe protection of an eagle's wings, to hatch a cockatrice. When neither the matter nor the manner of my writing gave advantage to the curious inquest of false surmise, the circumstances of the present time were strictly pondered; and if, among all the queens that either were or ever had been, one were found in common jealousy more offensive to the present state than all the rest, the same was made the only object of my speculation.

In short, Howard was accused of writing *A Dutiful Defense* not for Elizabeth but for her rival, Mary Queen of Scots. The argument of his treatise is truly general, its application limited to neither woman, yet his long attachment to the Stuart cause certainly lends point to the charge.

After all this, writes Lord Henry, "the sweetest spring began to empty and disgorge into an ocean of bitterness"—Elizabeth grew displeased—so, rather than provide more matter for his enemies, he abandoned the work. Yet since Elizabeth's detractors have continued to print their pasquils and libels, he has returned to the project: "I know not any man to whom this service doth more properly belong than to myself, who certainly without Your Majesty's unspeakable compassion of late had been of all men living of my birth and quality (as I believe) most miserable."

Ruin and Rhetoric

In 1590, Lord Henry greatly needed the queen's compassion. His second cousin Catherine, one of the wives of Henry VIII, serves as a reminder how well the turning of fortune's wheel is illustrated by the Howards, alternately exalted and scourged by the Tudors. Lord Henry was named for his father, the earl of Surrey whose Virgil is credited with introducing blank verse to English literature and in whose lyrics Sir Philip Sidney found "many things tasting of a noble birth, and worthy of a noble mind." Like many noble minds, Surrey's entertained dangerous political ambitions: one of the last acts of Henry VIII was to have him executed. The king also sent Surrey's father, third duke of Norfolk, to the Tower, where he stayed through the next reign. The family was removed from their palatial home, with the children placed under a guardian, until the accession of Queen Mary, who restored Norfolk's land and honors shortly before his death, upon which the dukedom passed to Thomas, Lord Henry's elder brother. Nor were the tumultuous changes experienced by Surrey's children limited to material circumstances. For instance, in the time of Edward VI, their tutor was John Foxe, the Protestant martyrologist. Under Mary, Foxe was replaced by John White, a devout Roman Catholic protégé of Gardiner's, soon awarded a bishopric. Norfolk seems to have honored Foxe to the end of his days, warning his children against papistry; Henry favored Bishop White and Catholicism.

After the accession of Elizabeth in 1558, family fortunes continued to rise for a season. But Lord Henry left Trinity after his brother became entangled in the affairs of the Scots queen, aspiring to marry her. Imprisoned in the Tower of London in the autumn of 1569, under house arrest a year later, back in the Tower by autumn of 1571, Norfolk was executed for treason the following spring. Beyond the fact that Lord Henry was imprisoned more than once in this period, we know little about his role.[13] The dedicatory epistle to *A Dutiful Defense* laments the execution of Norfolk, like other troubles, in general terms:

> After my return from the university, though I was but lately crept—or rather swept—out of the ruins of my house, Your Majesty most graciously admitted me to the kissing of your sacred hand. You regarded me with pity and relieved me with favor; you breathed life into the carcass of my starved hope with many likely tokens of far better hap; and, which I cannot forget to mention with unfeigned thankfulness, Your Highness gave me warning sundry times of silver hooks which were baited with devices and occasions of diverse kinds to draw me up (as it were) by the very jaws out of the streams of paradise.

Whether or not Howard was the innocent little fish his metaphor makes him out to be, and however sincere his thanks for the queen's advice, her warnings were apt. Ignoring them, however, he continued to work in various Catholic causes, not least that of Mary Stuart.

In the 1580s, Elizabeth and her ministers treated Roman Catholicism as an increasingly serious threat, especially when linked to a political program. Scattered documentary evidence suggests that when the Privy Council rounded up the usual suspects, Lord Henry was likely to be among them. In January 1581, we find him in the Tower accused of a variety of seditious activities, from openly defending "certain articles of papistry" to writing *A Treatise of Treasons* (1572).[14] Six months later, he was again (or still) in the Tower, suspected of spying and propagandizing for Catholic countries.[15] He had only recently shaken off these grave accusations when imprisoned in December 1583 for interrogation regarding the Throckmorton plot and the flight of his friends Charles Arundel and Lord Paget to France; a month later, Howard was reexamined.[16] In the same affair, the earl of Northumberland, William Shelley, and Howard's nephew Philip, earl of Arundel, were all three arrested. Never released, Northumberland died in captivity years later. Shelley was racked.[17] The earl of Arundel was released, then imprisoned two years later attempting to flee the realm, at which time the council had Lord Henry questioned still again. Arundel remained in the Tower, dying a martyr ten years later. Lord

Henry remained under suspicion even after the execution of Mary Queen of Scots, as appears from a letter in the Armada year complaining to Walsingham that "Some have gone about to kindle and revive those sparks of indignation in Her Majesty's conceit which I believed certainly to have been long since either satisfied with my tedious imprisonment, or slaked by the intercession of my honorable friends, or quenched by the proof of my devotion."[18] By the time of the epistle dedicatory to *A Dutiful Defense*, Howard and many of his family were devastated so completely that he refers to the events of the 1580s as "the last fall of my house," thus comparable to the "ruins" caused by the execution of Norfolk and of their father Surrey a quarter-century before him.

The precise nature and extent of Lord Henry's illegal activities pose difficult biographical questions we need not answer here, since the key point is that the queen and her leading ministers were deeply suspicious of him over many years, a fact that bears on *A Dutiful Defense* in a number of ways. For one thing, it means his papers were repeatedly searched and seized, and his comments about these incidents have a strong rhetorical interest. "My desks and coffers have been six times broken up, my papers rifled, and sundry books of notes conveyed away," he complains.[19] On one occasion, "this collection of arguments in defense of women's lawful interest" was even taken away and lost, its eventual return suggesting that providence had assigned Howard the task of defending Elizabeth.

> Thus, having once again recovered my notes (more pregnant with authority than easy to be read, which may be taken for another reason why they sped more luckily at so many frays), I resolved by the grace of God to take such a course in setting these small pieces of sweet wood together in a work of marquetry as it should no longer rest either in the hand of fortune or of emulation to forestall my purposes.

Marquetry—inlaid woodwork, often furniture—was a delicate craft much appreciated in Renaissance Europe that enjoyed a particular vogue in late Elizabethan England. (The finest is generally thought to be Italian *intarsia*, or pictorial marquetry, perhaps best known from the perspective panels in the Palazzo Ducale, Urbino.) "Sweet wood," scented fruitwood, is often favored for marquetry and recalls the more common image of the textual florilegium. Like Howard's reference to his "collection of arguments," his image of "a work of marquetry" represents the text as composed of reasons and examples first gathered from reading, then artfully set in place by the writer.

His next evidence for the providential nature of his undertaking carries the same rhetorical implications:

> Beside, it was not altogether void of prognostication that, ever since the first time wherein I devoted myself to the reading of good books, I was incited by a certain inward motion and secret instinct to refer all readings in the progression of my study to this happy head.

Similarly, in the dedicatory epistle to *A Defensative Against the Poison of Supposed Prophecies* (1583), Howard tells Sir Francis Walsingham that he had, by providence or prudence, collected matter relevant to that book since age sixteen. Lord Henry seems a paradigm of the Tudor humanists recently described by Mary Thomas Crane, filling commonplace books under this or that "happy head" in anticipation of occasions on which to frame the matter into a discourse fit for powerful patrons. Like them, Howard sought to turn his years of study to practical advantage. From the time he left Cambridge until he became a privy councilor in the reign of James I, he repeatedly sought favor by penning learned and "dutiful" works, a number addressed specifically to the queen.[20] Crane's analysis is notable for its provocative account of the ideological character of humanist discursive practices, with sixteenth-century rhetoricians theorizing reading and writing in a quasi-Derridean logic of supplementation that "allowed these men to present a double face to power." Correspondingly, their texts "are strongly marked by their author's position as a supplemental gatherer; they are best described not in terms of an author-centered imitative model, but as the products of a true intertextuality of fragments."[21] As we shall see, such is the case with *A Dutiful Defense*.

Emphasizing Howard's pathetic situation in 1590, the dedicatory epistle to *A Dutiful Defense* urges Elizabeth to accept his service and stop wasting his talent. One of the most striking passages praises her bounty and mercy for not having utterly destroyed him and for building his character by scourging him to the limits of endurance. He alludes to one of Surrey's "Tower" works, a translation from Psalm 119 published in *Tottell's Miscellany*:

> I confess with David in his thankful sonnet after long experience, which made his understading ripe, and with my father in the last thing that he wrote before his end, which made his judgment clear: "It is good for me that God," who knoweth what is fittest

for his creature—and Your Highness, that discerneth what is fittest for your subject—"hath thus humbled me."

Like God, the queen tests and humbles those she loves. Like the Psalmist, Lord Henry is older and wiser. More fortunate than his father, he lives under a merciful prince. Despite having been denied her presence for a decade, he yet hopes "that though I could not at the first procure a lease of favor for term of my life, yet at the last I may obtain a gracious reversion in respect of the fines which are already paid and answered after ten years' tragedies."

There is much more to the dedicatory epistle: detailed praise of Queen Elizabeth's accomplishments, for instance, and further pleas for mercy. But we have seen enough to grasp some of its general significance for Howard's defense of queenship. Now let us turn to the defense itself.

II

Tradition and Revision

In sixteenth-century Europe, both of God's books—Nature and the Bible—were commonly understood to give men all public authority as well as domestic superiority. Elizabeth Cady Stanton's introduction to *The Woman's Bible* (1895) provides a précis of a traditional Judaeo-Christian view:

> The Bible teaches that woman brought sin and death into the world, that she precipitated the fall of the race, that she was arraigned before the judgment seat of Heaven, tried, condemned and sentenced. Marriage for her was to be a condition of bondage, maternity a period of suffering and anguish, and in silence and subjection, she was to play the role of a dependent on man's bounty for all her material wants, and for all the information she might desire on the vital questions of the hour, she was commanded to ask her husband at home. Here is the Bible position of woman briefly summed up.

Such Bible-based subordinationism displays a "remarkable concordance" with classical writings on the inferiority of women, as Ian Maclean observes:

> The manner of Eve's creation suggests the lower status embodied in the *mas occasionatus* [defective male] theory; the first

sin recalls the jurist's belief in woman's *imbecillitas animi* [weakness of soul]; the curse of subordination to husband equates with woman's *deterior conditio* [lower status] in law; the 'Alphabet of the Good Woman' in Proverbs is consistent with Aristotle's division between conservative and acquisitive rôles in the household for woman and man.

This consensus of classical and Christian doctrines allowed scholars in the Renaissance to rely on a "synthetic, scholastic view" of women that was shared across disciplinary boundaries by doctors, lawyers, and theologians, with many elements common to popular thought. According to Maclean, this eclectic view—enshrined in the institutional practices of the learned professions—was "attacked for the first time as a whole" during the "half-century between 1580 and 1630," with the appearance of an impressive number of works "which propose, in a serious scholarly context, some revision in the nature and status of women."[22]

A Dutiful Defense of the Lawful Regiment of Women may best be read as participating in this attack. Even so, the relationship of Howard's treatise to other defenses of women needs careful evaluation. *A Dutiful Defense* challenges the traditional synthesis selectively and with a difference, for Lord Henry speaks in the name of conservative tradition, not feminist revision. His project could hardly be more different from a defense of the sort Constance Jordan characterizes as mounting an ideological critique of patriarchy by privileging experience over authority and undermining natural and divine law.[23] Rather, *A Dutiful Defense* seeks to reconcile queenship with patriarchy by relying upon the very traditions that Jordan's feminists attack: "In this question," writes Howard, "lies no hard or knotty part which hath not been broken up by the wedge of Holy Writ and hewn in sunder by the ax of ancient authority" (1.3). Such are the tools Howard uses to produce the most thorough and learned work in the entire queenship controversy, demonstrating that all the best authorities have always upheld a woman's rule as natural, lawful, and godly. From this perspective, upholding a queen's right does not encourage social change but, on the contrary, buttresses established order. The innovators are not her defenders but those who would dethrone her.

Ancient Authority and Malapert Discoursers

Given Howard's self-proclaimed reliance on traditional authorities, how can he be said to participate in the late sixteenth-century attack on the traditional synthesis described by Maclean? Given the pervasive misogyny of the authorities upon which he depends, how can he insist they all support a woman's right to rule? Both questions have the same answer: by his re-reading of the authoritative texts, which he reinterprets to construct a new synthesis in which divine law, civil law, and natural law all speak with one voice regarding the rule of queens.

Consequently, most chapters of *A Dutiful Defense* enter into disputations about how Church Fathers and more recent authorities explicate the Bible, about cruxes in civil law and associated commentaries, or about passing remarks on women from classical and Christian texts primarily devoted to other subjects. Howard's usual strategy is to bring texts and commentators into the fold as supporters of queenship. These appropriations are often (of necessity) ruthless, relying on every available means from selective quotation to misleading paraphrase: by such means, even Aristotle can be made to serve Lord Henry's turn! When it does fit Howard's purpose to acknowledge the existence of adversaries, he most often seeks to undermine their authority by historicizing their testimony or closely analyzing their texts. Such rhetorical and historical criticism requires circumstantiality:

> I must inquire of what credit or condition they were that declaimed in this sort, by what reason, to what end, and (as our civilian Cassius demandeth) *cui bono*: whether the country shall reap any good by their sharp tongues, or whether they are only bent to the furtherance of their own particular that utter them? (1.6)

For instance, as a historian, Buchanan comes in for just this treatment. One long chapter of *A Dutiful Defense* refutes the Kennedy speech in detail, then goes on to attack Buchanan's *ethos* using other passages of the *Historia* (especially its account of Flodden Field, a military victory for a Tudor queen regent as well as a great day for the Howard family).

As befits Howard's appeal to authority, much of his case is historical. Occasionally he appeals to memory of recent events, but most of his arguments concern places in authoritative texts, the "small pieces of sweet wood" gathered from such writers as Herodotus and Livy for the ancients, Eusebius and Sozomen for the early church, Paolo Emili and Carlo Sigonio for "modern" Europe, Francesco Alvares for Africa and Peter Martyr d'Anghiera for the New World. Like other works in the queenship controversy, Howard's treatise employs a rich rhetoric of exemplification.[24] One of the longest chapters presents detailed examples of female rule from "the records of all the kingdoms of the world," though Howard prefers Christian nations as being "of more reverend authority" (1.5). His range of examples—including many from medieval and Renaissance Europe, from Scotland to Poland—may well impress readers tired of Deborah, the daughters of Zelophehad, and other staples of the queenship controversy, though these too are discussed in due course.

Although Lord Henry addresses the commonplaces of the contemporary debate over women's rule, he very seldom mentions such works as *The First Blast*, even when countering their arguments in detail (e.g., at 3.1, where he answers Knox regarding Deborah). Such texts are accorded no authority. When he does name a participant in the debate, what follows is commonly an argument *ad hominem* that allows Howard to put forward his own testimony as a man of affairs. Thus he can get personal about Jean Bodin, "the French fashioner of commonweals," who visited England twice in 1581 to promote Elizabeth's proposed marriage to the French king's brother (an affair in which Lord Henry was also deeply involved). On the second visit, writes Howard, even this ardent advocate of the Salic law seems to have been convinced by the example of Elizabeth:

> Surely I am of the mind that if some of these directors lived among us, they would rest to rail and begin to wonder. For either Bodin (one of their best friends) became a new man at his being here with Monsieur, or he remaineth at this instant as he was before, which is an hypocrite (1.11).

Ordinarily, though, *A Dutiful Defense* portrays Knox, Goodman, and the others as a faceless threat, the generalized disorderly Other conjured up in so many official apologies for the Elizabethan regime. Refuting the enemies of queenship, Howard is much less likely to cite a particular source than to say "*They* allege . . ." and to deride and demonize *Them*. *They* are "the malapert discoursers of our time who, venturing their slender stock both of wit and learning for exchange of rotten wares, become for their labor bankrupt both in trade and honesty." *They* are "the cursed brood and generation of Cain," our sons of Belial and our Catilines, jugglers and libelers who color their sedition with the same arguments used throughout history by the "tyrants, usurpers, monsters, bastards, Achitophels, sultans, Turks, and murderers" who have greedily opposed female rule (1.6).

To the extent that Howard does portray his opponents more particularly, he most commonly does it to summon the specter of seditious Calvinists preaching popular sovereignty and tyrannicide. (The fact that their arguments against female rule were developed in tandem with doctrines of resistance served him well.) Knox and others had—with varying degrees of reluctance—acknowledged the rightfulness of Elizabeth's reign by praising her as a miracle: a Deborah, a Judith, a Daniel come to judgment. God had evidently raised her above that sex whose typical shortcomings they saw as better exemplified by her sister, Bloody Mary. Of course, only opponents of women's rule needed to make an exception of a good queen, and such an ad hoc answer carries little weight in the legitimist discourse of *A Dutiful Defense*, which places woman's rule firmly within the settled order of things. (Nor could making an exception of Elizabeth help Howard justify Mary Stuart, should he have wished to do so.) Howard only mentions the position when scornfully attributing it to Goodman, who "refused obstinately to recant his invective, protesting to Dr. Longworth that a woman might be called to authority by extraordinary grace, as Daniel was raised up against the judges, but not by ordinary means nor lawful succession" (1.7).

By One Law and in One Manner

By contrast, ordinary means and lawful succession are exactly the terms in which Howard's conservative discourse reconciles a woman's supreme political authority with patriarchy. Maclean observes that Renaissance writers are doomed to inconsistency when they try to "combine a conservative desire to maintain the fabric of society as it is with a radical reappraisal of woman's capacity for virtue."[25] How much more so a writer with Howard's rhetorical problem of affirming female virtue precisely in order "to maintain the fabric of society as it is"! How could the rule of one woman be justified without entailing the liberation of them all? To the extent that reconciling queenship with patriarchy requires Howard to assert women's fitness to rule, he must deny (or at least temper) some misogynist grounds for their subordination to men. Yet, since the terms of this reconciliation must not imply women's fuller participation in social and political life, he must be careful not to deny too much. Howard's task requires him to open wide vistas of women's competency, then to close down nearly every avenue for its exercise except one.[26]

That is exactly what he does. And as we examine how he does it, we will see the dynamic of the whole *Dutiful Defense*—a dynamic one might well describe as a downward spiral. Book One begins by arguing the spiritual equality of the sexes so forcefully that one recent commentator sees Lord Henry as a defender of "the independent woman" and "female autonomy" who "redefines the notion of woman and her social role."[27] Alas, this is to grab the elephant's leg and conclude that the animal is like a tree. True, Howard repeatedly affirms that women and men "have one creation, one capacity of grace, one virtue, one honor; they shall be either crowned or condemned in another life before one judge by one law and in one manner" (1.4). This may well sound like true sexual equality. At moments, he praises what he describes as specifically female virtues, such as an inclination to peace and pity, and he even entertains the idea that "if proportionably we like to compare those women that have governed in states and regiments with kings and emperors of equal suit, we may perhaps have cause to conclude with St. Basil that the weaker sex hath overcome the stronger" (1.7).

Patrimonial and Personal

The weaker sex, the stronger. The very terms in which Howard here praises women point to the basic problems. As his argument develops, he limits the implications of his seemingly liberatory rhetoric by increasingly emphasizing sexual difference. Biology and society take an ever greater toll. Howard's doctrine of spiritual equality can be restated, "The souls of women . . . differ not from men by sex as the bodies do" (1.13). The natural inferiority to be read off the female body is likewise inscribed in Scripture (e.g., women as the weaker vessels of 1 Pet. 3.7). Indeed, the spiritual equality of the sexes matters far less than we would expect, their physical difference more than we might hope:

> . . . though the stronger and more worthy sex be specified in that place of Paul [Ephesians 4.13] to show the glory of the state wherein both the sexes shall arise, yet this specification doth nothing derogate from their equality (1.7).

Even though both sexes may be equal in *one* respect, one is stronger and more worthy in *every other*:

> St. Paul hath used all these arguments . . . only to make proof that, of both sexes (being brought into comparison), the male ought to be accounted more excellent, which all men do acknowledge (3.5).

The usual implications follow: for example, "womanish" remains a term of opprobrium (3.12), while women who display martial virtue are "above their sex." Social practices that restrict women's education and participation in public affairs are explained as privileges, not privations, women being excused for sake of modesty and delicacy (2.3, 2.6). Nor need queens step down from this pedestal: they can leave the courts of law to lesser magistrates, and so on. Lord Henry assumes women to be subordinate in marriage, his main concern being to deny that every woman is thus subject to all men or that a queen must submit to her mate in matters of state. Now and then, like Aylmer before him, Howard uses language that suggests a more conventionalist perspective, referring to the male as "the stronger sex, *as we account it*" or to "women, *whom we count* the weaker" (1.9, 1.14, emphases added). But the gesture seems hollow. It never takes long for essentialist assumptions to resume control of the discourse.[28]

Thus the logic of Howard's position provides a dynamic for the whole treatise: a narrowing movement—from the assurances in Book One that women are men's spiritual equals, to the explanations in Book Two of why their exclusion from the law is an honor, and finally in Book Three to what is predictably the least "feminist" chapter (3.10), about whether women should be allowed to preach and administer sacraments. (They should not.) The idea that women are the spiritual equals of men may have far-reaching social implications for us, but not for Howard. To him, it means only that women are *capable* of practicing law, say, or serving as mayor—not that they should ordinarily be allowed to do so. On the contrary, men are ordinarily preferred with good reason: "We confess with Aristotle that women . . . are less apt to rule than men" (1.9; cp. *Politics* 1.12). Other things being equal, "where titles and pretensions are in all points equal and indifferent, the male ought worthier to be preferred because *in statu virile major dignitas*" (2.11). In the First Book, Howard produces a long list of elected queens; by Book III, he is explaining why it is always better to choose a man.

Ultimately, the distinction between inheritance and election is definitive: "What difference the civil laws have set down between offices that are patrimonial and personal is evident in proof, and that women are as ordinarily admitted to the first for their credit as excused from the latter for their privilege" (3.1). An individual who succeeds to the throne by blood cannot be presumed incapable because of her sex. Though most men are personally superior to her, she has an *absolute* right against which their *relative* superiority cannot prevail, any more than they ought to remove a king in his minority (cp. 3.12). Hence women's spiritual equality allows them to exercise public authority on the rare occasions they receive it. However, their

presumed physical inferiority and social "privilege" justify a patriarchal preference for male leadership, insuring that occasions of women's
rule remain rare, limited severely to cases of inheritance, most notably
the royal succession.

We may lament with Jordan that "Neither the presence of a woman
on the throne for the better part of the century nor the arguments for
the legality of her rule seem to have encouraged an acceptance of the
idea that women could assume magistracies or participate in political
life in other capacities."[29] But Howard strenuously denies that queenship
implies any such idea, and on this point Elizabeth seems to have shared
his opinion.

III

A great deal remains to be said about *A Dutiful Defense*, but more must
await another occasion. Having followed Howard's lead by attending
to the biographical context of his treatise, we might close with a glance
at his life after 1590. As we have seen, he presented *A Dutiful Defense*
as part of an open campaign to revive his fortunes and gain a place at
court. Whatever role the treatise played, the campaign succeeded spec-
tacularly. A sketch of Howard's life written about 1607 records that "In
Her Highness' later time she called him to the court, delighted in his
conversation, and greatly favored his virtues."[30] By the mid-1590s, he
had regained her good graces while serving Essex. When Essex fell,
Howard did not merely survive but prospered, transferring to Cecil's
patronage a project begun with Essex—once more "haling to the north
star" of the Stuarts by smoothing the way for the accession of King
James. In the process, Howard became one of the new king's most
trusted advisors, entering the last decade of his life as earl of
Northampton, a leading privy councilor and powerful patron.

Lord Henry's fortunes suffered one further reversal. As
Northampton, he sustained some old enmities and made new ones;
the policies he backed were not always popular, and his reputation as
a Catholic made him suspect to many in Stuart England; near the end
of his life, he was implicated in the scandalous murder of Sir Thomas
Overbury. As a consequence, he acquired an extremely bad reputation,
almost dark enough to rival the Machiavellian legend of his enemy
Robert Dudley, earl of Leicester, and the dark legends have come down
to us as the received ideas about each. Despite an occasional challenge, history has mostly allowed Howard's enemies to write his epitaph, which is a key reason why, as Kevin Sharpe writes, "the Earl of

Northampton's intellectual interests—in ethics, philosophy, history, and political thought—have lamentably been ignored."[31] Further study of his contribution to the queenship controversy will improve our appreciation of this neglected figure as well as our understanding of how an Elizabethan could theorize a woman's rule.

Acknowledgments

Thanks to the University of Iowa for a Semester Assignment; to the Newberry Library Center for Renaissance Studies, with the assistance of the National Endowment for the Humanities, for fellowship support; and to Renaissance Studies at Iowa. Thanks also to the British Library and the Public Record Office, London, for permission to quote manuscripts cited in the text. I owe much to their staffs and those of the Bodleian Library, Oxford; the Houghton Library, Harvard; the Folger Shakespeare Library, Washington; and the Huntington Library, Pasadena. Marcia Culver, Diana Greenway, Shirley Grubb, Constance Jordan, John L. Murphy, and Retha Warnicke all helped generously. Special thanks to Carole Levin, *semper eadem*.

Notes

1. Retha Warnicke emphasizes the exclusion of women from the royal succession in England before Mary Tudor: *Women of the English Renaissance and Reformation* (Westport: Greenwood, 1983), ch. 4.

2. Paula L. Scalingi, "The Scepter or the Distaff," *The Historian* 41 (1978): 75, emphasis added.

3. See James E. Phillips, "The Background of Spenser's Attitude Toward Women Rulers," *Huntington Library Quarterly* 5 (1941): 27–28; Scalingi, 71n; and Patricia-Ann Lee, "A Bodye Politique to Governe," *The Historian* 52 (1990): 261n. Pamela J. Benson's account appears to be based upon only the opening chapters of *A Dutiful Defense*, which greatly limits the cogency of her claims: see *The Invention of the Renaissance Woman* (University Park: Pennsylvania State University Press, 1992), ch. 9.

4. I have examined Bodl. ms. 903, Oxford; BL Harl. ms. 6257 and Lansd. ms. 813, London; Houghton fMS. Eng. 826, Harvard; and Newberry Case ms. fJ 5452.634, Chicago. Numerous other copies exist. Benson cites one at Pepys Lib., Magdalen College, Cambridge; Shirley Grubb uses BL Add. ms. 24,652 (see n. 12 below). I cite *Dutiful Defense* by section rather than folio (e.g., "1.7" refers to Book 1, Chapter 7) and have modernized spelling and punctuation for all early texts.

5. I have examined copies entitled (misleadingly) "An answer to the copy of a railing invective against the regiment of women" in BL Harl. ms. 7021 and Add. ms. 12,513. Numerous copies exist.

6. The oft-repeated tradition identifying the councilor as Lord Burghley is plausible, but I have been unable to trace this conjecture back beyond George F. Nott, who graces it with a "probably": *The Works of Henry Howard Earl of Surrey and of Sir Thomas Wyatt* (London, 1815; reprint, New York: AMS, 1965), 2: 439n.

7. Howard's *Defense of the Ecclesiastical Regiment in England, Defaced by T.C. in His Reply Against D. Whitgift* has a strong Trinity Hall connection. While Lord Henry was at Trinity, the queen replaced its master with John Whitgift, whose campaign to restore conformity included the expulsion of Thomas Cartwright (the "T.C." of Howard's title). As a recent master of Trinity wrote, Elizabeth later made Whitgift archbishop of Canterbury "to do to all England what he had done to our own College": G. M. Trevelyan, *Trinity College* (Cambridge: Cambridge University Press, 1943), p. 18. For Howard's academic career, see John Venn and J. A. Venn, eds., *Alumni Cantabrigienses* (Cambridge: Cambridge University Press, 1922), Pt. 1, 2:415.

8. Goodman, *How Superior Powers Ought to Be Obeyed* (1558), pp. 53–54. For *Second Blast*, see *Political Writings of John Knox*, ed. Martin Breslow (Washington: Folger, 1985), p. 159.

9. On the English reception of *De Jure Regni* in manuscript, see James E. Phillips, "George Buchanan and the Sidney Circle," *Huntington Library Quarterly* 12 (1948): 41–44; I. D. McFarlane, *Buchanan* (London: Duckworth, 1981), pp. 393–95. Linda Levy Peck identifies Buchanan as the target of Howard's fragments on kingly power in BL Titus C vi: see "The Mentality of a Jacobean Grandee" in *The Mental World of the Jacobean Court* (Cambridge: Cambridge University Press, 1991), pp. 148–168.

10. P. Hume Brown, *George Buchanan* (Edinburgh: David Douglas, 1890), p. 316; W. A. Gatherer, *The Tyrannous Reign of Mary Stewart* (Edinburgh: Edinburgh University Press, 1958), p. 4. Could Howard have seen the Kennedy speech in 1577? Much of the *Historia* was composed in the 1560s, with all but the last book completed by 1578; however, evidence of manuscript circulation is scarce (McFarlane, p. 418; Phillips, "Buchanan," 49–50). Without explanation, Benson (cited in n. 2 above) asserts that Burghley tried to trap Howard by charging him to answer the *Historia's* attack on Mary (pp. 232, 236).

11. When Howard did answer Knox's *First Blast*, he did so very differently: in a serial commentary that survives only in fragments, half in Howard's own hand (BL Cotton App. 27, fols. 83–103). The scope of the loss may be suggested by the fact that the remaining sections are numbered 36–43 and 90–92, and that no. 36 concerns Knox's second main point.

12. Howard alludes to the way Martin Marprelate uses Aylmer's *Harbor* to attack its author as a hypocrite. Martin notes approvingly that Aylmer's answer to Knox spoke sharply "against the callings of bishops and their usurping of civil offices and against their pride, pomp, and superfluity." Thirty years later, complains Martin, Aylmer as bishop of London embodies the very errors he had formerly criticized. See *Epistle*, esp. p. 3, and *Epitome*, sigs. D3–E3, in *The Marprelate Tracts* (1588; rpt. Menston: Scolar, 1967). Martin does not attack gynecocracy but says he expects to be accused of doing so, as indeed he was, a topic explored by Shirley Grubb in an inpublished paper.

13. In October 1571, Lord Henry pleads with Burghley to allow him to remain at Audley End (BL Cotton Titus C vi, 13). In March 1572, he writes to express gratitude for "release of my strait imprisonment" (f. 15), only to complain a month later about renewed confinement (Public Record Office, SP 12/86/143, 26 April 1572).

14. Thomas Norton reports the interrogatories to Walsingham in PRO, SP 12/147/5–6; several pages later is Howard's letter promising Walsingham to stop hearing mass. On *A Treatise of Treasons*, see Francis Edwards, S. J., *The Marvellous Chance: Thomas Howard, Fourth Duke of Norfolk, and the Ridolphi Plot, 1570–1572* (London: Rupert Hart-Davis, 1968), App. 3.

15. SP 12/151/96, 118–19; see also Charles Arundel's interrogation at 95–97v, 100–108v. For more about Howard's political activities in the 1570s and 1580s, see John Bossy, "The Character of Elizabethan Catholicism," in *Crisis in Europe 1560–1660*, ed. T. Aston (New York: Basic Books, 1965), pp. 223–46, and D. C. Peck's introduction to *Leicester's Commonwealth* (Athens: Ohio University Press, 1985). On the earl of Oxford's role in Howard's troubles, see D. C. Peck, "Raleigh, Sidney, Oxford, and the Catholics, 1579," *Notes and Queries* 223 (1978): 427–31. On a possible role for Giordano Bruno, see Bossy, *Giordano Bruno and the Embassy Affair* (New Haven: Yale University Press, 1991), pp. 29ff., 99–104. Bossy identifies Howard as the original of Polihimnio in Bruno's *De La Causa* and suggests that this portrayal as a misogynist forced Howard to write *A Dutiful Defense* (pp. 115–25).

16. BL Cotton Caligula C vii, fols. 349–50, 361–62 (signed answers without interrogatories): the first examiner is Lord Hunsdon, to whom Howard presented the Lansdowne manuscript of *A Dutiful Defense*. Howard admits to receiving a pair of letters from Paget, the first being (ironically) "congratulation of his deliverance out of trouble" (f. 361). For the persistence of his earlier problems, see letters to Walsingham dated 14 September 1582 (SP 12/155) and 29 February 1583 (SP 12/158/197).

17. A memo "to the lords in commission for the examining of such as are committed to the Tower" records the decision to rack Shelley, which is followed immediately by an item asking "Whether the Lord Henry Howard shall not be more straitly examined concerning a letter brought from the Scots queen to him by George Moore, which he denieth to have received," but the

lords defer the matter to Elizabeth (SP 12/168/29). On Arundel, see Arnold Pritchard, *Catholic Loyalism in Elizabethan England* (Chapel Hill: University of North Carolina Press, 1979), pp. 41–44.

18. SP 12/212/19, 7 July 1588.

19. For an important document regarding Mary Queen of Scots that was apparently taken from Howard during a 1583 search, see Edwards, *The Marvelous Chance*, p. 51n.

20. See Linda Levy Peck, *Northampton: Patronage and Policy at the Court of James I* (London: Allen and Unwin, 1982), pp. 12–13, and "Mentality" (cited in n. 8 above). There is no adequate account of Howard's life and works, but Peck's studies provide an excellent start. G. F. Nott's memoir (cited in n. 5), though an all-out attempt to rehabilitate its subject, is still worth consulting.

21. Mary Thomas Crane, *Framing Authority: Sayings, Self, and Society in Sixteenth-Century England* (Princeton: Princeton University Press, 1993), pp. 16–17.

22. Ian Maclean, *The Renaissance Notion of Woman* (Cambridge: Cambridge University Press, 1980), pp. 83, 89. Of the many surveys of early modern texts about women, the most philosophical are Maclean's book and Constance Jordan's *Renaissance Feminism* (Ithaca: Cornell University Press, 1990).

23. For example, Constance Jordan, "Women's Rule in Sixteenth-Century British Political Thought," *Renaissance Quarterly* 40 (1987): 426.

24. Among recent general studies, see especially John D. Lyons, *Exemplum* (Princeton: Princeton University Press, 1989) and Timothy Hampton, *Writing from History* (Ithaca: Cornell University Press, 1990). Glenda McLeod discusses catalogs of exemplary women in *Virtue and Venom* (Ann Arbor: University of Michigan Press, 1991).

25. Maclean, *Renaissance Notion*, p. 56.

26. The intractability of Howard's rhetorical problem is increased by the contradictions within the traditions on which he draws, contradictions systematic enough to appear in a thinker as different as Calvin. See John L. Thompson's excellent *John Calvin and the Daughters of Sarah* (Geneva: Librairie Droz, 1992).

27. Benson, *Invention*, pp. 233, 240.

28. The contrast between essentialism and conventionalism remains useful in such a context but should be evaluated in light of the critique by Diana Fuss, *Essentially Speaking: Feminism, Nature, and Difference* (New York: Routledge, 1989).

29. Jordan, "Women's Rule," 423–24. On women under Elizabeth, see especially Allison Heisch, "Queen Elizabeth I and the Persistence of

Patriarchy," *Feminist Review* 4 (1980): 45–56; Mortimer Levine, "The Place of Women in Tudor Government," in *Tudor Rule and Revolution*, ed. D. J. Guth and J. W. McKenna (Cambridge: Cambridge University Press, 1982), pp. 109–110.

30. BL Add. ms. 6298, f. 285.

31. Kevin Sharpe, *Sir Robert Cotton: History and Politics in Early Modern England* (Oxford: Oxford University Press, 1979), p. 79.

Catherine de Médicis, a la cruauté de conduire Charles IX à Montfaucon, contempler le corps sanglant de Coligni.

Catherine de Médicis. By permission of the Newberry Library.

The Blood-Stained Hands of Catherine de Médicis

Elaine Kruse

From Eve to Hillary Rodham Clinton women have been attacked for having undue and thus, dangerous, influence over men. In modern American culture, Presidents' wives who have played any state role have been roundly criticized. During the 1992 American presidential race, *The American Spectator* dubbed Hillary Clinton "the Lady Macbeth of Little Rock"; *Human Events* magazine called her "the Evita Perón of American politics." One week into the Clinton presidency, Hillary's friends gave her a witch's hat, a playful warning that her assignment to draft health-care reform would open her up to the image of "the wicked witch of the West Wing."[1]

Whenever a president appeared to be weak, attacks mounted. When Nancy Reagan was perceived to be protecting her ailing husband from reporters and feuding with Chief of Staff Don Regan, she was dubbed the "dragon lady."[2] William Safire sniped:

> What Nancy says goes. This is not Rosalyn Carter, the "Steel Magnolia," stiffened her husband's spine; this is an incipient Edith Wilson, unelected and unaccountable, presuming to control the actions and appointments of the executive branch.[3]

These images of First Ladies indicate the ongoing paranoia about women exerting political influence from behind the scenes, demonstrating Joan Scott's contention that gender is not only a basic element of social relations founded on perceived differences between the sexes, but also a primordial means of signifying power relationships.[4]

Similarly, the representation of women in early modern France betrayed deep anxiety surrounding women and power. Whether witch or queen, danger became inherent in what John Knox coined "the monstrous regiment of women."[5] The historical reading of Catherine de Médicis, Queen of France during the sixteenth-century wars of religion, serves as a touchstone for the imaging of women, in particular, the gender construction of powerful women and the stereotypes developed about them.

Catherine was successively Queen (as wife to Henri II, who reigned from 1547 to his accidental death in 1559), Queen-Mother under sons Francis II (r. 1559–60), Charles IX (r. 1560–74), and Henri III (r. 1575–1589), and Queen-Regent during the minority of Charles IX (1560–63) and in the interim between the death of Charles IX and the return of the future Henri III from Poland (1574–75).

The portrayal of Catherine as the Wicked Queen—dangerous foreigner, evil woman, and political manipulator—demonstrates how xenophobia, the witch-craze, and power relations were used to gender the political discourse during the chaotic years of religious warfare and dynastic instability. The legend of Catherine de Médicis became a weapon, both to undermine later queens or queen-regents and to rouse partisan fury against the Catholic Church and/or the monarchy. Two centuries later, the Catherine de Médicis legend in its most virulent form served, first, as a veiled attack and then, as overt courtroom rhetoric, against another queen, Marie Antoinette. Tried and executed in October 1793, nine months after the execution of her husband, Louis XVI, by the French revolutionaries, she was charged with being a foreigner imbued with tyrannical politics, the lewd perverter of her own son, and the traitor to the nation who led her husband astray. The queen became the ultimate example of woman as other, the justification for the exclusion of women from participation, first from the throne, then from all public life.

The original legend reflected the preoccupations of the sixteenth century; its longevity suggests its utility against all women. The equation: women + power = danger, is grounded in misogynist theological, biological, and political arguments. The exclusion of women from public roles in the established Christian Church was reinforced by Tertullian, an early Church father, who wrote:

> . . . do you not know that you are Eve? God's sentence hangs still over all your sex. . . . You are the devil's gateway. . . . It was you who coaxed your way around him whom the devil had not the force to attack.[6]

Biological theories from the Greeks to the Renaissance held that women were "other," defective males, dominated by carnal passions.

CHARLES IX. AND CATHERINE DE' MEDICI. — Page 354.

Charles IX and Catherine de Médici. Reproduced from the collection of the
University of Nebraska Library.

Women were deemed irrational, bound by their reproductive role, and physically weak.[7]

Similarly, political theory advantaged men. The Salic law, which in French private law prevented women from inheriting landed family property, was falsified in the fifteenth century through insertion of a forged clause in order to exclude women from succession to the throne.[8] Sarah Hanley argues that Renaissance jurists, uneasy about the inherent weakness of the legal objection, developed a natural law argument to legitimize male right: a marital regime model of government based on "biogenetic notions of seminal theory and male generative capacity." Linking family formation and state building, their premise was that just as husbands through seminal transmission create the family line, so "kings likewise create royal heirs who perpetuate monarchy." A queen of France was "foreign seed," capable of reproduction but incapable of seminal creation. In order to reinforce this contention, they drew on the image of Catherine de Médicis to develop a "misogyny code," used against successive queens and queen-regents.[9]

The legend of the Wicked Queen portrayed Catherine de Médicis as an upstart Italian; a monstrous mother; a lusty, demonic woman; an ambitious Machiavellian politician; and the vicious perpetrator of the Saint Bartholomew's Day massacre. The focus of the legend, the massacre, occurred in the context of the 1572 wedding of Marguerite de Valois, Catherine's daughter, and sister to the reigning Charles IX, to Henry of Navarre, scion of the Protestant branch of the royal family. Catherine tried unsuccessfully to end religious warring through arranged truces, such as the Peace of St. Germain (1570). The marriage was her plan to unite the two factions and calm the passions of years of atrocities on both sides. Among the Protestants in Paris for the wedding was Gaspard de Coligny, lord of Chatillon and Admiral of France, a prominent Protestant leader and bitter enemy of the Catholic Guise family. On Friday morning, August 22, four days after the wedding, an assassination attempt against Coligny miscarried when he bent over to adjust his shoe as a shot was fired from a window, wounding him. Tensions escalated between the three major parties: Catholic, Protestant (known as Huguenots), and crown, with rumblings of a Huguenot retaliation against the parties responsible. On Saturday night a royal order went out to murder the wounded Coligny and other leading Protestants before trouble erupted.[10] The ensuing massacre spread to the streets of Paris, a rabidly Catholic city, and ultimately to provincial cities, resulting in the deaths of thousands of Huguenots.[11]

Numerous tracts, particularly the *Marvelous Discourse on the Life, Actions, and Misconduct of Catherine de Médicis, Queen Mother,* launched the legend of the Wicked Queen following the massacre.[12] What started as a scurrilous attack by political adversaries has since taken on mythic proportions, a legend perpetuated by ideologue and historian alike in the centuries that followed.[13] Seventeenth-century royal historian Scipion Dupleix stressed her ambition; Voltaire, her superstition; nineteenth-century historian Jules Michelet, her total wickedness: "She reeks of death." American historian Ralph Roeder in the 1937 biography, *Catherine de Medici and the Lost Revolution,* intoned, "She became a medium through which all the negative and destructive forces of life were free to work." Garrett Mattingly, in *The Armada* (1959) depicted her as an unnatural mother, claiming she and the Duke of Guise drove "the poor, weak, half-crazy young king into an act that would haunt him the rest of his short life."[14]

The longevity of the legend suggests ongoing paranoia about powerful women. Catherine de Médicis became the villain in what Robert Kingdon describes as a coordinated publishing strategy begun in 1574. Kingdon argues that the *Marvelous Discourse* was part of a political attack on the Valois throne at the weak moment of the regency after Charles IX died. Although probably a Protestant tract, Kingdon claims it was used as propaganda to justify and encourage civil war by both Protestants and Catholics against the crown. Michel Reulos suggests an earlier scenario: that although the King originally took credit for the massacre, this put in question his role as *roi judiciare,* so propagandists changed the accountability to the Queen-Mother as a foreigner.[15]

A major justification of exclusion of Queens from ruling was anti-foreign bias. The attacks on Catherine de Médicis picked up on anti-Italian xenophobia directed against her since the 1530s. The Venetian ambassador Michiel, reporting on the atmosphere in France after the attempt on Admiral Coligny's life, wrote:

> They call this arbitrary way of proceeding, without form of trial, the way of tyranny, and they attribute it to the Queen, as an Italian, a Florentine, and of the house of Medici, of tyrant blood (they say). She is consequently thoroughly detested, as is also, on her account, the whole Italian nation.[16]

The *Marvelous Discourse* began with an attack on her background: first of all Italian, worse than that Florentine, and vilest of all, a Medici.

Catherine de Médicis is Italian and Florentine. Amongst the nations, Italy takes the prize for cunning and shrewdness; in Italy, Tuscany; and in Tuscany, the city of Florence.... Now when a person without a conscience has the art of deception, as often seen in that country, imagine how much evil you can expect. And besides, Catherine comes from the house of Médici.[17]

In Jacques Auguste de Thou's *History of the Bloody Massacres* (1604), he explained Charles IX's perfidy, "being by nature of an Italian genius, and well-instructed by his Mother in the policies of her country." And of Catherine herself,

it cannot be, but that a woman who is a foreigner, and an Italian, descended of the race of Popes ... and of a Florentine and guileful nature, should study all extremities against her enemies.[18]

Catherine was denounced as a Médici on two scores in the *Marvelous Discourse*. First, the Médicis were portrayed as *parvenus*, virtually unknown in early Florence, who took their name from a man who was a *medicin* (doctor). Also, the legend stressed that their ancestor, Silvestre, was champion of the populace over against the nobility; that they made their money through banking and usury; and that they became masters of the city through various forms of corruption.[19] Thus, Catherine was tarred with the brush of being from an upstart family, with no noble heritage, which rose to power through dirty politics.

Her critics ignored her French noble blood; indeed, she was a cousin by marriage to her husband. Catherine's mother was Madeline de la Tour d'Auvergne, descended on her father's side from the dukes of Aquitaine and the counts of Auvergne, and on her mother's side, a direct descendant of Saint Louis himself and a princess of the blood. Certainly, her French pedigree was impeccable. Yet, Jean Heretier, in his 1959 biography, *Catherine de Médici*, would refer to her "tidy bourgeois mind," intent on marrying her children into the royal houses of Europe.[20]

But even more damning was the fact that she was the daughter of the man to whom Machiavelli had dedicated *The Prince*. François Hotman and others of the "politique" party used Machiavelli as the "very embodiment of tyranny, atheism, and intolerance." Following the massacre, stories circulated that Catherine considered this book as her bible, raised her children on it, and that the future Henri III carried it in his pocket. Suggestions were made that the murder of Coligny and the massacre were direct applications of the eighth chapter of *The Prince*.[21] The anonymous tract *Wake-Up Call for the French and their Neighbors* (1573) blatantly charged that Catherine had followed Machiavellian principles throughout her dealings with the Protestants.

In the religiously sensitive sixteenth century, the legend of the wicked foreign queen took on the added physiognomy of the "witch": the woman alone, uncontrolled by father or husband, sexually predatory, practicing evil arts (*maleficia*) to exercise her will or to wreak vengeance, and servant of Satan.[22] The writer of the *Marvelous Discourse* argued that there were signs that Catherine was dangerous from birth. Turning the nativity story on its head, the legend reported that menacing stars stood over the place where she was born. Supposedly, her parents consulted leading astrologers, who warned that "if she lived, she would be the cause of great calamities, and ultimately the total ruin of the house and place into which she married." Her parents were shocked, but determined to raise her and avoid disaster, vowed never to marry her.[23] No historical evidence of such a prediction exists; rather, her mother died of childbirth fever within fifteen days of her birth, and her father of syphilis and consumption within the month.

Catherine became the ward of her uncle, the Médici pope Clement VII, after her parents' deaths. When Florence was under seige, he placed her in a convent for protection. The writer of the *Marvelous Discourse* painted that incident as evidence of Catherine's malignity, bringing disaster on her native city. The city council, according to this account, knew of the prediction; some suggested she be placed in a basket and hung on the ramparts, so the enemy cannon could blow her away; others thought she should be placed in a brothel when she was of age; and others, that she be placed in a convent for the rest of her life. The Protestant perspective was apparent when the writer intoned: "the final suggestion, seemingly the kindest, was in fact the cruelest."[24]

According to the legend, when Clement arranged the marriage of Catherine and Henri, duke of Orleans, second in line to the French throne, he brought about the tragic fate of France. The legend blamed Catherine for the death of Francis, Henri's older brother.[25] This was only the first in a series of untimely deaths laid to Catherine's "murder Italian style." Poisoning was believed to be a device of Italian tyrants, such as the Borgias, as well as a female weapon, for women prepared, served, or supervised the feeding of household and guests. Catherine was accused of what might be termed *maleficia* throughout her career: of poisoning her opposition, ranging from family members to the entire army of the Prince of Condé.[26] Henri of Navarre's mother, Jeanne d'Albret, reluctant to agree to the ill-fated wedding, was supposedly the victim of poisoned gloves.[27] The rumormongers even suggested that Catherine de Médicis was responsible for her own children's deaths. Gilbert Burnet, writing *A Relation of the Massacre* in late seventeenth century England, said of Charles IX's death, that it was "a long sickness . . . believed the effect of a lent Poison given him by the Queen-Mother . . . "[28]

The witch image applied as well to Catherine's married life. The first ten years of the marriage were childless. According to the legend, she was on the verge of repudiation when she introduced Diane de Poitiers into the household as a diversion for her husband. In fact, Diane had served as lady-in-waiting at the court for many years. The young prince fell in love with this woman, twenty years his senior, several years after marrying Catherine. Although Catherine tolerated the royal mistress throughout her husband's lifetime, she was not enamored of the situation. Diane supposedly suggested her own physician to help cure the young couple's sterility. Catherine subsequently gave birth to ten children, seven of whom lived to adulthood. The *Marvelous Discourse* attributed this turnabout to "the methods we have all heard about," an inference of women's secret knowledge.[29] Other writers claimed she had tried many different potions, which explained the fragile constitution of her sons, reiterating the calumny of kings victimized by the royal mother.

The writer of the *Marvelous Discourse* claimed that Catherine corrupted her children deliberately, surrounding them with a licentious court: (Charles IX would have been) "a naturally good prince, if she had not used ever means to corrupt him."[30] She was blamed with introducing her sons to cockfighting, designed to make them cruel. Her children were depicted as weak and morally misshapen, and the blame placed on Catherine. In the English reprint of the *Marvelous Discourse* of 1693, it said of Charles IX: (he) "was as ignorant of affairs as when he was a pupil, and the Queen would have him understand no more than a mute in a play."[31] The royal mother became the "unnatural mother," destroying or dominating her children for her own ambitions, then betraying and abandoning them. Or, she became the "dangerous mother," sacrificing the good of the state for the sake of her children.

Catherine was not only the Bad Mother; she was also the Bad Woman. A poem from the *Wake-Up Call* described the Peace of St.

Germain as the child of the Cardinal de Lorraine and his "whore" Catherine:

> My father was a devil in dis-Guise
> Assuming the habit of a priest,
> A deadly monster professing all vice,
> Stirring up trouble, a terrible beast,
> Coupling with that high born whore,
> Descended from the buggers of Italy,
> Nursed by the milk of a horrible fury.[32]

Rumors were spread that the Cardinal of Lorraine

> visited the Queen-Mother at midnight wearing only a night-shirt, and that the valet guarding the door warned that any-one telling would find his life in danger.[33]

Sexual danger carried over into the accounts of the massacre, where mutilations of the bodies frequently included castration.[34] Catherine was depicted as taking her son's hand to lead him out to gloat over the castrated corpse of Coligny. Another story claimed that Catherine inspected the body of Sire de Soubise to see why he had been "impotent to live with a woman." Castration and prurient interest linked Catherine with the sixteenth-century image of the witch who delighted in stealing men's penises.[35]

That the dangerous woman, the witch, was in league with the Devil seemed self-evident in what was portrayed as Catherine's vicious vendetta against pious Christians. Her peace forays were denounced as Catholic duplicity. To the Protestant mind, any connection with magic was tantamount to heresy, and Catherine was known to rely on astrologers.[36] Thus, Catherine, as presented in the *Marvelous Discourse*, became the image of the witch in every respect: an outsider, isolated as a widow, identified by astrologers as evil, knowing secret arts, practicing *maleficia* upon her enemies, consorting with the devil in the form of the Cardinal of Lorraine, lewd, and exercising power through indirect and secret channels.

The images of foreigner and witch facilitated blaming Catherine for the Saint Bartholomew's Day massacre. The Protestant accounts painted her as a duplicitous, demonic Papist, intent on destroying the Huguenots. They alleged that she encouraged the marriage of Henri of Navarre and Marguerite as a ploy to draw all leading Huguenots to Paris for a premediated slaughter. They claimed she plotted to kill Coligny and convinced an unstable Charles IX to order the massacre.

Catherine became the Lady Macbeth of French history: ambitious, amoral, and acting through indirect channels to perpetrate political assassinations.

Was Catherine guilty of planning the Saint Bartholomew's Day massacre? Little evidence supports such a contention. The wedding was intended to reconcile the opposing religious factions. Plans included elaborate banquets and artistic productions in Renaissance style. As the Venetian diplomat, Cavalli, commented in the *Relazione* of 1574, premeditation was unlikely because "there were so many mistakes."[37] Historians still disagree on who to blame for the assassination attempt and for the murder of Coligny and others at court. The standard claim that Catherine ordered the assassination because she saw Coligny as a rival for power does not stand up under scrutiny of his long absence from court. However, Catherine may well have decided to eliminate Coligny after the aborted assassination, justified as a regalian right to protect the state.[38] The Venetian ambassadors reported

> that the Queen-Mother replied (to Queen Elizabeth) that they were compelled to make further executions to set their affairs right, and moreover, that princes were under no obligation to keep their promises to their subjects.[39]

Henri IV later observed, "What was the poor woman to do . . . ? I'm surprised she didn't do worse things."[40] But the raging massacre in Paris and other cities was a popular phenomenon, commonplace in the context of the religious wars.[41] Yet, Catherine became the villain of all the bloodletting.

The legend of wicked Catherine de Médicis became a vehicle for calumny against other queens. The most successful propaganda campaign was that launched against Marie Antoinette in the decade preceding the French Revolution.[42] Like Catherine, Marie Antoinette was a foreigner, a young, vivacious girl when she came to court, and barren in the early years of marriage, creating anxiety over the royal succession. She became influential in a court rife with factionalism. The legend of Catherine de Médicis proved particularly useful to suggest the failings of the monarchy, and particularly, the Queen.

In 1783 Marie Genevieve Charlotte Thiroux d'Arconville published *History of Francis II* in which she viciously attacked Catherine:

> Catherine de Médicis, a woman without character, combined all the weaknesses and vices of every type . . . using them as needed for her insatiable ambition and satisfaction;

She continued in that vein to suggest to suggest that Catherine flitted endlessly between opposing factions and was "irresolute, false, inconstant, and coldly cruel."[43] This resurrection of the legend appears to have been a veiled attack on Marie Antoinette in the charged political atmosphere of the 1780s.

The Queen as evil influence was reinforced by Marie-Joseph de Chenier's play, *Charles IX*, first performed on 4 November 1789, four months after the fall of the Bastille, and continued over the objections of the king in 1790. The legend was evoked from the outset with Henry of Navarre claiming his mother had been poisoned and Coligny regretting the "Medici" influence, the poisoned breath surrounding Charles IX from the cradle.[44] The reluctant king struggled against Catherine's argument that the massacre was necessary, and revoked the order, only to find that the executions had begun. "You have ruined me!. . . . I dare to ask: is it you who reigns?"[45]

The attack on foreign queens became overt with the article, "Manifesto of French patriots on the marriages of our kings," published in *Révolutions de Paris* in December 1790 and reprinted as *The crimes of the Queens of France, from the beginning of the monarchy until Marie Antoinette.* The author, Louise de Keralio, argued that all of the "misfortunes, wars, devastation, and oppression" of France had been due to the marriages of kings to foreign women, "compacts between despots." The original article included capsule biographies of queens from Louise de Savoie to Marie de Médicis, emphasizing the following on Catherine:

> What can we say of this queen, whose name alone awakens the idea of villainy and the most consummate hypocrisy? Our families have still not recovered from the profound and innumerable evils this Italian brought on us. The reign of this woman is the image of hell. Try to imagine a crime whose theory and practice were not in use in the court of Charles IX, of Francis II, and of Henri III; you will not find one.

Catherine de Médicis became the central example of the foreign, criminal queen in this diatribe against Marine Antoinette. The article concluded: "It is time we had a king totally French, with a French father and a French mother."[46]

Three years later Marie Antoinette, the "widow Capet," was being tried for treason. The accusation against her stated:

> In the fashion of Messaline, Brunehilde, Fredegonde, and Médicis, who qualify as former queens of France, and whose

names are so odious that they ought to be effaced from the annals of history, Marie Antoinette . . . has been the scourge of France and a bloodsucker of the French.[47]

The case against Marie Antoinette was based on the same kinds of charges laid to Catherine, although the witch image had become secularized. As a foreigner, she had sacrificed France for her own interests. As an unnatural mother, she had perverted her son, teaching him to masturbate and forcing him to commit incest with her. And as a politician, she had influenced the rightful king to carry out policies detrimental to the French people and encouraged the enemies of France.[48]

Like Catherine de Médicis, Marie Antoinette was attacked for political reasons, with the charges carrying the same weight of misogyny. Between the lines lay the fear of women exercising power, whether it be overtly political or through their roles as wives and mothers. At the historical moment in which men claimed equality in political life, killing the "Father" and proclaiming the fraternity of the sons, women were deemed other, dangerous, and incapable of political rights.[49]

Both Catherine de Médicis and Marie Antoinette were viewed in the past as powerful women, devious and evil. By the same means, women were written out of political life well into the twentieth century. The measure of modern society will be equity for women in all levels of power, finally eradicating the legacy of myth and misogyny.

Notes

1. Garry Wills, "A Doll's House?" *New York Review of Books*, vol. 39, no. 17, 22 October 1992, pp. 6–10; Eleanor Clift, "Battle Scars," *Newsweek*, 8 February 1993, p. 14; Howard Kurtz, "Lady MacBeth or Cinderella? Mrs. Clinton Makes News for Starved Press," *International Herald Tribune*, 28 November 1992.

2. "The Week of the Dragon," *Time*, 16 March 1987, p. 24.

3. William Safire, "First Lady's Interference Damaging Reagan's Image," *New York Times*, 3 March 1987.

4. Joan Wallach Scott, "Gender: A Useful Category of Historical Analysis," in *Gender and the Politics of History* (New York: Columbia University Press, 1988), pp. 28–50. See also Natalie Zemon Davis, "Women on Top," in *Society and Culture in Early Modern France: Eight Essays* (Stanford: Stanford University Press, 1975).

5. John Knox, *Works*, ed. David Laing, vol. 4 (Edinburgh: James Thin, 1895), and *First Blast of the Trumpet against the Monstrous Regiment of Women* (1558).

6. Tertullian, *De Cultu Feminarum*, quoted in Julia O'Faolain and Lauro Martines, *Not in God's Image* (New York: Harper, 1973), p. 132.

7. Ian Maclean, *The Renaissance Notion of Woman* (New York: Cambridge University Press, 1980), chap. 3.

8. On the Salic Law, see Ralph Giesey, "The Juristic Basis of Dynastic Right to the French Throne," in *Transactions of the American Philosophical Society*, New Series 51:5 (1961): 17–22.

9. I am indebted to Sarah Hanley for this theoretical model, found in her preface "The Masks of La Loi Salique in the Quest for Male Right and Female Exclusion from Monarchic Government" for *Des Femmes dans l'Histoire: La Loi Salique* (Paris: Côtes Femmes Éditions, forthcoming).

10. For a complete description of the wounding, murder, and mutilation of the body of Coligny, see Robert Kingdon, *Myths About the St. Bartholomew's Day Massacres, 1572–1576* (Cambridge: Harvard University Press, 1988), pp. 28–33.

11. Natalie Zemon Davis, "The Rites of Violence" in *Society and Culture*, pp. 152–87; Janine Estèbe, *Tocsin pour un massacre. La saison des Saint-Barthélemy* (Paris, 1968).

12. *Discours merveilleux de la vie, actions, et deportements de la reyne Catherine de Médicis, declarant tous les moyens qu'elle a tenus pour usurper le gouvernement du royaume de France et de ruiner l'estat d'iceluy* (1574) attributed to Henri Estienne. M. L. Cimber and F. Danjou, ed. *Archives curieuses de l'histoire de France depuis Louis XI jusqu'à Louis XVIII* (Paris, Beauvais, 1836) 1re série, tome 9, pp. 1–113. Robert Kingdon discusses the authorship of this tract and its intent in *Myths*, pp. 200–213. Other important tracts include *Le Reveille-matin des François, et de leurs voisins*, attributed to Nicolas Barnaud, Hugues Donneau, Theodore de Beze, or perhaps even François Hotman ('Edinburgh' [Basile], 1574); and Pierre de l'Étoile, *Journal du Regne du Roy Henri III* (Paris, 1719).

13. Nicola Mary Sutherland, *Princes, Politics, and Religion, 1547–1589* (London: Hambledon Press, 1984), chapter 13—"Catherine de Médici: The Legend of the Wicked Italian Queen," pp. 237–48; Philippe Joutand, Janine Estebe, Elizabeth Labrousse, and Jean Lecuir, *Le Saint-Barthelémy ou les resonances d'un massacre* (Neuchatel, 1976).

14. Scipion Dupleix, *Histoire générale de France*, vol. 3 (Paris, 1634); Voltaire, *Essai sur les moeurs et l'esprit des Nations et sur les Principaux faits de l'Histoire, depuis Charlemagne jusqu'à Louis XIII* (n.p., 1770); Ralph Roeder, *Catherine de'*

Médici and the Lost Revolution (New York: Viking, 1937), p. 472; Garrett Mattingly, *The Armada* (Boston: Houghton Mifflin, 1959), p. 230.

15. Robert M. Kingdon, *Myths*, pp. 201–2; Michel Reulos, "La Saint-Barthelémy: Thème Politique ou Thème Religieux?" *Revue d'Histoire littéraire de la France*, 73, no. 5 (Sept–Oct, 1973):778–783.

16. Giovanni Michiel, in Sir Henry Austen Layard, *The Massacre of St. Bartholomew, illustrated from State Papers in the Archives of Venice* (London: Spottiswoode & Co., 1887), p. 27.

17. *Discours*, p. 5.

18. Jacques Auguste de Thou, *The History of the Bloody Massacres of the Protestants in France in the Year of Our Lord, 1572* (London: John Lieu, 1674).

19. *Discours*, pp. 5–13.

20. Jean Heretier, *Catherine de Medici*, trans. Charlotte Holdane (New York: St. Martin's Press, 1963), p. 299.

21. Donald R. Kelley, "Murd'rous Machiavel in France: A Post Mortem," *Political Science Quarterly* 85 (December 1970):552–53, citing *De iusta Henrici tertii abdicatione e Francorum regno* (Lyon, 1591); II:33 and Franciscus Portus, *Ad Petri Carpentarii virulentam epistolam responsio* (s.l. 1573), pp. 31–32.

22. Joseph Klaits, *Servants of Satan: The Age of the Wtich Hunts* (Bloomington: Indiana University Press, 1985), p. 16.

23. *Discours*, p. 13.

24. *Discours*, p. 14.

25. *Discours*, p. 16.

26. In the English translation, *The History of the Life of Katherine de Médicis, Queen Mother and Regent of France* or *The Exact Pattern of the Present French King's Policy* (London: John Wyat, 1693), Wyat selected which legends to perpetuate.

27. Nancy Lyman Roelker, *Queen of Navarre, Jeanne d'Albret, 1528–1572* (Cambridge: Harvard, 1968), p. 391. The tale of poisoned perfumed gloves was used in more than one instance in the legend.

28. Gilbert Burnet, *A Relation of the Barbarous & Bloody Massacre of about One Hundred Thousand Protestants, Begun at Paris, and Carried On Over All France by the Papists in the year 1572* (London, 1678).

29. *Discours*, p. 17. Roman d'Amat and R. Limouzen-Lamothe, *Dictionnaire de Biographie Française*, vol. 11 (Paris: Librairie Latouzey, 1967), p. 248.

30. *Discours*, p. 22.

31. *The History of the Life of Katherine de Médicis*, p. 55. Catherine used her role as mother as a symbolic strategy to fortress her position. See Rachel Weil, " 'The Crown has Fallen to the Distaff': Gender and Politics in the Age of Catherine de Medici, 1560–1589," *Critical Matrix*, vol. 1, no. 4 (Princeton, 1985): 1–38.

32. *Reville-Matin des François et de leurs voisins*, I, 13, translated in Donald R. Kelley, *The Beginning of Ideology: Consciousness and Society in the French Reformation* (Cambridge: Cambridge University Press, 1981), p. 287.

33. Pierre de L'Étoile, *Journal du Regne de Henri III*, p. 56. The *Reveille Matin* included a tale of the cardinal being tricked into accepting a painting showing him engaged in an orgy with Catherine de Médicis and the Duchess of Guise.

34. Kingdon, *Myths*, p. 38, drawn from Simon Goulart, *Mémoires de l'estat de France sous Charles neufiesme. Contenans les choses plus notables, faites et publiées tant par les Catholiques que par ceux de la Religion, depuis le troisiesme édit de pacification fait au mois d'Aoust 1570 iusques au regne de Henry troisiesme. Réduits en trois volumes, chascun desquels a un indice des principales matières y contenus . . . à Meidelbourg. Par Henrich Wolf* 3 vols. (Geneva: Vignon, 1576).

35. Hans Baldung Grien's wood carvings depicted women engaged in ecstatic, sensual delirium; others showed nests filled with penises stolen by the witches. Linda Chults, "Baldung and the Witches of Freiburg: The Evidence of Images," *Journal of Interdisciplinary History* 18, no. 2 (Autumn 1987): 249–276.

36. Robert W. Scribner, "The Reformation, Popular Magic, and the 'Disenchantment of the world,' " *Journal of Interdisciplinary History* 23, no. 3 (Winter 1993):475–494. Catherine's connection with astrologers is described as malevolent in the anti-Papist work by Eugène Defrance, *Catherine de Médicis, ses astrologues et ses magiciens envouteurs, documents inédits sur la diplomatie et les sciences occultes du XVIe siècle* (Paris: Mercure de France, 1911).

37. Cavalli, *Relazione*, p. 42.

38. Barbara Diefendorf supports N. M. Sutherland's contention that Catherine had nothing to gain in disrupting her carefully laid plans to end religious strife by a strike against Coligny. She argues that the accused assailant, Maurevert, may well have been acting on his own or on the orders of the Guise family. The decision to kill the Huguenot leaders was a "preemptive strike," probably due to rumors of a planned Huguenot retaliation. Barbara Diefendorf, *Beneath the Cross: Catholics and Huguenots in Sixteenth-Century Paris* (New York: Oxford University Press, 1991), pp. 93–99. Compare to Kingdon, *Myths*.

39. Cavalli, *Relazione* in Layard, *The Massacre of St. Bartholomew*, p. 17.

40. Claude Groulard, *Mémoires de Messire Claude Groulard ou Voyages par lui faits en cour* in Claude Bernard Petitot, ed. *Collection complète des mémoires relatifs à l'histoire de France,* séries 1, vol. 49 (Paris:1821–27), p. 384.

41. Barbara Diefendorf, "Prologue to a Massacre: Popular Unrest in Paris, 1557–1572," *American Historical Review* 90 (1985):1067–91.

42. See Lynn Hunt, *The Family Romance of the French Revolution* (Berkeley: University of California Press, 1992), pp. 103–111, on the pornography and libellous tracts used to destroy the queen's reputation, and Sara Maza, "L'Image de la souveraine: femininité et politique dans les pamphlets de l'affaire du Collier," in Harvey Chisick, ed. *The Press in the French Revolution* (Studies on Voltaire and the Eighteenth Century) (Oxford: Voltaire Foundation, 1991), pp. 363–378.

43. Marie Genevieve Charlotte Thiroux d'Arconville, *Histoire de François II* 2 vols. (Paris: Chez Belin, 1783), p. 47. Summarized in Sutherland, *Princes,* p. 240.

44. Marie-Joseph de Chenier, *Charles IX; tragédie en cing actes* (Paris: Les Bons Livres, 1870), p. 3, 5. I am indebted to Frans C. Amelinckx for alerting me to this play.

45. Chenier, *Charles IX*, p. 36.

46. "Manifeste des patriotes français-Du mariage de nos rois," *Révolutions de Paris* no. 76 (18–25 Décembre 1790):564–569. Although published under the name of Louis Proudhomme, *Les Crimes des reines de France* was the work of Keralio, as noted in Lynn Hunt, "The Many Bodies of Marie-Antoinette: Political Pornography and the Problem of the Feminine in the French Revolution," in *Eroticism and the Body Politic*, ed. Lynn Hunt (Baltimore: Johns Hopkins, 1991), pp. 108–130, and footnote 42, pp. 129–30.

47. Charles Ostyn, "Le procès de Marie Antoinette," *La Révolution française* 6 (1984):644–46 contains the complete transcription of the trial. The *Discours* had compared Catherine to Brunhilda, as was Marie Antoinette in this trial. In 1587, Pierre de Belloy had recounted "bad queen" tales of Chrotilde [*sic*], Fredegonde, Bruechilde, Judith, Blanche (mother of Saint Louis), Isabeau de Bavaire, and Louise de Savoie: "in France, women are excluded from succession to the throne: their governing has been disastrous (funeste) for us in the past; and the French have had nothing but regret and discontent over their rule." *Examen du discours publié contre la maison royalle de France, et particulièrement contre la branche de Bourbon, seule reste d'icelle, sur la loy salique, & succession du royaume. Par un Catholique, apostolique, romain, mais bon François, & tres fidèle suiet de la couronne de France* ([Paris], 1587), pp. 248–53.

48. The political ramifications of the attack on Marie Antoinette are discussed by Elizabeth Colwill, "Just Another Citizen? Marie-Antoinette on Trial, 1790–1793," *History Workshop Journal* 28 (Autumn 1989):63–87.

49. Joan Landes, *Women and the Public Sphere in the Age of the French Revolution* (Ithaca: Cornell University Press, 1988).

The order and the manner of the burning of Anne Askew. From John Foxe
Acts and Monuments. By permission of the Folger Shakespeare Library.

Expert Witnesses and Secret Subjects: Anne Askew's *Examinations* and Renaissance Self-Incrimination

Elizabeth Mazzola

> Then he asked me, why I had so few words? And I answered,
> "God hath given me the gift of knowledge, but not of utterance."
> Anne Askew, *Examinations* (Foxe 541)

I. Introduction

My theme is autobiography, in particular a subject's decision not to write one. If the evidence for this choice is, by its nature, unavailable, we have found other ways to claim it. One useful method is proposed by Freud. In 1906, a year after he published his first major case history, "Fragment of an Analysis of a Case of Hysteria" (or, as it is more commonly known, "Dora"),[1] he addresses a seminar on criminology, where he comments on some of the similarities between criminals and hysterics.[2] Since Foucault we have learned to perceive the ways both parties transgress society's rigidly defined codes of normal behavior,[3] but for Freud, the likeness has more to do with what the subject knows, not what he does. As he explains: "In both cases we are concerned with a secret, with something hidden. But in order that I may not appear paradoxical, I must point out the difference at once. In the case of the criminal, it is a secret which he knows and hides from, but in the case of the hysteric it is a secret from him, a secret he himself does not know" (18). The problem therefore is epistemological, not legal or medical: it concerns the ways reason knows itself,[4] and not how it outlaws and punishes irrationality. Moreover, the procedure Freud outlines specifies no effort to expose the hidden knowledge; instead, the aim of the examiner is simply to extract it. Within both the courtroom and the clinical setting, the possession of knowledge rightfully belongs to the apparatus which can remove it.

In making the analogy between criminals and hysterics, Freud refers to a male hysteric, although in a memorandum to Fliess he claims that men are much less inclined to hysteria.[5] This thinking also suggests why women, whom Freud maintains are more passive sexually,[6] are less likely to be criminals and constitutionally less-suited, at least consciously, to keep secrets. As it so happens, our stories are filled with female characters who cannot keep secrets, like Midas' wife who, in some versions of the tale, cannot help exposing the secret that her husband has the ears of a donkey; or Philomena, whose tongue was cut out by her sister's husband, but who still manages to weave the story of her rape into a tapestry. Margery Kempe might also fit into this category: generally, such women expose information men already know. There is a larger body of women, though, who may die without telling their secrets: Shakespeare's fictional sister; many rape victims; authors like Mary Sidney or Margaret More Roper, who prefer to translate books instead of write them; or women whose diaries or memoirs we have only now recovered, hundreds of years after they were written.[7]

But there is a third category which I want to explore in this essay, made up of women whose knowledge does not signify our own— women who have secrets but who, given the chance, refuse to tell them. For example, we are not even allowed to imagine the undisclosed knowledge of sixteenth-century Protestant martyr Anne Askew. Twice Askew is questioned for heresy, once before a packed London crowd—the first gentlewoman to be publicly tried there; during her second examination, she is placed on the rack by two magistrates (again, a torture from which women were usually spared); finally, she is sentenced to death. But despite her rigorous and exhausting interrogations (sometimes lasting more than four hours), and even when she is tortured, Askew never betrays anything but the Protestant faith to which she adheres, reveals no concealed information besides her extraordinary mastery of Scripture, and refuses to share the names of any other members of her sect.[8]

Askew is not marginalized or repressed by the authorities who try her for heresy, but chooses instead to keep quiet: her silence, then, is very different for anonymity. We have a record of this silence in the *Examinations*, her first-person account of the two trials, published by Protestant propagandist and Bishop John Bale, and then reprinted in John Foxe's massive Protestant hagiography *Acts and Monuments*. But the *Examinations* discloses as little as Askew does on the stand. It comes to us as an early and almost uncertain work of autobiography, recapitulating rather than explaining Askew's testimony, as if she's still defending herself before her readers. Thus, she strikes us as a subject who cannot be told, a self that remains a secret.

As a consequence, readers need to approach Askew not as an object but as a subject of knowledge, as someone who knows something which we do not.[9] This reorientation Askew actively seeks out, as when, early in the *Examinations*, her response sharply deflects the question back onto her accusers: "First Christopher Dare examined me at Sadler's Hall, being one of the quest, and asked, if I did not believe that the sacrament hanging over the altar was the very body of Christ really. Then I demanded this question of him, Wherefore was St. Stephen stoned to death? and he said, he could not tell. Then I answered that no more would I assoil his vain question" (Foxe 538). What Askew seems to know is oppositional, lodged in the gaps or cracks in the ecclesiastical authorities' own learning. This formulation, however, implies that Askew's knowledge is limited by and dependent upon her accusers': as if the Freudian unconscious originated solely from the analyst's frustration. But the point is that Askew also knows who they think. She refuses to unburden her conscience (Foxe 540) and thus comply with her accusers' strategy to pin her to heresy charges. She will not even permit them to hypothesize about her. At one point, Bishop Bonner tells her: " 'Then you drive me, . . . to lay to your charge your own report, which is this: you did say, He that doth receive the sacrament by the hands of an ill priest, or a sinner, receiveth the devil, and not God.' To that [Askew] answered, 'I never spoke such words: but as I say now again, that the wickedness of the priest should not hurt me, but in spirit and faith I received no less than the body and blood of Christ" (Foxe 540). Every occasion to reveal herself serves instead as one to proselytize, to sharpen her doctrine, to elaborate her position.

A year after her death, when Bale prints the two examinations which have been smuggled to him (and gives us the only version of her account which we now possess), he also supplies a commentary explaining how Christ has made strong "a gentlewoman very young, dainty and tender" (Bale 140), "most deliciously brought up" (Bale 209), his "elucydacyon" comparing her to the holy maids Lydia, Cecilia, and Blandina. In other words, Bale makes plain Askew's meaning to the world, something she refuses to do for her examiners. Askew's rhetorical resistance was apparently recognized by Foxe, however, for although in his huge project he combines hearsay, propaganda, oral legends, government records, religious documents, and sermons,[10] his version of the *Examinations* leaves out Bale's commentary, as if Foxe had decided to let Askew "speak for herself."

Nowadays, of course, one's own testimony is hardly taken to be "authoritative"; and little information about personal experience is assumed to be objective, much less self-evident. In current trials, a psychologist may serve as an "expert witness" for either the defense or the prosecution, because there is nothing exculpatory about a doctor's forensic skill or the medical testimony one might provide about a patient. These secrets, in other words, explain very little. The doctor may be just one of many experts, including lie detectors, character witnesses, and more innocent bystanders, since we expect facts to be produced, not to already exist. In contrast with these practices, although no witnesses appear at either of Askew's two trials, no one besides Askew would be useful to the process anyway, since legal procedures in the sixteenth century relied little on evidence and did not stipulate that juries be open-minded.[11] Because a confession was all that was required to convict someone, one might have to be extracted, if necessary. Despite the fact that—or because—an outcome was typically preordained, Askew adopts the roles of all these players at once and serves as witness, judge, and jury; she not only provides testimony about her beliefs, but also about her credibility: in response to questions she finds absurd, she just smiles (Foxe 538); and at one moment of frustration, she answers: "What I had said, I had said" (Foxe 539).

Askew's self-reliance might be contrasted with the example offered by Freud's hysterical patient Dora. Through analysis, Freud sets his patient's interpretations against his own, and ultimately renders his only witness' testimony implausible and untrustworthy. But what is also instructive about this case is that Dora abandons analysis after eleven weeks and, rather than admitting her affection for her seducer (or for Freud), independently draws an admission from her seducer that she had not imagined the episode, that he had indeed propositioned her ("Dora" 238). If the subject matter in question has now become, more explicitly, herself, like Askew, Dora asserts a "right to know," "independent of and autonomous from the methods and presumptions regulating the prevailing (patriarchal) forms of knowledge."[12]

II. Making a Sign Talk

It is within the fissures between autobiography and clinical description, and in the spaces between free association and sworn testimony, that we need to locate Askew's *Examinations*, the personal record of her trial which stands in place of a diary or memoir, an account which keeps its subject secret. Yet the plasticity of these accounts, particular those of female experience—as well as their tendency to collide—arguably suggests "a time before what some would call patriarchy," that is, "an imaginary perspective from which to establish the contingency of the history of women's oppression."[13] Judith Butler claims that a "medicolegal alliance" for regulating identity had not yet emerged in the sixteenth century[14] when Askew tells her story; when Freud's Dora cuts the telling of her own story short, we can see that the coalition is firmly in place. In a sense, then, the problem is an historical one. As Stephen Greenblatt described the efforts of Montaigne and Hamlet to represent themselves as subjects who know themselves: "Because of subsequent developments, we associate Protestantism with a still more intense self-scrutiny. . . . But significantly, among the early Protestants we find almost no formal autobiography and remarkably little personal testimony. . . . There is a powerful ideology of inwardness but few sustained expressions of inwardness that may stand apart from the hated institutional structure."[15] But I would like to suggest that the problem is an epistemological one too, because it concerns the ways a subject might be learned.

Just as in her testimony, Askew reveals very little in her *Examinations*, the title of which suggests that there might be correct—as well as incorrect—modes of autobiographical investigation. She makes no mention of domestic events, her two children, or any private feelings and, like Julian of Norwich's *Showings*, her text discloses almost nothing; it is a surface which repeatedly discounts inner life.[16] But compared to Julian's text or to Margery Kempe's autobiography of the "creature," the *Examinations* is not a project which requires the sponsorship of male patrons or partners, like Jesus, a husband, or an analyst. Explaining that, as a woman, "she knew not the course of schools" (539), Askew instead uses the autobiographical format to challenge the grounds of her examiners, as if ontology might crush epistemology, and epistemology overcome ontology.[17]

But this project to know herself in secret begs serious questions. To what extent, for instance, is Askew really free to disagree with official rulings? What is her opposition worth? And, given a woman's status during this time, why would she be placed on trial? In other words, what might a court expect to learn from women, when it denied them the right to speak in nearly every other forum? To what could women possibly attest, except phallocentric subordination and the knowledge that excluded them?

Like Dora, who was only eighteen when she began her sessions with Freud, Askew was twenty-four when she was tried for heresy. Like Dora, she initially appeared to hold few objections to the process for procuring the truth. In fact, Askew was in London seeking to obtain a divorce when she was first brought in for questioning. During her second trial she exclaimed: "My lord! I wish that all men knew my conversation and living in all points: for I am sure myself this hour, that there are none able to prove any dishonesty by me. If you do know any that can do it, I pray you bring them forth" (Foxe 541). In addition, although she repeatedly asks questions of her own in response to her accusers', this is a stalling, defensive move on her part employed by many persecuted heretics, which also reveals the extent to which she and her accusers agree on what's worth knowing.[18] When she is forced to sign a confession as a condition for release after her first examination, she also includes a disclaimer, so that this document, too, reflects her thinking (Foxe 543).

In contrast to Joan Kelly-Gadol's claim that the same Renaissance machinery which made male individuality visible rendered female individuality invisible,[19] sixteenth-century legal machinery provided a means to make women visible and invisible all at once: like religious discourse,[20] we might even see this machinery as liberating because it allows women's voices to be heard. But what do we hear? It would be too facile merely to evaluate Dora's and Askew's efforts in terms of a contest between *male reason* and *female experience;* that interpretation obscures how both texts also represent what Dora and Askew know, especially about themselves. In particular, Askew discards her husband's name, refuses to settle for a verdict which displeases her, and seeks to write in her *Examinations* an account of her trials which will challenge the official version of them.[21]

Jonathan Goldberg likewise outlines the ways trials might permit "slippage which allow vocalization," so that "voicing" gets dislodged from specific (and gendered) voices in a liberating, expansive moment within the theatrical space. In *The Merchant of Venice*, for instance, "the play fully problematizes the notion of the law and that Portia has a voice *within* the law; not that it constricts and denies her, not that she must submit to the father, but that she *becomes* the father precisely

because the law is not the father's and not exclusively a male terri-
tory."[22] Goldberg highlights the pretense that a court might indeed
learn from Askew: in order to hear testimony—or evidence introduced
by the condition of personhood, such as having a point of view—the
court must take the self, even the selves of women, as givens. But
what he fails to note is that if the self is offered as a basis for knowledge, its testimony is instantly taken as incriminating. Even Portia, as
Goldberg himself notes, comes to court disguised as a man, a precau-
tion so that she does not have to defend herself in this forum. In a
footnote Goldberg adds:

> Legally, it is true, women in Renaissance England were bound
> and powerless except in very special circumstances. . . . Yet
> Renaissance legal theory is full of holes and attempts to place
> women in the law ran into all sorts of difficulties. [W]ithin the
> most conservative discourses of the Renaissance, contradic-
> tion are rampant, and 1580–1630 seems to be the period in
> which the elaborate syntheses, which marked and limited the
> place of women, begin to crack because of its own internal
> contradictions, as well as the pressures of history and alterna-
> tive discourses.[23]

But this suggests that if women fall through the "cracks" or appear
through the "holes" of such discourse, they might be registered there
as mistakes or accidents which ought to be either corrected or ignored.

Actually, it is for this reason that women routinely appear "in the
law." In many accounts of witch trials, Renaissance women seem remarkably at ease, possibly indicating the extent to which these trials
duplicated everyday practices of patriarchal scrutiny, judgment, and
condemnation.[24] In fact, women readily offer themselves up as evidence at these times. Anne Boleyn exclaims in the Tower: " 'I can say
no more but nay withyowt I shuld oppen my body' and ther with
opynd her gown."[25] Shakespeare's Hermoine similarly states in *The
Winters Tale:* "Since what I am to say must be but that / Which contradicts my accusation, and / The testimony on my part, no other /
But what comes from myself, it shall scarce boot me / To say 'not
guilty': mine integrity, / Being counted falsehood, shall, as I express
it, / Be so receiv'd."[26]

As if to fault them for calling her in the first place, Askew suggests
that the problem with the patriarchy is precisely that it cannot get its
facts straight. This critique appears during the first examination, when
the disputants make a brief foray into the "woman" question:

> Then the bishop's chancellor rebuked me, and said that I was much to blame for uttering the Scriptures. For St. Paul, he said, forbade women to speak or to talk of the word of God. I answered him that I knew Paul's meaning as well as he, which is, in 1 Cor. xiv., that a woman ought not to speak in the congregation by the way of teaching: and then I asked him how many women he had seen go into the pulpit and preach? He said he never saw any. Then I said, he ought to find no fault in poor women, except they had offended the law (Foxe 538).

This exchange is only part of Askew's larger project to educate her accusers about their epistemological faults, that is, their failure to consider the evidence she represents herself, as when she later corrects another examiner:

> Then took he my book out of my hand, and said, 'Such books as this, have brought you to the trouble that you are in. Beware,' said he, 'beware, for he that made this book, and was the author thereof, was a heretic, I warrant you, and burned in Smithfield.' And then I asked him, if he were certain and sure that it was true which he had spoken. And he said, he knew well the book was of John Frith's making. Then I asked him if he knew well the book was of John Frith's making. Then I asked him if he were not ashamed to judge of the book before he saw it within, or yet knew the truth thereof. I said also, that such unadvised hasty judgment is a token apparent of a very slender wit. Then I opened the book and showed it him. He said he thought it had been another, for he could find no fault therein. Then I desired him no more to be so unadvisedly rash and swift in judgment, till he thoroughly knew the truth: and so he departed from me (Foxe 540).

III. Making the Body Listen

During Askew's second trial, her accusers now strive to catch these errors, primarily by casting a wider net, and identifying what Askew knows with what she is. Elaine Beilin describes a more sober, even grave tone to these proceedings[27]; but unlike the aim of the first examination, which was to muzzle Askew, the interrogators this time seem to want their subject to speak. Askew reports: "Then had I divers rebukes of the council because I would not express my mind in all things as they would have me" (Foxe 544). She is faulted for her silence, for drawing on parables, or for speaking like a parrot: for hiding secrets, not for being one. So her accusers turn to her body as the vehicle or location for these secrets, as if it is her body which holds them. During this second examination, moreover, they employ torture, not as a means to punish her, but as an epistemological procedure which obtains the truth by "unmaking" her body.[28] Knowledge might be produced on a more pliant subject-matter, when bodies do not have to talk but can simply signify, and in the middle of a grueling interview, the two magistrates take off their gowns and rack Askew themselves: "Then they did put me on the rack, because I confessed no ladies or gentlewomen to be of my opinion, and thereon they kept me a long time; and because I lay still, and did not cry, my lord chancellor and Master Rich took pains to rack me with their own hands, till I was nigh dead" (Foxe 547–48). Yet Askew still refuses to cooperate. After being removed from the rack, she continues to proselytize even though she's unable to get off the floor because of her pains. A week later and still too pained to walk, she is carried in a chair to Smithfield where, unable to stand, a chain is wrapped around her waist and the stake and she is burned along with three other men.

In contrast to the sixteenth-century ecclesiastical authorities who take advantage of this second chance to try Anne Askew, Freud botches his only opportunity to treat Dora, and she abruptly terminates their sessions without apparent relief of her symptoms. But Freud has come to see her as an opponent whose testimony he must ignore, because she refuses to either present her body or to represent his knowledge. As he writes:

> When a patient brings forward a sound and incontestable train of argument during psycho-analytic treatment, the physician is liable to feel a moment's embarrassment, and the patient may take advantage of it by asking, 'This is all perfectly correct and true, isn't it? What do you want to change in now that I've told it you?' But it soon becomes evident that the patient is *using thoughts of this kind, which the analysis cannot attack,* for the purpose of cloaking others which are anxious to escape from criticism and from consciousness (188) (my emphasis).

Just as Bale's text converts Askew's *Examinations* into a self already established as a container for God's knowledge, Freud explains his patient as comprehending the sexual knowledge he knows.[29] In the requirement that physical evidence offered by women be supplemented verbally in rape trials is the same belief that women's testimony can be shown to be at odds with their experience.[30] Later laws against self-incrimination[31] will recognize this duality, but when the self does not really exist except, as Marguerite Waller claims, for a small and masculine minority,[32] the secrets it contains must seem vast enough for everyone else. Besides, such provisions are easily overturned: even in 1905 Freud can assert the claims of science or the "rights of the gynecologist" ("Dora" 175) in exposing Dora's confidences. Perhaps these rights have always belonged to the body which knew how to articulate them; in the sixteenth century, "[s]o resolutely did Catholic authorities insist on their control over the heretical body," Mark Breitenberg comments, "that several Protestants who had died previously were exhumed and publicly burned.[33] Similarly, Askew is reconstituted by Bale and later Foxe as a model for the patriarchy, "a singular example of christian constancy for all men to follow" (Foxe 550).

The remains produced once more to be punished by Catholic authorities clearly demonstrate that what is known about the self has little to do with any knowledge of the body. Such an opposition, reproduced and feminized and embodied in the nineteenth century by hysteria[34] has precursor, Catherine Clement[35] argues, in witch trials. One difference, however, between Askew's crimes and Dora's illness is found in the official determination of the doctor that self-knowledge is now private and worthless. In contrast to either Askew or her accusers, the hysterical self Freud treats must cease to see herself as an object of epistemological debate; in its place, Freud allots to Dora unrecognized jealousy, pride, unconscious motives, "gynaecophilic currents of feeling" and a secret, rather technical vocabulary of anatomical terms ("Dora" 210, 224).[36] If *Studies on Hysteria*, as Janet Malcolm maintains, might be characterized as "the story of the gradual transformation of a naively blundering hypnotist into the composed founder of psychoanalysis,"[37] Freud's account of Dora reconstitutes his subject as a catalog of his mistakes.

There is a period between Askew's execution and Dora's therapy, during which philosophy invents itself as a subject that has no body, but completely certain of the reality it unfailingly registers on the *tabula rasa*. When Dora dreams, this subject is caught in a mirror, and the mistake reflected there must be excised once again.[38] Earlier, Anne Boleyn's trial and execution had recorded this dilemma because the evidence which explained her could only be used against her: recent historians have suggested seeing the queen as the victim of a pact to protect Henry against charges of impotence,[39] or the possibility that one of the king's two bodies was flawed. The adultery charge included not one but five lovers (including her brother), and the indictment read, rather vaguely, that Anne had stated she would marry one of them after the king died,[40] so the perception that reason and history were not identical is explained by the queen's indifference. And like Dora, Anne Boleyn is subjected to this operation "while fully awake."[41] At her trial, she said "I believe you have reasons . . . upon which you have condemned me: but they must be other than those that have been produced in court."[42] But for the same reason Henry relies on it to discredit female testimony, Freud ultimately rejects the seduction theory presented in his earliest paper on hysteria.

Although those two examples point to the ways privacy is allocated to women in exchange for their secrets, I do not mean to imply that this epistemological compromise is always gendered, or that men might always know more or suffer less. But everywhere around them—as their autobiographies suggest—is evidence of what they think: evidence that explains women is more frequently buried underneath. Even Anne Askew can tell Nicholas Shaxton, her former associate, who he is. Preaching the sermon while the fires at Smithfield rage, he had urged Askew to recant as he did (Foxe 547); but she tells Shaxton a secret, something he does not know, about himself—she says it would have been better had he never been born.

Notes

The First Examinacyon of Anne Askew (1546) and *The Lattre Examinacyon of Anne Askew* (1547), published by John Bale and reprinted in *Select Works of Bishop Bale* ed. Henry Christmas (Cambridge: Cambridge University Press, 1849). John Foxe combined the two accounts under the title the *Examinations* and printed it without Bale's commentary in *The Acts and Monuments*, Vol 5. 1563. Reprint (New York: AMS Inc., 1965), pp. 537–550.

1. Peter Gay, ed., *The Freud Reader,* Reprint (New York: W. W. Norton and Co., 1989).

2. "Psychoanalysis and the Ascertaining of Truth in Courts of Law," in *Collected Papers, Vol. 2. Clinical Papers. Papers on Technique,* ed. Joan Riviere (New York: Basic Books, 1959), pp. 13–24.

3. See for instance, *The Order of Things: An Archaeology of the Human Sciences* (New York: Vintage Books, 1973); and *The Birth of the Clinic: An Archaeology of Medical Perception* trans. A. M. Sheridan Smith (New York: Pantheon Books, 1973).

4. Elizabeth Grosz, "Bodies and Knowledges: Feminism and the Crisis of Reason," in *Feminist Epistemologies*, ed. Linda Alcoff and Elizabeth Potter (New York: Routledge, 1993), p. 189.

5. "Draft K," *The Freud Reader*, p. 96.

6. "Draft K," *The Freud Reader*, p. 96.

7. Catherine A. MacKinnon explains how this silence typically works: "No law silences women. This has not been necessary, for women are previously silenced in society—by sexual abuse, by not being heard, by not being believed, by poverty, by illiteracy, by a language that provides only unspeakable vocabulary for their most formative traumas, by a publishing industry that virtually guarantees that if they even find a voice it leaves no trace in the world." *Towards a Feminist Theory of the State* (Cambridge: Harvard University Press, 1989), p. 239.

See also Margaret Patterson Hannay, Introduction, *Silent But for the Word: Tudor Women as Patrons, Translators and Writers of Religious Works*, ed. Margaret Patterson Hannay (Kent, Ohio: Kent State University Press, 1985), pp. 1–14; for a study of female autobiographical impulses and the way historiography ignores them, see Sidonie Smith, *A Poetics of Women's Autobiography: Marginality and the Fictions of the Self* (Bloomington: Indiana University Press, 1987).

8. Efforts were made by her accusers to link Askew with a group surrounding Catherine Parr. For details and relevant background information, see Derek Wilson, *A Tudor Tapestry: Men, Women and Society in Reformation England;* Elaine Beilin, "Anne Askew's Self-Portrait in the *Examinations*," in *Silent But for the Word*, pp. 77–91; and Retha M. Warnicke, *Women of the English Renaissance and Reformation* (CT: Greenwood Press, 1983).

9. See Grosz, "Bodies and Knowledges," p. 206.

10. 387. Mark Breitenberg, "The Flesh Made Word: Foxe's *Acts and Monuments*," *Renaissance and Reformation* 25, 4 (1989): 381–407.

11. See W. S. Holdsworth, *A History of English Law*, vol. 4 (London: Methuen & Co., Ltd. 1924); Margery Stone Schauer and Frederick Schauer, "Law as the Engine of State: The Trial of Anne Boleyn," *William and Mary Law Review* 22, no. 1 (1980): 49–84.

12. See Grosz, "Bodies and Knowledges," p. 188.

13. Judith Butler, *Gender Trouble: Feminism and the Subversion of Identity* (New York: Routledge, 1990), p. 35.

14. Butler, *Gender Trouble*, pp. ix, 32.

15. *Renaissance Self-Fashioning: From More to Shakespeare* (Chicago: University of Chicago Press, 1980), pp. 85, 87.

16. See Mary G. Mason, "The Other Voice: Autobiographies of Women Writers," in James Olney, *Autobiography: Essays Theoretical and Critical* (Princeton: Princeton University Press, 1980), pp. 208–09, 211.

17. See MacKinnon, *Towards a Feminist*, p. 241.

18. Greenblatt, *Renaissance Self-Fashioning*, pp. 76–77.

19. Joan Kelly-Gadol, "Did Women Have a Renaissance?" in *Becoming Visible: Women in European History*, ed. Renate Bridenthal and Claudia Koonz (Boston: Houghton Mifflin Co., 1977), pp,. 137–65.

20. See Ellen Macek, "The Emergence of a Feminine Spirituality in *The Book of Martyrs*," *Sixteenth Century Journal* 19, no. 1 (1988): 63–80.

21. Wilson, *A Tudor Tapestry*, p. 229.

22. Jonathan Goldberg, "Shakespearean Inscriptions: the voicing of power," in *Shakespeare and the Question of Theory*, ed., Patricia Parker and Geoffrey Hartman (New York: Methuen, 1985), pp. 120–121; 116–1347.

23. Goldberg, "Shakespearean," p. 137, n10.

24. For this reason, perhaps, David Bergeron seems so quick to dismiss it. With some confidence he states: "Patriarchy, obviously, is a given in Shakespeare's world. . . . Does not this presumed situation reflect both the practicalities of the theater and the realities of the political and social world in Jacobean England?" "Hermione's Trial in *The Winter's Tale*," *Essays in Theater,* 3,1 (1984): 12, n3.

25. In fact, G. W. Bernard takes this statement as one of the most telling pieces of evidence of the queen's adultery. See "The Fall of Anne Boleyn," *English Historical Review* (1991): 604–605.

26. *The Winter's Tale*, Act 3, Sc. 2, lines 22–28. ed. J. H. P. Pafford (London: Methuen, 1963).

27. Beilin, *Anne Askew's Self-Portrait*," p. 88.

28. See Grosz, "*Bodies and Knowledges*," p. 198; John H. Langbein, *Torture and the Law of Proof: Europe and England in the Ancient Regime* (Chicago: University of Chicago Press, 1977); and *Prosecuting Crime in the Renaissance: England, Germany, France* (Cambridge: Harvard University Press, 1974). See also Ian Maclean, *The Renaissance Notion of Woman: A Study in the Fortunes of Scholasticism and Medical Science in European Intellectual Life* (Cambridge: Cambridge University Press, 1980), pp. 69–81; and Holdsworth, *A History of English Law*.

29. And in this kind of educational experience, only the doctor will learn something. Freud writes: "From the very beginning I took the greatest pains with this patient not to introduce her to any fresh facts in the region of sexual knowledge; and I did this, *not from any conscientious motives*, but because I was

anxious to subject my assumptions to a rigorous test in this case. Accordingly, I did not call a thing by its name until her allusions to it had become so unambiguous that there seemed very slight risk in translating them into direct speech. Her answer was always prompt and frank: she knew about it already. But the question of *where* her knowledge came from was a riddle which her memories were unable to solve. She had forgotten the source of all her information on this subject" (186). See also Toril Moi, "Representation of Patriarchy: Sexuality and Epistemology in Freud's Dora," in *In Dora's Case: Freud—Hysteria—Feminism*, ed. Charles Bernheimer and Claire Kahane, 2d ed. (New York: Columbia, 1990), p. 194.

30. See Frances Ferguson, "Rape and the Rise of the Novel," *Representations* 20 (Fall 1987).

31. Schauer, "Law as the Engine," p. 75, n129 suggests the privilege dates from the middle of the seventeenth century, and notes a reference in 1619 that "neither was a mans fault to be wrung out of himself (no not by examination only) but to be proved by others." See also Holdsworth, *A History of English Law*, pp. 193–94.

32. "Academic Tootsie: The Denial of Difference and the Difference it Makes," *Diacritics* (Spring 1987) 17:1 2–20, and "The Emperor's New Clothes: Refashioning the Renaissance," *Seeking the Woman* (Knoxville: University of Tennessee Press, 1989), pp. 160–83.

33. Breitenberg, "The Flesh Made Word," p. 402.

34. Freud, "Dora," p. 22.

35. Bernheimer, Introduction, Part One, *In Dora's Case*, p. 4.

36. Freud tells us that he has learned not to trust the testimony of the patient, although he must still rely on it to contradict her. For example, he remarks that when she was 14, Herr K. kissed her: "This was surely just the situation to call up a distinct feeling of sexual excitement . . . But Dora had at that moment a violent feeling of disgust. . . ." In a footnote he adds "The causes of Dora's disgust at the kiss were certainly not adventitious, for in that case she could not have failed to remember and mention them. I happen to know Herr K., for he was the same person who had visited me with the patient's father, and he was still quite young and of prepossessing appearance" (183–84).

37. Janet Malcolm, "Reflections: J'appelle un chat un chat," *In Dora's Case*, p. 319.

38. As Butler claims: "If there is something right in Beauvoir's claim that one is not born, but rather *becomes* a woman, it follows that *woman* itself is a term in process, a beginning, a constructing that cannot rightfully be said to

originate or end. As an ongoing discursive practice, it is open to intervention and resignification" (33).

39. Schauer and Schauer "Law as the Engine," p. 71. Neil Hertz similarly comments on the "structures of complicity between doctors and husbands, that keep the sexual etiology of the neuroses a well-kept, smoking room secret" (240). "Dora's Secrets, Freud's Techniques" in *In Dora's Case.*

40. Schauer "Law as the Engine," pp. 61, 64; Bernard, "The Fall of Anne Boleyn," p. 584. Bernard tries to appear cautious, however, in pronouncing his verdict: "Perhaps the safest guess for a modern historian is that Anne had indeed committed adultery with Norris, and briefly with Mark Smeaton; and that there was enough circumstantial evidence to cast reasonable doubt on the denials of others. It must also be remembered that not everyone involved was tried and punished" (606). Cf. Retha M. Warnicke, "Sexual Heresy at the Court of Henry VIII," *The Historical Journal* 30, no. 2 (1987): 247–68. Warnicke cites dates when reputed lovers could not possibly have been with the queen as evidence of the ease with which evidence was attached to her body (259–60).

41. Malcolm, "Reflections," p. 319.

42. Schauer and Schauer, "Law as the Engine," p. 70.

Mary Baynton and Anne Burnell: Madness and Rhetoric in Two Tudor Family Romances

Carole Levin

In the reign of the Tudors, there were a number of cases of people calling attention to themselves for their claims to be more than they seemed. They claimed the identity of one of the Tudors themselves— Mary or Edward—or that they were the child of a king or queen. Freud has called those who believe they are not their parents' children— but instead the child of someone of much higher status, someone famous and special, a noble or a monarch—a family romance.[1] It suggests the need to establish some identity and sense of value beyond the usual one received by one's own background and a search for a parent who in imagination is more exalted and generous, of a much higher social status, than the reality.[2] Such emotional instability could happen at any time—in our own age as well as earlier ones. But it appears especially worthy of comment in the sixteenth century.

During the Renaissance, women did to a certain extent exercise political power and transcend the limitations imposed by gender. Social and economic class status permitted some women to overcome gender barriers. Although powerful queens and some aristocratic women left their mark upon the age, most women of the Renaissance were disempowered. There were few avenues to political power open to illiterate lower-class women. Belief in a family romance could well give the person a sense of power to speak beyond the realms usually allowed by class or gender. While there were many males who either were suffering from delusions or were conscious impostors, this essay focuses on two women, Mary Baynton and Anne Burnell. For both of these women of lower status, such beliefs and behaviors gave them, at least briefly, a voice. For both of them, however, the cost was high. In 1533 Mary Baynton claimed to be the Princess Mary, daughter of Henry VIII. Over fifty years later Anne Burnell, who was truly a butcher's daughter, claimed she was the daughter of Philip II of Spain. These delusions and/or impostures gave these lower-class women a voice and the possibility of a greater arena. For Mary Baynton this meant brief money and support and then punishment. For Anne Burnell, the belief she was the king's daughter allowed her to frame her experiences in a way that gained her both notoriety and also pain, before she also vanished from the annals of recorded history. Distinctions of status were very powerful in Tudor England. How one dressed, the work one did, the appropriateness of certain behavior patterns, and the ability to articulate a perspective, all depended on one's social class, though there were strains on these efforts to maintain order.[3]

Despite the distinctions of status, there was, moreover, also in Tudor England at the least the possibility of the re-invention of self. Identity could have a fluidity and uncertainty inconceivable today, or at least popular fiction, drama, ballads, and folk tales suggested this alternative. It was all too easy for someone to appear in a new place and invent a new identity. The most dramatic examples of this are Lambert Simnel and Perkin Warbeck, who in the reign of Henry VII claimed to be the nephew and the younger son of the former king, Edward IV. In less politically charged ways, husbands could also simply desert their wives and go to a new town and establish a new identity.[4] With no passports or identity cards, the Tudor state had little means of controlling its population. The drama of the late sixteenth and early seventeenth century was filled with plot devices of characters returning after being believed dead, such as Hermione in *The Winter's Tale* or Marina in *Pericles*. In *Twelfth Night*, Viola in a sense *becomes* her brother Sebastian when she assumes the identity of the boy, Cesario.[5] While clearly people then as now could distinguish between fiction and reality, between a folk story and their everyday life, and they knew that what they saw on stage was fantasy, these motifs provided a context for a belief system that could accommodate a view that someone was not the person they appeared.

Another factor that created an appropriate context for impostors was the fragmentation of family relations at the top of society—with the very monarch. Henry VIII had six wives in his search for a son and stable succession. Perhaps his desperation led to feelings of fragmentation for others. And none of his children—Edward, Mary, or

Elizabeth—had children at all. Elizabeth ruled alone—neither daughter, wife, nor mother, with no surviving siblings—for forty-five years. Elizabeth I created family tropes in her political rhetoric in an attempt to allay some anxiety her aloneness created.[6] Despite this rhetorical stance, one tends to agree with Francis Bacon on how separate Elizabeth was from family. "Those that continue unmarried have their glory entire and proper to themselves. In her case was more especially so; inasmuch as she had no helps to lean upon in government, except such as she had herself provided; no own brother, no uncle, no kinsman of the royal family, to share her cares and support her authority."[7] Being well and truly queen without aid not only enhanced Elizabeth's reputation for self-sufficiency but also might have made her appear isolated and vulnerable; it caused great worry over what would happen to England if anything happened to Elizabeth. And problems of identity might be especially extreme at the stressful times of national crisis.

Furthermore, people in Tudor/Stuart England were well aware of mental instability. Especially after 1580 there were many reported cases of melancholy. As Michael MacDonald has pointed out, people in the Tudor/Stuart age were as convinced as we are today that social and psychological stress could disturb the balance of someone's mind and destroy their health. There were many warnings that fear and grief, especially if sudden and intense, could possibly cause madness. A seventeenth-century proverb warned that "oppression makes the wise man mad."[8] One may wonder even more about the wise woman.

National fear and grief might well also cause madness; an insecure government could respond to such an aberration with harshness. In late 1533 in the north of England, an eighteen-year-old woman, Mary Baynton, was arrested and examined for impersonating Mary. She had gone around begging money so that she might use it to seek the protection of Emperor Charles V. She explained to her listeners that her aunt and namesake Mary, the French queen, had once read a book of prophecies and had told her, "Niece, Mary, I am right sorry for you, for I see here that your fortune is very hard. Ye must go a-begging once in your life, either in your youth or in your age." Temperamentally inclined to get something unpleasant out of the way immediately, she decided to do it in her youth. It is not clear from the examination whether Mary Baynton really believed she was the Lady Mary or had merely figured out a clever scheme for gaining money, but she was apparently successful enough at finding people to accept her claim to bring her to the attention of the magistrates. We might note that here is a young woman not only claiming to be the Princess Mary, but also claiming that her authority for what she is asking came from another woman, Mary, sister of Henry VIII. Henry had attempted to divorce his wife Catherine because he claimed that he must have a son—a daughter could not rule. Yet here was a woman who not only took over the daughter's role but emphasized the line of power coming through the female to sanction her public behavior. Mary Baynton's imposture allowed her to obtain funds under false pretenses; for the people who helped her there was the expression that a woman could be powerful. Yet for a lower class woman the identity of royalty was necessary to give her that power. The year 1533 was, of course, a particularly stressful one not only for the Lady Mary but for those who believed in her cause: Archbishop Cranmer had finally declared the marriage between her parents invalid, and Henry as a free man had publicly announced his marriage to Anne Boleyn, who later that year gave birth to Elizabeth.[9]

Perhaps Mary Baynton so identified with the Princess Mary that she had in a sense become her, at least in her own mind. Perhaps she only recognized how powerful the image of Mary was for some people and exploited this belief. Though our evidence is still fragmentary we do know more about Anne Burnell than Mary Baynton, enough at least to know that Burnell was not involved in misleading people to swindle them out of their money.

During the reigns of Mary and Elizabeth there were rumors that their brother Edward was still alive and pretenders actually claimed to be Edward. The anxiety of the English government and its people during the period immediately before the Armada manifested itself in a number of similar cases.[10]

A case that had implications for our understanding of the restrictions of gender and the implications of mental illness also occurred around the time of the fear of a coming Spanish Armada in August 1587, though of course it was delayed for a year. A woman named Anne Burnell came to the attention of authorities for claiming that she was the daughter of Philip II of Spain, and that magically had appeared on her back the arms of the kingdom of England. Her family had already seen its share of trouble. The previous year her husband, Edward, had been imprisoned for a time, possibly for some connection with the Babington conspiracy or perhaps for debt. Whatever the cause of Burnell's imprisonment, it made him wary of getting into more trouble, and caused him to seek advice about his wife's delusions.[11] What seemed to trigger Anne's delusion was the news that Sir

Francis Drake had just captured the Spanish ship the *San Felipe* in the Azores and brought its wealthy cargo back to Plymouth. When Drake returned to England people wondered if perhaps his exploits would delay the coming of the Armada Philip was threatening to send.[12]

Anne Burnell's claims that she was Philip's daughter came to the attention of the Privy Council, and they asked James Dalton to examine Anne and the people with whom she and her husband had spoken. Dalton was a Counsellor of the City and was treasurer of Lincoln's Inn. He served as a Member of Parliament for most of Elizabeth's reign. John Neale describes Dalton as a formidable champion of conservatism, and notes that as he got older and more established he had "shed the radical sympathies of his youth." In Parliament Dalton was clearly associated with the queen's party, not with those who upset Elizabeth by demanding further religious reforms. Neale concludes, "Authority found in him an able champion." Dalton may have been chosen for this task since he already knew Anne Burnell. In fact, he and his wife Mary had Anne live with them for several weeks so she would be under safeguard and observation. Dalton was a wise choice as his loyalty to Protestantism and the queen were beyond question.[13]

One issue that greatly concerned the authorities was whether Anne Burnell claimed to be the daughter of Philip *and* Mary, thus making her (in her own eyes) legitimate and the actual queen of England, or whether she claimed to be only the daughter of Philip. John Warner testified that Edward Burnell had come "unto the house of this examinate request[ing] to speake with him." That Drake had brought the Spanish treasure ship to England, made Anne, claimed her husband, convinced that King Philip "would not be longe after & further that she was the daughter of king Philip and it mighte be Queene Mary was her mother and she had the armes of England on her bodye." John's wife Avis was present during the conversation and affirmed the truth of her husband's report.[14]

But people who had spoken with Anne herself gave a slightly different story. Johan Fenton, wife of John Fenton, testified that about six weeks past "she hearde the said Anne Burnell say that she was king Phillips child but she denyeth that she heard her say that she was Queene Maryes daughter." Her husband did add that "the said Anne Burnell hath toulde them that she had on her bodye the marks of the Armes of England." But on "veiweinge the body of the said Anne [he] could perceive no such thing." Elizabeth and Thomas Bradeshawe each testified at Anne Burnell's request. Elizabeth had heard Anne "saye that she was kinge Phillips child" but not of Mary. Anne had told the Bradeshaws as well about the marks on her back but neither claimed to have actually seen them.

Dalton also publicly and for the record examined Anne Burnell herself. She claimed to be king Philip's child but "denied that ever she said Queen Mary was her mother or it mighte be she was her mother or any . . . [and] she thanckd God she never had so litle witts as to thinke it possible." Anne also affirmed as she had told others that she had the arms of England on her back. It is interesting that while Anne was certainly delusional, she had a perception of herself as not being so irrational as to think that she was the daughter of the late queen. To her mind the belief about Philip made perfect sense—though one might wonder why, if she was the daughter of Philip but not Mary she would have on her body the arms of England, rather than Spain. We might wonder, too, why the assertion of her parentage was not enough for Anne. She had to believe there was a physical manifestation of her specialness. Clothing, as was mentioned earlier, was a clear marker of status, and the number of royal proclamations on the subject in Elizabeth's reign suggest both the importance of regulation and how often the rules were potentially flouted.[15] For Anne to dress like a king's daughter would be both too costly and also illegal. It could be demanded that she remove such clothing. But the marks that appeared on her skin were both beyond her control and volition, and, also, indelible. These marks are a rhetoric of sign that proclaimed Anne's uniqueness, in her own eyes at least, beyond anything that she could *say*. Though Anne called herself a Spanish king's daughter, her deepest need may have been to demonstrate her connection to English royalty.

Dalton asked Anne what first put the idea she was King Philip's child into her head. She explained that eight years past she was visiting her mother-in-law in the county of Nottingham and had spoken with a woman known as the witch of Nuttall. This witch informed Anne that she was "a Spaniarde birde & that she had marks above her, which would appeare hereafter & that she did not knowe her owne father for it was a wise childe that did." Anne was so impressed with this intimation that she gave the "said witch a bande that was about her necke & a bracelett of amber from her arme." Later when she was in London she happened "to be in company of a gentleman that was said to be very well learned who falling in talke with her said she was proude but if she knewe her self she would be the proudest woman in the realm." This made Anne call to mind what the witch had said and she told this to the wise man. The fortune teller made Anne promise she would never reveal him and, with this assurance, "then he toulde her that the best spaniard that ever came in England was her father & toulde her that she had markes aboute her yt should appeare greater hereafter." Anne "from that time she took the veiwe hereof in a glass" and began to see the marks promised her. This language used by the "wise man" was the stock in trade of fortune tellers, and we can imagine that many people heard similar prognostications and shrugged them off. Burnell, however, was so susceptible to such suggestions that she altered her entire life.

According to Anne's testimony, her husband Edward was not very sympathetic to her claims. "Since Witsontide her husbande upbradeinge her with the basenes of her parentage her father beinge one Kirkall a Butcher in Eastcheape in London who died xiiii yeares past & her mother long before." Anne responded that she might be more of a gentlewoman than any Burnell in England and told him to look on her back and this would prove it to him. Anne's delusions may well have reflected her unhappy marriage and the inferior status she felt within it. At first, however, all Edward could see on Anne's back were veins. Later he had a different, but even more derisive, response. "Aboute a fourthnight after he looked on her backe & she asked him why he laughed & he said because she was branded on the backe as one of the Queene greate horses was on the Buttocke."

Anne claimed that she had been told eight years previously that she was the daughter of Philip of Spain, but she did not announce it until 1587. We might wonder why this delusion came at this time. It certainly was not the death of her actual father because he had died fourteen years before and her mother had predeceased him. It may have been the imprisonment of her husband the year previously as well as the uncertain political situation. Perhaps what caused Burnell's delusions is less significant than the concern these delusions caused the Privy Council.

James Dalton's wife, Mary, was far more sympathetic to Anne than Edward Burnell was. Mary said she thought Anne was a gentlewoman and that she had "a good likinge of her both for her modest & good behaviour & also her gentlewomanlye qualities." Even before Anne had been ordered to stay at the Daltons "before this time very often & many times . . . hath invited her into her house." Mary did testify that Anne claimed to be the daughter of Philip but "beinge demanded wheather ever she hearde her saye Quene Mary was her mother or the like words she sayeith she never hearde her saye any such wordes nor toulde that to be her meaninges: but that if she were his childe she was a bastard." This should have mediated some of the danger of what Anne Burnell said. Philip fathering bastards while king consort of England may have demonstrated his potency but hardly his loyalty to Mary. And a bastard child had no legal standing. Though Anne insisted she was the daughter of Philip, and claimed the English royal arms, she never asserted this made her queen.

Anne kept her word and did not reveal the name of the "wise man" to the authorities, but he was apparently Thomas Watson, later a friend of Christopher Marlowe and possibly a Catholic sympathizer. While Anne had not named her "wise man," one of her friends, Elizabeth Bradshaw, did. Dalton examined Watson, but while he agreed that he and Burnell had talked eight years ago, and she had told him the witch's prophesy of being of good birth, he denied he had told her anything, or that she had claimed to be Philip's daughter. Watson was thus dismissed. Charles Nicholl says of Watson's role in the incident, "This is a story of an unscrupulous young man and an unfortunate old woman. Watson's actions are amusing on one level, a jape, but they have a hard edge. He trades on his learning, on the mystique it has for those who lack it. There is the overtone of charlatanism, of phoney magic and mumbo-jumbo. It is a piece of theatre, with Watson giving his best in the role of the 'soothsayer.' The whole thing plays like a comedy, but the comedy has a victim."[16]

James Dalton himself tried to do the best he could for Anne Burnell. He was asked to furnish his opinion of the "behaviour of the gentlewoman & likelyhoode of the truth of the matter." Dalton explained that he "ever thought very well of her for her modestye & good behaviour." While Dalton could not deny Anne's claims that she was Philip's daughter he agreed it was unlikely she had claimed to be Mary's as well. Dalton also suggested that Anne's wits had become disordered because of her worry "about her husband being for a time a prisoner in the kinge bench," and the "evell acquaintaunce" she had made at that time. Dalton proved a strong advocate for Anne, explaining that "since she came to my howse her behaviour hath bin very good & vertuous much given to prayer & abstinence & to good gentlewomanlye exercises all the day without resorte to her of anye or goeing abrode but in my wiues company." Dalton was certainly concerned about her both for her own sake and for the possibility her delusions could be used by others for political reasons. "She seemeth much enclined to melancholye & I am not without doubte of worse effectes of that humor specially if she should come amonge such evell people as woulde feede her humor as amonge such it seemeth she hath bin to much alreadye." The possibility that Anne's delusion could be used by people trying to attack Elizabeth's government may well have been the real danger. Dalton only felt pity for Anne herself. "It semeth that her wittes be troubled & through greate misery & penury... [and] are greatelye decayed: she is weake & taketh no rest a nightes."

Apparently Dalton's explanation and advocacy carried the day and nothing was done to Anne Burnell at the time. Five years later, however, the response was much less benign. Reginald Sharpe has argued that the continuation of the war and the threatened renewal of a Spanish invasion in 1592 imposed a great strain on the citizens of London and presents Anne Burnell's delusions as one example of this strain, though it does not appear that Sharpe was aware of Burnell's problems in 1587. Certainly it appears by 1592 her delusion had hardened and she was again investigated by the Privy Council. By now Anne's husband was dead; he had died in 1587, the same year as her earlier examination. We can only speculate on how being a widow had impact on her mental state.[17] Word was sent to the Lord Mayor of London "to cause the said An Burnel to be carefullie viewed and seen by some discreet and experimented phisicion and surgeon, whether the armes of England and Spain be naturallie upon... her back or otherwize, and thereupon to make true certifcat unto us what shalbe found." This order of the Council suggests that they believed it might be at least possible that such marks might be on her back. The late sixteenth century was one of those transition periods where such mystical, visionary manifestations were still believed as possible, but physical proof was now required.[18] The Council also considered very seriously what to do if her claim proved false, showing concern not only about Anne herself but whoever else might be either misled by her or using her delusions for their own ends. "For yt is meant (if the matter shall apeare to be false or that there hath bin had practis therein) that due punishment shalbe inflicted both on the said An Burnel and on such as are parties thereunto. And therefore yt were good for the better bolting owt of the truth your Lordship be verie circumspect herein, carefullie examining such persons as may probablie be suspected to be privie and acquainted herewith upon oath or otherwize."[19] In the last decade and a half of Elizabeth's reign, there were many seditious comments, threats against the queen, and unrest.[20] The delusional Anne Burnell might be perceived as dangerous if others supported her claims.

The Council was soon convinced of Anne's culpability, but the only other person they also blamed was her young maid servant Alice

Digges. Digges is the one person who claimed she indeed did see the English arms on Anne's back. "She hathe affirmed that she sene uppon the back of Ann Burnell the picture of a lyon with certeine redd crosses adjoyning to the same. Both were ordered to be whipped through the streets of London."[21] Though the Council did not show mercy or understanding to Anne Burnell, they did to Alice Digges when they learned that, instead of "a woman servant of some more yeares" she was "but a yong gerl of thirten yeres, and [not] likly to be participant of the practice of the said Ann Burnell." They suggested to the Lord Mayor that "you shall doe well to cause notice to be given to her parentes that they may appoynt some fitter place for her educacion then with a woman of such impudencie and infamie as the said Ann Burnell is."[22]

Anne Burnell was whipped through the streets of London in December 1592 as punishment and warning. Earlier in the reign William Cartwright, brother of the Puritan Thomas Cartwright, had claimed to be the true king kept from his place by Elizabeth. He had been simply kept under restraint. Anne Burnell's sentence was far more harsh and more public. Elizabeth's government felt the need to create a theatre of punishment that also served to warn others what might happen if they emulated Anne Burnell. Her case received enough interest and publicity for a ballad about her to be registered that same month, published by Edward White: "shewinge how a fond woman falsely accused her self to be the kinge of Spaines daughter and beinge founde a lyer was for the same whipped through London. . . . beinge known to be a butchers daughter of London, a ballad." The punishment of Anne Burnell is also recorded in the 1615 edition of John Stow's *Annals*.[23] We might wonder if it was simply the generosity of James Dalton that kept Anne Burnell from being punished this way in 1587, but it does seem that by 1592 Elizabeth's government was that much more sensitive to any such perceived threat. It is suggestive that only the year before, in 1591, William Hacket's delusions—that he was Jesus Christ and king, and was so proclaimed by his followers—had been treated with utmost severity; he had been executed as a traitor.[24]

We can only speculate on why these people made such claims. Mary Baynton's claims netted her some money but also got her in trouble with authorities. Sixty years later Anne Burnell paid dearly for her delusion, but it again gave this "butcher's daughter" a voice she had never had before. Catherine Belsey has argued that for those women accused of witchcraft their time of execution "offered women a place from which to speak in public with a hitherto unimagined authority which was not diminished by the fact that it was demonic." One might argue that these impostures also gave both women and men of lower class the same chance for a public voice, though at sometimes horrific cost. Christopher Hill has suggested that "madness itself may be a form of protest against social norms, and that the 'lunatic' may in some sense be saner than the society which rejects him." But the chance of a public voice and the move beyond expectations of class and gender were not the only reason for such a delusion or the explanation of why it caused such concern.[25]

In 1587 Mary Stuart's execution finally ended her presence in England, and the attendant assassination plots against Elizabeth. But though Mary Stuart's death removed one danger, Philip II's threatened invasion of England in a holy war provided another. Though the English felt victorious over the defeat of the Armada in 1588, the threat of further Spanish invasions intensified the strains of the 1590s, as did the economic problems of disastrous harvests, taxation, inflation, and excessive food prices. Elizabeth, now in her sixties, still refused to name an heir. Anne Burnell suffered from the delusion that she had the importance of being the daughter of the king of Spain. Her own family relations were such she needed to create a "family romance" to feel important, and to believe that marked on her very skin was the magical proof of her assertions. She could have been ignored, or left as a figure of mockery or pity. By 1592 England was in an even more vulnerable position than it had been five years earlier, and for Anne, this was her second time in trouble; they had let her off easily once before. The harshness meted out to Anne Burnell expresses much of the insecurity of late Elizabethan England. Elizabeth Tudor, despite her rhetoric of family relations, was isolated. Anne Burnell's claim of royal parentage exposed that isolation. The only real danger Anne Burnell might pose would be if she were the focus point of others' disatisfaction, and cleverer, saner minds had made use of her. But both her class and her gender made this improbable, and, in fact, the only one ever to believe her was a thirteen-year-old servant maid. Anne herself never asserted that her royal parentage should give her political position. Though earlier in the century a butcher's son, Thomas Wolsey, had risen to be Cardinal and Archbishop of York, the realm of Henry VIII's last daughter had no space for the delusions of Anne Burnell, who was only the butcher's daughter.

Notes

1. Sigmund Freud used the term "family romance" to discuss a particular psychological phenomenon, one where people thought they were the children of someone famous instead of the child of their parents. The term recently has been made popular by such scholars as Lynn Hunt, *The Family Romance of the French Revolution* (Berkeley and Los Angeles: University of California Press, 1992); and Gary Waller, *The Sidney Family Romance: Mary Wroth, William Herbert, and the Early Modern Construction of Gender* (Detroit: Wayne State University Press, 1993) in their recent books. Hunt, however, used it to discuss a much broader psychological interpretation of the French Revolution. Waller is correct that when we use the term we must take gender into account. Though Waller is bringing a Freudian interpretation to the Sidneys, he is also using the term in a much broader context than Freud's original meaning. Camille Paglia may have begun this popularization of the term. In *Sexual Personae* she argues that "We each have an incestuous constellation of sexual personae that we carry from childhood to the grave and that determines whom and how we love or hate. Every encounter with friend or foe, every clash with or submission to authority bears the perverse traces of family romances." But while this may be true, and Paglia refers to "Freud's brilliant theory of 'family romance,' " this is in fact much broader than Freud's definition. Camille Paglia, *Sexual Personae: Art and Decadence from Nefertiti to Emily Dickinson* (Yale University Press; reprint New York: Vintage Books, 1991), p. 4. In this essay, I am using "family romance" in the more precise way that Freud did. My thanks to Ruth Elwell for her help in understanding this terminology. A version of this paper was presented at the December 1992 American Historical Association Meeting in Washington D.C. I would like to express my appreciation of the other panelists, Elaine Kruse, Mary Elizabeth Perry, Maarten Ultee, and Esther Cope for their valuable comments.

2. For more on the term "family romance," see Reuben Fine, *A History of Psychoanalysis* (New York: Columbia University Press, 1979), p. 425; and Henri F. Ellenberger, *The Discovery of the Unconscious: The History and Evolution of Dynamics Psychiatry* (New York: Basic Books, 1970), pp. 507–08.

3. Karen Newman, "Dressing Up: Sartorial Extravagance in Early Modern London," *Fashioning Femininity and English Renaissance Drama* (Chicago: University of Chicago Press, 1991), pp. 109–27; Peter Stallybrass, "Patriarchal Territories: The Body Enclosed," in Margaret W. Ferguson, Maureen Quilligan, and Nancy J. Vickers, eds., *Rewriting the Renaissance: The Discourses of Sexual Difference in Early Modern Europe* (Chicago: University of Chicago Press, 1986), pp. 123–42.

4. Laurence Stone, *Family, Sex, and Marriage in England, 1500–1800,* abridged edn. (New York: Harper and Row, 1979), p. 35.

5. For a very useful discussion of identity in the Renaissance and its implication for this play, see Stephen Greenblatt, "Psychoanalysis and Renaissance Culture," in Patricia Parker and David Quint, eds., *Literary Theory/Renaissance Texts* (Baltimore: Johns Hopkins University Press, 1986), pp. 210–24.

6. See Lena Orlin's essay, "The Fictional Families of Elizabeth I," in this collection for more on this issue.

7. Francis Bacon, *Works*, ed. James Spedding, 14 vols. (London: Longman and Co., 1858), Chap. 3, p. 310.

8. Michael MacDonald, *Mystical Bedlam: Madness, Anxiety, and Healing in Seventeenth-Century England* (Cambridge: Cambridge University Press, 1981), p. 72; Vieda Skultans, *English Madness: Ideas of Insanity, 1580–1890* (London, Boston and Henley: Routledge & Kegan Paul, 1979), p. 18.

9. James Gairdner and R. H. Brodie, ed., *Letters and Papers of the Reign of Henry VIII* (London: HMSO, 1864–1932), VI, 1193. See also, Carolly Erickson, *Bloody Mary* (Garden City, NY: Doubleday, 1978), p. 106.

10. For more on rumors of Edward's survival and other examples of males who thought they were related to Elizabeth, see Carole Levin, "Queens and Claimants: Political Insecurity in Sixteenth Century England," *Gender, Ideology, and Action: Historical Perspectives on Women's Public Lives*, ed. Janet Sharistanian (Greenwood Press, 1986), pp 41–66, and *"The Heart and Stomach of a King": Elizabeth I and the Politics of Sex and Power* (University of Pennsylvania Press, 1994), chapter five.

11. Mark Eccles, *Christopher Marlowe in London* (Cambridge: Harvard University Press, 1934), p. 154; Cynthia Chermely, " 'Nawghtye Mallenchollye: Some Faces of Madness in Tudor England," *The Historian*, vol. 49, no. 3 (1987): 325.

12. That year Drake destroyed some of the Spanish fleet at Cadiz. He then heard that ships rich in cargo were somewhere near the Azores and could possibly be taken. The *San Felipe* was reputedly among the greatest in fleet and was the greatest prize Drake and the English had taken in eight years. Its cargo included great quantities of spices and other goods such as ebony, silk, jewels, china, and gold silver. "The capture of the *San Felipe* had 'made' the 1587 voyage. The attack at Cadiz . . . may have disrupted Spanish preparations for the Armada, but in the eyes of most English contemporaries the dazzling fortune brought home in the carrack was the perfect consummation of the adventure." John Sugden, *Sir Francis Drake* (London: Barrie & Jenkins, 1990), p. 216. Also, the departure to the Azores as well as the attack on Cadiz helped slow the preparations for the Armada since Philip sent his fleet after Drake to try to protect the treasure ships returning from the East.

13. F. A. Inderwick, ed., *A Calendar of the Inner Temple Records* (London: Published by order of the Masters of the Bench and Sold by Henry Sotheran

and Co.; Stevens and Haynes; Stevens and Sons, Ltd., 1896), p. 473; P. W. Hasler, *The History of Parliament: The House of Commons, 1558–1603* (London: Her Majesty's Stationary Office, 1981), Chap. 2, pp. 8–9; *The Records of the Honorable Society of Lincoln's Inn: The Black Books, I, 1422–1586* (Lincoln's Inn, 1897), p. 408; Stow, *Annals of England*, 1615 edn., p. 728; John Neale, *Elizabeth I and Her Parliaments, 1584–1601* (London: Jonathan Cape, 1957), pp. 24, 245, 326.

14. *Lansdowne Manuscript*, vol. 53, no. 79. The *Lansdowne Manuscript* used on microfilm at the Folger Shakespeare Library.

15. F. A. Youngs, Jr., *The Proclamations of the Tudor Queens* (Cambridge: Cambridge University Press, 1976), pp. 163, 164.

16. Charles Nicholl, *The Reckoning: The Murder of Christopher Marlowe* (London: Picador, in association with Jonathan Cape, 1993), p. 188.

17. For more on the status of widows, see Charles Carlton, "The Widow's Tale: Male Myths and Female Reality in Sixteenth and Seventeenth Century England," *Albion*, vol. 10, no. 2 (Summer, 1978): 118–29; Louise Mirrer, ed. *Upon My Husband's Death* (Ann Arbor: University of Michigan Press, 1992); Barbara J. Todd, "The Remarrying Widow: a Stereotype Reconsidered," *Women in English Society, 1500–1800* (London and New York: Methuen, 1985), pp. 54–92. Stone discusses the difficulties for sixteenth-century widows. *Family, Sex, and Marriage*, pp. 136–37.

18. See for example, Judith Brown, *Immodest Acts: The Life of a Lesbian Nun in Renaissance Italy* (New York: Oxford University Press, 1986).

19. Reginald R. Sharpe, *London and the Kingdom* (London: Longmans, Green, and Co., 1894), Chap I, p. 552; *Index of Wills Proved in the Prerogative Court of Canterbury, Vol. IV, 1584–1604, and Now Preserved in the Principle Probate Registry, Somerset House, London.* Compiled by S. A. Smith, M.D., ed. Edward Alexander Fry (London: British Record Society, 1902; Public Records Office). The Edward Burnell who died in 1587 appears to be Anne's husband. It was certainly not the Edward Burnell who died ten years later. This Anne Burnell is also a different person from the Anne Burnell mentioned in the Inquisition after the death of Elizabeth Kennett. Edward Alexander Fry, ed., *Inquisitions Post Mortem of the Tudor Period for the City of London, Part III, Elizabeth, 1577–1603* (London: the British Record Society, 1908), pp. 130–31; John Roche Dasent, ed., *Acts of the Privy Council of England*, New Series (London: His Majesty's Stationary Office, 1890–1943), pp. 23, 331.

20. See Levin, *"The Heart and Stomach of a King,"* chapter four.

21. Whipping was a common punishment, especially for theft. J. A. Sharpe, *Crime in Early Modern England, 1550–1750* (London and New York: Longman, 1984), pp. 63–70. This punishment had the added element of public humiliation.

22. *Acts of the Privy Council of England,* ed. John Roche Dasent (London: H.M.S.O., 1890–1923), 23, pp. 366–67.

23. Hyder E. Rollins, *An Analytical Index to the Ballad-Entries in the Registers of the Company of Stationers of London* (1924 reprint, by the University of North Carolina. Hatboro, Penn.: Tradition Press, 1967), pp. 209–210; John Stow, *Annals of England faithfully collected out of the most authenticall authors, records, and other monuments of antiquitie, from the first inhabitation until this present yeare 1592* (London: R. Newbery, 1615), p. 764.

24. For more on Hacket, see Curtis Charles Breight, "Duelling ceremonies: The strange case of William Hacket, Elizabethan messiah," *Journal of Medieval and Renaissance Studies* vol. 19, no. 1 (Spring, 1989): 35–67; John Booty, "Tumult in Cheapside: The Hacket Conspiracy," *Historical Magazine of the Protestant Episcopal Church* 42 (1973): 293–317; Thomas, *Religion and the Decline of Magic,* pp. 133–35; Richard Bauckham, *Tudor Apocalypse* (Oxford: the Sutton Courtenay Press, 1979), pp. 191–207; Patrick Collinson, *The Elizabethan Puritan Movement* (London: Jonathan Cape, 1967), pp. 405–31.

25. Catherine Belsey, *The Subject of Tragedy: Identity and Difference in Renaissance Drama* (London and New York: Methuen, 1985), pp. 190–91; Christopher Hill, *The World Turned Upside Down: Radical Ideas During the English Revolution* (Middlesex, England: Penguin, 1972), p. 16.

VVHEN YOV SEE ME,
You know mee.
Or the famous Chronicle Hiſtorie of King
HENRY the Eight, with the birth and vertuous
Life of EDVVARD *Prince of Wales.*

As it was played by the High and Mighty Prince of Wales *his
Servants.*

By SAMVEL ROVVLY, Servant to the Prince.

LONDON
Printed by *B. A.* and *T. F.* for *Nath: Butter,* and are to be ſold at his
ſhop in *S. Pauls* Church-yard, neare St. *Auſtins* Gate.
1632.

Henry VIII, From *When You See Me, You know me.* By permission of the
Folger Shakespeare Library.

Queenship in Shakespeare's *Henry VIII*: The Issue of Issue

Jo Eldridge Carney

In 1644, the inimitable recorder of seventeenth century culture, Samuel Pepys, wrote in his diary: "Went to the Duke's house, the first play I have been at these six months, according to my last vowe, and saw the so much cried-up play of 'Henry the Eighth,' which, though I went with resolution to like it, is so simple a thing, made up of a great many patches that, besides the shows and processions in it, there is nothing in the world good or well done."

Fortunately, Pepys gave the play a second chance; four years later, another entry in his diary reads: "After dinner my wife and I to the Duke's playhouse, and there did see 'King Henry the Eighth,' and was mightily pleased, better than I expected, with the history and shows of it."[1] In both cases, Pepys notes the pagaentry of the play; like many of his contemporaries, he views *Henry VIII* as spectacle.

Since the seventeenth century, critical discussion of *Henry VIII* has focused on other issues: on the probable occasion for which Shakespeare wrote the play, the elaborate marriage celebrations in 1613 for Princess Elizabeth, daughter of James I; or on the question of authorship—specifically whether Shakespeare wrote the play himself or collaborated with Fletcher; or on the allegorical theme of the inevitable rise and fall of Fortune's wheel.

More recently, critics have begun to examine character—principally, the eponymous Henry, Wolsey, Buckingham, Katherine of Aragon, and Anne Boleyn—with some illuminating results. Such character analysis, however, can be problematic, for the focus in this play is not on individual characters. As R. A. Foakes argues in his notable preface to *Henry VIII*, Shakespeare's latest plays have a different purpose than

189

the earlier histories, tragedies, and comedies: "The last plays show neither concentration of interest on one or two central characters, nor concentration on a problem. As in some of the histories and dark comedies, there is no central character, and several, perhaps six or more, share an equally important status. . . . The total effect, the almost visionary whole is more important than what happens to the individual or the development of character."[2] Foakes further argues that in this case it is the *idea* of king that supersedes character, and that the events and characters in the play are secondary to the larger exploration of kingship itself.

I would agree with Foakes but extend his argument by saying that insofar as Shakespeare is concerned in *Henry VIII* with the idea of kingship, he is also addressing the idea of queenship, presenting what it means to be a queen, and illustrating the nature and limitations of the role. So perhaps it is not surprising that Pepys and other seventeenth-century chroniclers of the play say so little about individual character and instead emphasize the spectacle and historical presentation. In *Henry VIII*, there are three separate queens—Katherine of Aragon, Anne Boleyn, and Elizabeth, who only appears as an infant in the final scene of the play, but is the raison d'être for all that precedes. The three queens are crucial to the play's events, but they are less significant as individual characters and more important as links in the great chain of the succession. Historically, Katherine of Aragon, Anne Boleyn, and certainly Elizabeth wielded a significant amount of power during their reigns, but in Shakespeare's account, their capacity for procreation is far more important than their ability to rule.

Most critical discussion of the queens in this play has centered on the differences between Katherine and Anne. Katherine is more aggressive: she complains to the King about Wolsey's taxation of the commoners, she protests the treatment of Buckingham, and she defends herself in the divorce trial, delivering one of the most eloquent speeches of the entire play. If most of her attempts to exercise power are ultimately ineffective, at least she is daring enough to try. Anne, on the other hand, is relatively passive; she complies with Henry's wishes and is never seen as disruptive or disagreeable, which is something of a contrast with the historical record.[3]

There are other differences as well: Katherine is more direct, more straightforward in her rhetoric, while Anne is more playful and ambiguous in her conversations. Katherine is on the descending side of Fortune's Wheel; Anne is on the ascendancy. Katherine is associated with death, Anne with fertility and life.[4] And yet, for all of their obvious differences, differences that are often emphasized by stage performances,[5] their similarities are more essential. Any individual features that Katherine and Anne might possess are subsumed into the larger idea of queenship, and of course, Elizabeth is presented without any specific characteristics whatsoever. Elizabeth's lack of definition is particularly noteworthy: historically, this fascinating, complex monarch would have been the queen most prominent in Shakespeare's memory. We have no doubt that Shakespeare could create unique, interesting female characters, and his failure to do so in this play seems quite deliberate. In Shakespeare's *Henry VIII*, all the world is a Tudor stage, and the roles of the queens are clearly circumscribed.

What, then, does it mean to be a queen in Shakespeare's version of Henry VIII's reign? With a nod to Samuel Pepys, we might first note that in this play, both queens are overwhelmingly connected with pageantry and spectacle: Katherine's public appearance at the divorce trial and her elaborate dream vision, Anne's dancing at Wolsey's ball and her coronation. Their scenes are often large, grand tableaux, rather than small, intimate settings. Critics have commented on the importance of spectacle in this play, but it is important to emphasize how much this spectacle specifically centers on Katherine and Anne, and, at the end, even Elizabeth. Being a queen entails an acceptance of the attendant pomp and circumstance, a willingness to represent royalty and display.

Second, the idea of queenship in *Henry VIII* implies a superiority over other women. This superior status does not necessarily manifest itself in obvious display of power or in unkind treatment of other women, but being a queen does mean avoiding the weak customs of the general lot of women. When Katherine becomes frustrated at the proceedings of the divorce trial, she says to Wolsey:

> Sir,
> I am about to weep, but thinking that
> We are a queen, or long have dreamed so, certain
> The daughter of a king, my drops of tears
> I'll turn to sparks of fire.   (2.4. 67–71)[6]

Katherine recognizes that ordinary women might cry under duress, but that weeping is not considered appropriate behavior for a queen. Indeed, later in the play when Wolsey finds himself fallen out of Henry's favor, he tells Cromwell that his misery has forced him to weep, "to play the woman" (3.2. 430). When Katherine insists, then, that she will turn her own sorrow to "sparks of fire," Wolsey reminds her that anger is equally unacceptable for a queen. He seems shocked at the queen's display of wrath, since she has previously shown "disposition gentle" and "wisdom / o'ertopping woman's power" (2.4. 85–86): in other words, her previous acquiescence has heretofore been a sign of her superiority "o'ertop" the usual lot of women who presumably do not possess the power to control their unruly tempers.

This distinction between queenly demeanor and ordinary female behavior is again emphasized in act 3, scene 1, when Wolsey and Campeius visit Katherine to persuade her to resign herself to Henry's wish for a divorce. As she sits with her serving women doing needlework, she tells the men, "Your graces find me here part of a housewife" (3.1. 24). Katherine suggests that, exiled from the court and its ceremony, she is reduced to doing needlework like other women. In fact, Katherine of Aragon was an accomplished seamstress who insisted on making Henry's shirts.[7] In this play, however, Shakespeare suggests that needlework is not an activity usually undertaken by a queen, in order to emphasize the difference between queenly behavior and ordinary housewifery. Katherine further insists that since she has "fall'n from favor," she is just "a poor, weak woman," "a woman, friendless, hopeless." By the end of the scene, she is referring to herself in the third person; once she is stripped of her official trappings as queen, her very identity is called into question.

The most important feature uniting Katherine and Anne, and ultimately Elizabeth, however, is that their principal obligation as queen is to produce an heir to the throne, ideally a male heir. This inability is precisely what leads to Katherine's downfall as queen, and subsequently, Anne's demise as well. Within the confines of this play, Shakespeare gives Henry every benefit of the doubt in presenting him as a man whose conscience is truly troubled over the lack of a male heir. In more than one speech, Katherine insists that she has been the perfect wife: affectionate, submissive, patient, obedient. Indeed, as she lists her virtues we are reminded of another Shakespearean Katherine and another Shakespearean queen: Kate's final speech in *The Taming of the Shrew* and Hermione's final appeal to Leontes in *The Winter's Tale*. Even Henry calls Katherine "the primest creature that's paragoned o' the world" (2.4. 25). When she walks out on the divorce trial, Henry calls out after her:

> Go thy ways, Kate;
> That man i' the world who shall report he has
> A better wife, let nought in him be trusted,

For speaking false in that; thou art alone—
If thy rare qualities, sweet gentleness
Thy meekness saintlike, wifelike government,
Obeying in commanding, and thy parts
Sovereign and pious else, could speak thee out
The queen of earthly queens.   (2.4. 131–139)

In spite of his ostensibly heartfelt admiration for his wife, however, Henry has no qualms about divorcing her, because she failed in the most essential task of queenship. It is not enough to be a paragon of virtue: you must also ensure the succession to the throne.

Shakespeare does not disguise the fact that Katherine is no longer sexually attractive to the King. Henry tells Wolsey that he regrets divorcing "so sweet a bedfellow." Katherine suggests, however, that she is hardly Henry's sweet bedfellow when she says to Wolsey: "Alas, 'has banished me his bed already, / His love, too, long ago. I am old, my lords, / And all the fellowship I hold not with him / Is only my obedience" (3.1. 118–121). Shakespeare emphasizes, however, that more fatal to Katherine than her failure to attract Henry is her failure to produce a son,[8] which Henry describes at the divorce trial:

First, methought
I stood not in the smile of heaven, who had
Commanded nature, that my lady's womb,
If it conceived a male child by me, should
Do no more offices of life to't than
The grave does to th' dead: for her male issue
Or died where they were made, or shortly after
This world had aired them. Hence I took a thought
This was a judgment on me.   (2.4. 184–192)

Although Henry may seem to be generously accepting a share of the responsibility for the unsuccessful delivery of a male heir, a closer reading indicates that he is placing the blame on Katherine. According to Henry, he has successfully executed his role in begetting a male child, but then "my lady's womb" did "no more offices of life to't than / The grave does to the dead." Analogizing the womb to the grave, Henry suggests that his contribution to the procreative process has been active and life-affirming, while Katherine's part has been passive, neglectful, and thus, fatal. The unsuccessful pregnancies now become "her male issue:" the shift in the possessive pronoun to "her" clearly suggests that this failure to produce is Katherine's fault, not Henry's.

Furthermore, in suggesting that heaven's "judgment" has deliberately deprived him of a son because of past misconduct, he is not, of course, referring to any of his adulterous liaisons, but to his marriage to Katherine. She must bear the blame not only for her own inability to deliver a male heir, but she is also the cause of Henry's troubled conscience, and hence, his divine punishment.[9]

Like Katherine, Anne's success as a queen is predicated upon her reproductive abilities. While Shakespeare tones down the popular view of Anne as wanton witch, she is described as beautiful and sexually enticing. Her beauty, however, is only a desirable asset insofar as physical attraction leads to procreation, and the successful delivery of a male heir to the throne. Wolsey objects to Henry's choice of Anne as his new wife, arguing that her beauty alone is not sufficient reason to make her a queen: "It shall be the Duchess of Alencon, / The French King's sister; he shall marry her. / Anne Bullen? No; I'll no Anne Bullen's for him; / There's more in't than fair visage" (3.2. 85–88). Although Wolsey's objections to Anne are political, he is right in suggesting that being a queen involves more than a pretty face; it means providing Henry with a son.

Others besides Wolsey recognize that Anne's attractions are inseparable from her potential as a mother to a prince. When Lord Chamberlain announces to Anne that Henry is endowing her with the title of Marchioness of Pembroke, he says, in an aside:

> I have perused her well;
> Beauty and honor in her are so mingled
> That they have caught the kind: and who knows yet
> But from this lady may proceed a gem
> To lighten all this isle.   (2.3. 73–79)

Another of Henry's intimates, the Duke of Suffolk, echoes this attitude later in the play when he remarks of Anne:

> She is a gallant creature, and complete
> In mind and feature. I persuade me, from her
> Will fall some blessing to this land, which shall
> In it be memorised.   (3.2. 49–52)

There is no question that Anne's principal attraction is her probable fertility.

Anne herself seems well aware that this is the principal responsibility of queenship. In a scene which has no precedent in any of his sources, Shakespeare shows Anne talking privately with one of her ladies-in-waiting, called here simply "Old Lady." It is a scene reminiscent of the rather bawdy conversations between Juliet and her Nurse, or Desdemona and Emilia; here, the Old Lady counters Anne's somewhat feigned naiveté with an earthly bluntness, and their conversation is weighted with references to sexuality and childbearing.

When Anne expresses her sympathy for Katherine and insists, "By my troth and maidenhead, I would not be queen," (2.3. 23–24) the Old Lady immediately rejects Anne's demure protestations and argues that Anne, like any woman, would love to be queen, that the "eminence, wealth, and sovereignty" (2.3. 29) of queenship would be worth the inevitable loss of one's maidenhead. When Anne protests that she could not even bear the responsibility of being a Duchess, the Old Lady scolds her, ". . . if your back / Cannot vouchsafe this burthen, 'tis too weak / Ever to get a boy" (2.3. 42–44). "To get a boy," to bear a son, is the burden of a queen, and the Old Lady reminds Anne that she would accept the burden of Queenship not only for her own selfish gain, but also for the sake of the country, specifically for the country's secure succession. She tells Anne: "In faith, for little England / You'd venture an emballing" (2.3. 46–47). The word "emballing" is of course noteworthy: although the word ostensibly refers to being invested with the ball and sceptre as the physical symbols of royalty, the sexual connotations of the word make its usage here delightfully appropriate.

Finally, the association between Anne's queenship and her fruitfulness is underscored in the elaborate depiction of her coronation. Anne, now the object of adoration and celebration, is given no lines in this particular scene; there is no need for her to say anything. She is a symbol of beauty and fertility, a vessel, pure icon; as one gentleman describes Anne to another gentleman, the emphasis on her sexuality is evident: "Believe me, sir, she is the goodliest woman / That ever lay by man" (4.1. 69–70). He refers not only to her attractiveness, but specifically to her role as Henry's bed partner.

This focus on sexuality and fertility is even more evident in the response of the mass of spectators. As Anne simply sits enthroned in stately passivity, the crowd goes wild:

> Hats, cloaks,
> Doublets, I think, flew up, and had their faces
> Been loose, this day they had been lost. Such joy
> I never saw before. Great-bellied women,
> That had not half a week to go, like rams

> In the old time of war, would shake the press
> And make 'em reel before 'em. No man living
> Could say 'This is my wife' there, all were woven
> So strangely in one piece.   (4.1. 71–81)

The people are so excited at the sight of Anne that they are literally casting their clothing into the air. The reference to "great-bellied women" is particularly significant: revelling in Anne's reflected glory, the women in the crowd, their deliveries imminent, are all "woven so strangely in one piece." They have no individual identity and are defined completely by their fertility. In fact, Anne Boleyn was five months pregnant at the time of her coronation; Shakespeare, tactfully choosing not to include this fact in his presentation of events, displaces the queen's pregnancy to the spectators who are pressing to be as one with her, and Anne's association with childbearing is preserved.[10]

Once Anne delivers the Princess Elizabeth, she essentially disappears from the play—her task is completed. This dispensability is alluded to by one of Anne's enemies, Stephen Gardiner, Bishop of Winchester. When he hears that the Queen is enduring a difficult, potentially fatal labor, Gardiner replies: "The fruit she goes with / I pray for heartily, that it may find / Good time, and live: but for the stock, Sir Thomas, / I wish it grubbed up now" (5.1. 21–23). The Queen can be uprooted and destroyed; all that matters is the harvest.

Of course the problem here is that the fruit that Anne produces is also female: the future Queen Elizabeth I. In another scene that has no precedent in Shakespeare's historical sources, Shakespeare, in another diplomatic tour de force, finds a way to manage the disappointing absence of a male heir. Queen Anne may not have delivered a boy, but the baby is said to be as much like a male as possible, and, in her femaleness, she is at least the means of bearing future male offspring.

When the Old Lady comes to tell the King about Elizabeth's birth, he asks impatiently, "Is the Queen delivered? / Say ay, and of a boy" (5.1. 162–163). The crafty woman responds, "Ay, ay, my liege, / And of a lovely boy: the God of heaven / Both now and ever bless her! / 'Tis a girl, / Promises boys hereafter . . . 'tis as like you as cherry is to cherry" (5.1. 163–169). In an attempt to flatter the King, or earn a larger tip, the Old Lady assures Henry that Elizabeth is exactly like him, "as cherry is to cherry," an echoing of the fruit imagery used by Gardiner. While trying to erase Henry's obvious disappointment that the child is a girl, the Old Lady simultaneously tries to sublimate Elizabeth's femaleness and turn it to good use by presenting the new princess as a future mother to young princes. Elizabeth has only just entered the world, and already her potential as a childbearer is being celebrated.

Fertility is further associated with Princess Elizabeth in the christening scene, one that parallels Anne's coronation scene. Just as the London populace that witnessed the pageantry of Anne's crowning was presented as wild, high-spirited, sexually charged, and excessively fertile, the crowd pressing to watch the procession of Elizabeth's christening is untamed, unruly, and supremely uninhibited.

As the porter strains to control the throngs, he wonders why they are so excited: " . . . have we some strange / Indian with the great tool come to court, the women so / besiege us? Bless me, what a fry of fornication is at door! On / my Christian conscience, this one christening will beget a / thousand, here will be father, godfather, and all together" (5.3. 30–34). The passage is fraught with sexual references, beginning with the innuendo of the phrase "the great tool" in referring to the purported physical attributes of the Indian, who was often brought over from the New World and displayed in his native garb as a public curiousity. The colorful phrase "a fry of fornication" is even more blatant in its suggestion of a veritable swarm of animalistic sexual activity, threatening an "invasion at door." Finally, the Porter's outburst ends with a prediction that the young princess and eventual queen, by her very presence, will encourage rampant coupling and conceiving. Whereas the emphasis on fertility in Anne's coronation scene has some historical validity, the same emphasis is entirely on Shakespeare's comic addition in Elizabeth's christening scene. That he chooses to associate the infant Elizabeth with procreation again underscores his view of the function of queenship in *Henry VIII*.

In spite of the Porter's inability to suppress the rabblerousers, the elaborate spectacle of the christening proceeds flawlessly, and the splendid pageantry culminates in Cranmer's encomiastic prophecy of Elizabeth's reign. He promises she will be a virtuous, strong queen, beloved by her people, that her kingdom will enjoy peace and prosperity. But the most significant of Elizabeth's many accomplishments has nothing to do with foreign or domestic policy: what matters is her ability as queen to provide an heir to the throne. Shakespeare again manages to maintain this connection in spite of the fact that he is presenting a Virgin Queen, a woman who never married or bore a child:

> as when
> The bird of wonder dies—the maiden phoenix—
> Her ashes new create another heir
> As great in admiration as herself,
> So shall she leave her blessedness to one . . .
> Wherever the bright sun of heaven shall shine,
> His honour and the greatness of his name
> Shall be, and make new nations. He shall flourish. (5.4. 39–52)

Elizabeth, Cranmer proclaims, will be like the maiden phoenix, whose sacred ashes will produce another heir, James. The phoenix was a popular image in the literary figuration of Elizabeth, although the image usually referred to self-generation; here it is James, the long-awaited male heir, who is born from Elizabeth's ashes.

Interestingly enough, this emphasis on the succession eliminates one Queen entirely: Mary Queen of Scots, James' real mother. She is written out of the play just as she was written out of any direct part in the actual succession. The purpose of this scene, then, appears to be to celebrate Elizabeth, and by suggestion, her namesake, Princess Elizabeth Stuart, for whose marriage celebrations this play was probably written: in fact, the underlying purpose of this scene is to celebrate her father, King James, and the return to male rule.

As we examine the connection between Queenship and bearing an heir to the throne, we must briefly consider another *Henry VIII* play: Samuel Rowley's *When You See Me, You Know Me.* This popular play was published in 1605 and then reprinted in 1613, most likely for Princess Elizabeth's wedding festivities; it focuses largely on the antics of Henry's court fools, Will Somers and Patch, though it does address some of the more prominent events of Henry's reign.

This play was certainly on Shakespeare's mind when he wrote his version of *Henry VIII.* It is generally agreed that Shakespeare relied heavily on Holinshed's *Chronicles of England* and Foxe's *Acts and Monuments* as his historical sources for *Henry VIII*, but Rowley's play must be considered as a literary source.[11] In the Prologue to the play, Shakespeare reminds the audience that this work is se-rious, in contrast to Rowley's play: "Only they / That come to hear a merry, bawdy play, / A noise of targets, or to see a fellow / In a long motley coat guarded with yellow, / Will be deceived" (13–16).

Yet for all of the rowdy jesting and clowning it contains, Rowley's play does consider some of the same issues that concerned

Shakespeare. Shakespeare's play may differ from Rowley's in tone and historical focus, but central to both works is the emphasis on queenship and fertility. Rowley's work resumes where Shakespeare's ended, or, since Rowley wrote his play first, perhaps we should say that Shakespeare wrote the prequel to Rowley. Rowley ignores both Katherine and Anne and begins his play with the reign of Jane Seymour, specifically with her lying-in and her labor pains. Queen Jane's function as childbearer is obvious from the opening scene, in which the King, thrilled about the imminent birth of his child, exclaims:

> God a-mercie Jane, reach me thy Princely hand.
> Thou art not a right woman, goodly, chief of thy sex,
> Methinks, thou art a Queen superlative.
> Mother a God, this is woman's glory,
> Like good September vines, loden with fruite.
> How ill they did define the name of women,
> Adding so foul a proposition:
> To call it woe to man: tis woe from man.[12]

Like Shakespeare, Rowley defines his queen as superior to the general lot of women. Both dramatists also draw upon the natural imagery of the harvest to describe the primary function of women.

Henry then calls for his fool, Will Somers, to cheer Jane; Will jokes about her large size, but adds that the important point is for her to "bring thee a young Prince." When her labor pains grow stronger and Jane has to leave the room, Henry calls after her: "Now Jane, bring me but a chopping boy, / Be but a Mother to a Prince of Wales / And a ninth Henry to the English crown, / And thou makest full my hopes." From Fool to King, the message to the Queen is clear: deliver a male heir to the throne.

Rowley then takes interesting liberties with the historical record: Henry is told that Jane is having such a difficult labor that he must choose between her life and the life of the child. Henry is torn by the decision he is asked to "resolve":

> To lose my Queen, that is my sum of bliss,
> More virtuous than a thousand Kingdomes be;
> and should I lose my Sonne (if Sonne it be)
> That all my Subjects so desire to see,
> I lose the hope of this great Monarchy.
> What shall I doe?

In actuality, Jane Seymour did indeed endure intense labor, and die twelve days later of septicemia, but Henry never had to make such a choice at the actual time of the baby's delivery.[13] In choosing to add such a dilemma to this scene, Rowley not only adds dramatic suspense to the plot, he also undercores the very issue of queenship and reproduction.

In this case, Henry finally gives orders that Jane should be saved but he only arrives at this decision after some equivocation and some nudging from his sister Mary to "Remember the Queen, my Lord." When Queen Jane dies, Henry is appropriately but briefly grieved; he reminds the court, however, that they should rejoice in the new heir, Prince Edward, saying, "One Phoenix dying / gives another life," the very image Shakespeare appropriated in his tribute to Elizabeth. Jane has fulfilled her task, and she disappears from the play.

As different as these two plays are, there is one significant similarity: the queens in Shakespeare's *Henry VIII* and Rowley's *When You See Me, You Know Me* are presented as conduits, royal vessels for the safe and successful bearing of a male heir. The reigns of Katherine of Aragon, Anne Boleyn, Jane Seymour, and certainly Elizabeth Tudor were historically important in their own ways, but neither Shakespeare nor Rowley chooses to focus on their contributions to the Tudor monarchy. The issues raised in connection with these queens are not the Reformation or international diplomacy or the Spanish Armada. As far as the presentation of the queens is concerned, there is only one issue: the issue of issue.

Notes

1. Samuel Pepys, *The Diary of Samuel Pepys*, ed. R. C. Latham and W. Matthews, 9 vols. (Berkeley: University of California Press, 1976), vol. 5, p. 2, vol. 9, p. 403.

2. R. A. Foakes, ed., *King Henry VIII*, Arden Edition of Shakespeare, (London: Methuen, 1957), p. xli.

3. For a historical view of Katherine, see the biography of Garrett Mattingly, *Catherine of Aragon* (Boston: published 1941); for a more recent account, see Antonia Fraser, *The Wives of Henry VIII* (New York: Knopf, 1992).

Historical accounts of Anne are generally more problematic, but readers should begin with John Foxe's *Book of Martyrs*; Foxe offered a generous account of Anne as a saintly queen, but his view was soon supplanted by more critical responses. For recent accounts of Anne, see E. W. Ives, *Anne Boleyn* (Oxford: Blackwell, 1986); and Retha M. Warnicke, *The Rise and Fall of Anne Boleyn* (Cambridge: Cambridge University Press, 1989).

4. See Linda McJ. Micheli, " 'Sit By Us': Visual Imagery and the Two Queens in *Henry VIII*," *Shakespeare Quarterly*, 38 (1987): 452–466; Kim Noling, "Grubbing Up the Stock: Dramatizing Queens in *Henry VIII*," *Shakespeare Quarterly*, 39 (1988): 291–306; and Hugh Richmond, "The Feminism of Shakespeare's *Henry VIII*," *Essays in Literature* 6 (1979): 11–20.

All three authors discuss the individual characters of Katherine and Anne, but Micheli specifically examines how the visual imagery and non-verbal gestures associated with the queens establish meaning and relationships in the play; Noling argues that the patriarchal urge for a male successor undermines the queens' power; and Richmond argues that the queens' strong presence in the play displays a "distinctly Shakespearean feminism."

Like Noling, I disagree with Richmond's emphasis on the queen's power and I agree with her own emphasis on the queens as "a means of producing kings of England." My article, however, focuses more specifically on the sexual imagery of the language in the play, and on Rowley's "sequel."

5. See the review of the 1986 production of *Henry VIII* at Stratford, Ontario by Herbert S. Weil, Jr., *Shakespeare Quarterly*, 38 (1987): 237–238; Weil refers to "the husky frank arguments of Katherine," and "the final scenes of Anne . . . who seems unsure of her right to be present." Micheli refers to other productions; see Micheli, 454.

6. All references to *Henry VIII* are from *The Oxford Shakespeare*, Stanley Wells and Gary Taylor, gen. eds., Wells and Taylor refer to the play as *All is True*, "the title by which it was known to its first audiences." When the play was printed in the 1623 Folio it was called "The Famous History of the Life of King Henry the Eighth."

7. See Eric Ives, *Anne Boleyn*, p. 175.

8. There is some debate about the exact number of children Katherine of Aragon bore. It is generally agreed, however, that she suffered several miscarriages; in addition, three babies, two of whom were male, were stillborn or died shortly after birth, and two babies, one of whom was male, died within a few months of birth. The only surviving child was, of course, Mary Tudor.

See also J. Dewhurst, "The alleged miscarriages of Catherine of Aragon and Anne Boleyn," *Medical History* 28 (1984): 49–56.

9. For an analysis of Henry's conscientious objections to his marriage and his motives for divorce, see J. J. Scarisbrick, *Henry VIII* (Berkeley: University of California Press, 1968), especially pp. 150–155.

10. In her book *The Rise and Fall of Anne Boleyn*, Retha Warnicke notes that Anne's fertility was openly celebrated during the coronation festivities. Many of the verses written by Nicholas Udall and others for the occasion specifically refer to her fruitfulness: i.e., "May heaven bless these nuptials, and make her a fruitful mother of men children!" Anne's pageantry at the time was, accord-

ing to Warnicke, "one of her most noticeable features during her coronation." Although many writers chronicled Anne's coronation, the crowd response appears not to have been as universally joyous as Shakespeare describes it. See Warnicke, *The Rise and Fall*, chapter 8.

Jasper Ridley, in his biography *Henry VIII: The Politics of Tyranny*, also comments on Anne's coronation: "It was watched by thousands of interested, but silently hostile spectators." Ridley, p. 212.

11. See *Narrative and Dramatic Sources of Shakespeare*, ed. Geoffrey Bullough, vol. 4 (New York: Columbia University Press, 1962), pp. 437–443. Although many recent critics have seen little connection between the two plays, I agree with Bullough's assessment of the resemblances between the two works.

12. Samuel Rowley, *When You See Me, You Know Me*, ed. F. P. Wilson, Malone Society Reprints, 1952.

13. See Antonia Fraser, *The Wives*, p. 280.

The AUTHOR's

PREFACE

To the READER.

TO out-run those weary hours of a deep and sad *Passion*, my melancholy *Pen* fell accidentally on this *Historical Relation* ; which speaks a *King*, our own, though one of the most *Unfortunate* ; and shews the *Pride* and *Fall* of his *Inglorious Minions*.

I have not herein followed the dull *Character* of our *Historians*, nor amplified more than they infer, by *Circumstance*. I strive to please the *Truth*, not *Time* ; nor fear I *Censure*, since at the worst, 'twas but one *Month* mis-spended ; which cannot promise ought in right *Perfection*.

If so you hap to view it, tax not my *Errours* ; I my self confess them.

20 *Feb.* 1627.   E. F.

THE

Author's Preface page, *The History of the Life, Reign, and Death of Edward II, King of England.* Reproduced by permission of the Folger Shakespeare Library.

Reform or Rebellion?: The Limits of Female Authority in Elizabeth Cary's *The History of the Life, Reign, and Death of Edward II*

Gwynne Kennedy

Variously described as a protodrama, a play, a marriage "of prose and verse, of biography and the drama," a biographical narrative, and a history, Elizabeth Cary's *The History of the Life, Reign, and Death of Edward II* also belongs among early modern political works that theorize models of sovereignty and subjection.[1] In *The History of Edward II*, two sets of subjects, a group of noble men (the barons) and Edward's wife (Queen Isabel), act according to a form of obedience favored by the narrative and clearly opposed to the absolutist view of subjection ascribed to the king. As a result, the conflicts between Edward and his subjects in Cary's text are also contests between alternate theories of sovereign-subject relations. The implicit analogy between household and commonwealth that organizes *The History of Edward II* breaks down, significantly, when the consequences of giving the same right of limited resistance to Edward's barons and Edward's wife become apparent.[2] Both parties seek only the king's reformation, but the barons' failed armed uprising against Edward is deemed "innocent," whereas Isabel's successful capture of Edward without a battle is harshly condemned. As this essay will show, the account of Isabel's victory in *The History of Edward II* reveals deeply ambivalent attitudes about female authority, attitudes complicated by negative emotions, notably anger, which make the queen's intentions and exercise of political power especially problematic. The essay begins with a short summary of Edward II's career and the context for *The History of Edward II*, before turning to Cary's concept of obedience and its enactment by the barons and Queen Isabel.

Edward II's reign (1308–1327) began uneasily with his recall of Pierce Gaveston, banished by Edward I. Edward II's homoerotic relationship with Gaveston, whom he elevated to high rank and considerable power, alienated several influential noblemen (Cary's barons). The king's perceived disregard for state business and refusal to curtail Gaveston's influence led these nobles twice to demand Gaveston's banishment, and, after his second recall, to kill him. The influence of a new favorite, Hugh Spencer, made for Edward's continuing unpopularity and drove the barons to arms to enforce their demand for Edward's reformation and his favorite's removal. They were defeated in battle, and many of them were executed.

Queen Isabel subsequently went to France, either to negotiate a peace treaty with her brother Charles, the French king, or to enlist his support against Spencer; there is no consensus among Renaissance histories. Promised and then refused aid from Charles, Isabel eventually returned to England with a small army of Heinault soldiers, the heir apparent Prince Edward, and Roger Mortimer, her lover and one of the original barons. Commoners and nobles quickly rallied to Isabel, and the king and Spencer were captured without a battle, though accounts differ as to how and where. Spencer was executed; Edward was deposed, imprisoned, and later murdered. Mortimer and Isabel ruled for her son, crowned Edward III, until he removed them from power. Mortimer was tried and executed for Edward II's murder, and Isabel spent the rest of her life under a sort of house arrest.[3]

Cary wrote *The History of Edward II* soon after converting to Catholicism in the fall of 1626. Her conversion had unanticipated public consequences for herself, her marriage, and her relations with Charles I. Without her doing, news of her action reached the king, who urged her to recant; when Cary refused, she was ordered confined to her household. Cary's Protestant husband reacted to the news with extreme hostility. From Ireland, where he was acting as Lord Deputy, Henry Cary ordered all but one of her servants dismissed, cut off financial support, had the children taken from her, and the house stripped of its contents. Cary lived in desperate circumstances for several weeks until her release, but afterwards she was still forbidden access to the king, and it was many months before her situation improved even marginally. While various parties petitioned Charles to provide her relief, Henry Cary sent letters to him and others denouncing his wife and adamantly denying her support. Elizabeth Cary's mother meanwhile refused to aid or support her daughter. As several scholars have noted, Cary's sympathetic account of Isabel's experiences in France has similarities to Cary's own situation around the time she wrote *The History of Edward II*.[4]

In Cary's history, the standard for sovereign behavior is first articulated by Edward I, in his dying words to his son, "Royal Actions must be grave and steady, since lesser Lights are fed by their Example: so great a Glory must be pure transparent" (6). There is a similar insistence on spotless virtue and the exemplary role of kingship after Edward II engineers Spencer's recall from banishment ("The actions of a Crown are exemplar, and must be perfect, clean, upright, and honest" (68)) and again after Edward's deposition ("The Royal Glory should be pure, and yet transparent, suffering not the least eclipse or shadow" (139)).[5] Edward II is repeatedly censured for disregarding these principles, and although the text stops short of arguing that a sovereign's corruption justifies disobedience, it does acknowledge a connection. "The heart of the Subject as it is obliged, so it is continued by the Majesty and Goodness of the King: if either prove prostitute, it unties the links of Affection; those lost, the breach of Duty succeeds, which hunts after nothing but Change and Innovation" (158). When a ruler "degenerate[s] from his Wisdome and Greatness," explains the text shortly after, "it by degrees varies the integrity of the heart, and begets a liberty of Speech; which falls often on the actions of Revolt and Tumult" (159)

As these passages suggest, Cary's history shows a particular concern for the consequences of Edward's misrule on the affective aspects of subjection. The sovereign's virtue makes submission easy, but his moral corruption changes willing obedience into forced compliance. In that case, subjects lose even the appearance of agency (of voluntary submission) and also their "integrity of the heart," thus producing an internal split between the subjects' desires/interests and their duty. Emotions comprise an area of autonomy for subjects and must be rightly valued by those who are owed obedience. "Of all others, it is the most erroneous fond opinion, which conceits Affections may be won and continued in a subordinate way. They are the proper Operations of the Soul, which move alone in their own course, without a forc'd compulsion" (63). Edward, "believing the bare Tye of Duty was enough" (9), fails to appreciate either the affective elements of submission or the relation between his exemplary role and political stability.

Cary's Edward II errs also by refusing to allow any restrictions on his royal will, as we see, for example, when he informs the barons that his relationship with Spencer is none of their concern: "Seek not to bar me of a free election, since that alone doth fully speak my Power: I may in that endure no touch or cavil, which makes a King seem lesser than a Subject" (59). The text does not support his absolutist position, but instead offers the possibility of legitimate resistance, disagreement, and expression of self-interest within subjection—that is, some opportunity for a subject to negotiate his/her interests and to make legitimate, though limited, demands on a sovereign whose actions are harmful. Such an opportunity devolves from the mutual obligations or "reciprocal correspondence" of sovereign and subject: "The *power Majestick* is or should be bounded; and there is a reciprocal correspondence, which gives the *King* the obedience, the subject equal right and perfect justice, by which they claim a property in his actions; if either of these fall short, or prove defective by wilful errour, or by secret practice, the State's in danger of a following mischief" (68). This stake or "property" in sovereign conduct provides some grounds for subjects to criticize and even take direct action to reform sovereign errors and to protect themselves. The members of Parliament who vote for Edward's deposition, for instance, "had just cause to restrain [him] from his Errours, but no ground or colour to deprive him of his Kingdom" (131).

This model of obedience is tested out in Edward's confrontations first with his nobles and later with his wife. Cary's history affirms the barons' right to influence Edward's actions and supports their efforts to reform him, because they intend neither to challenge Edward's authority nor to overthrow him. Their objections to the king's "neglects of the State-affairs, and the forgetfulness of the civil and ordinary Respect due to his great Barons," the result of Edward's involvement with Gaveston, are presented as justified from the start (18). The mixture of public and private interests articulated in the lines above are sufficient grounds in Cary's text to insist that Edward curtail his favorite's influence. After demanding and receiving the king's consent to Gaveston's banishment, the barons, "whose innocent aims had no end but Reformation, depart content" (23). They later return "well and strongly attended" and "boldly" require Edward to banish Gaveston again, but their actions are not improper challenges to Edward's authority. On the contrary, the text approves their "just Indignation" at the king's apparent incorrigibility (27). When the "enraged" nobles finally seize and behead Gaveston, the text directs its criticism toward corrupt courtiers like Gaveston and does not pass judgment on his executioners (30–32).

Cary's account even represents the barons' armed uprising against Edward in a favorable light, minimizing the transgressive nature of their actions in several ways. The nobles' recourse to arms is depicted as a last resort, after other efforts have failed, and Edward shows no sign of amending his behavior. Unlike Grafton's *Chronicle*, *The History of Edward II* casts Edward's party as the aggressors instead of the nobles, and Cary's Spencer elects to be "the first Invader" (69). Responsibility for initiating the battle belongs with the king's forces in Cary's version, for the barons' army retreats without engaging Edward's troops, as a result of some bad strategic decisions and Spencer's unexpected initiative. Their inefficient withdrawal encourages the king's army to attack; consequently, the barons' fight looks more like self-defense than an offensive measure to press their demands. Martial heroic language further counteracts a reading of the battle as unlawful rebellion. The brave barons fight like "inraged Lions" and "act Wonders," until "wearied, not o'ercome, they yield to Fortune, and by a glorious Death preserve their Honour" (71). They are "brave Arches" with "angry Swords"; one of them falls when "Heroick Bloud, not Valour, fail'd him" (71). Edward's rash execution of the defeated nobles, made even more heinous after an appeal for mercy by one of his own lords, also seems to deflect attention from the barons' questionable use of force against Edward.

Some concluding comments on the uprising explain the text's constant defense of the barons and its sympathetic portrayal of the conflict. These remarks describe active resistance that may resemble but not actually *be* rebellion:

> it is clear, when they [nobles] had him [Spencer] at their mercy, that they sought not bloud, but reformation; and assuredly in this their last act [the battle], which was rather *defensive* than otherwaies, their intentions towards the *Crown* were innocent. In all respects (saving the levy of their Arms, which was done onely to support it with more Honour) as things fell out afterwards, it had been happy for the *King* if he had lost this Battel, and they had prevailed ... (74).

What makes the barons' armed opposition "rather *defensive* than otherwaies" is their "innocent" intent. Despite appearances, they seek Edward's reformation, not his overthrow, and consequently, their limited actions conform to the model of subjection discussed earlier and do not constitute a breach of obedience. The parentheses and emphatic phrases ("it is clear," "assuredly," "in all respects") rhetorically indicate the difficulty of describing opposition that does not signify a renunciation of obedience or outright rebellion. They may also indicate discomfort at approving such aggressive opposition, as "saving the levy of their Arms" is no small exception.[6] Nevertheless, the barons' intentions justify what could otherwise be mistaken for treasonous conduct.

Like the nobles, Queen Isabel first appears as one of Edward's virtuous, wronged subjects. For much of Cary's history, Isabel is portrayed as a long suffering wife, "one of the goodliest and fairest Ladies of that time" and a "Jewel" who is "not . . . rightly valued" by her husband (18–19). The queen, too, acts to defend a mixture of public and personal interests that supports rather than challenges the social order. In her case, Isabel's efforts to reform her husband and marriage gain legitimacy because they uphold the superiority of heterosexual marriage and heteroerotic desire, while affirming the gender roles that sustain them. Edward's homoeroticism thus offers Cary's Isabel an authoritative site from which to speak and act as an unduly wronged, neglected wife.

The queen, however, does not deliberately challenge Edward's authority or criticize him directly. Cary's depiction of Isabel's escape to France illustrates a mode of indirect confrontation with male authority that is characteristic of the entire work. The queen's flight occurs near the middle of the history and is the moment when Isabel first emerges as a significant figure in the text; her increased presence corresponds to her assumption of an active role in her own defense and Edward's reformation. Unlike other treatments of this event, Cary's account casts Spencer rather than Edward as Isabel's adversary and frames the conflict as one between queen and favorite. Because Spencer stands in Edward's place, the authority Isabel defies and the man she outwits is not her husband but a lesser substitute, and so Isabel's wifely obedience is not directly in question. This arrangement, moreover, enables Isabel to criticize Edward through his surrogate, for Cary invents a misogynistic Spencer who dangerously undervalues Isabel's intelligence and courage, as Edward has failed to value Isabel according to her worth. When the queen outmaneuvers Spencer and escapes safely to France, a triumph she clearly relishes, she also undermines his misogynistic views of herself and women's nature.

The text's references to divine intervention in Isabel's successful escape (92) and in her later safe return to England (115) seem to give the queen's actions a special sanction. Her initial success in gathering local support also implies the justness of her cause. Once the people realize Isabel desires not "to rifle, but reform the Kingdom, they come like Pigeons by whole flocks to her assistance" (117–18).

Nobles and commoners swell her numbers "like a Ball of Snow increas'd by motion" (118). Yet the very ease and speed of Isabel's advance gradually become disquieting. As her power increases, and with it the likelihood of Edward's capture, the text suggests a more equivocal attitude toward Isabel's enterprise. The queen retroactively sanctions the mob's murder of Bishop Stapleton (though done without her knowledge) because "it ran with the sway of the time, and the Queens humour" (122–23). Her supporters, now the "heady monster Multitude" (122), demand instant justice, the death of the elder Hugh Spencer (Edward's ally), with a "confused clamour" (125) that betrays their irrational, vengeful, and fickle natures. An angry, pitiless Isabel oversees his execution (126) as remorselessly as she has pursued Edward, "the Prey... her Haggard-fancy long'd for" (123).

These negative remarks lead up to a decisive change in Isabel's hitherto virtuous character the moment she captures Edward and Spencer. Once in control, Isabel is an ambitious, very angry, and vengeful woman:

> The Queen, having thus attained to the full of her desire, resolves to use it to the best advantage: Ambition seis'd her strongly, yet resigneth to her incensed Passion the precedence. (127–28)

Isabel directs her "incensed passion" at Spencer, not the king (whom she sends off to prison), and treats the favorite with "insulting joy," "base derision," and "a kinde of insulting Tyranny, far short of the belief of her former Vertue and Goodness" (128). The text describes at some length Isabel's abuse of her newly acquired power (128–130), particularly her cruel handling of Spencer, which argues "a Villanous Disposition, and a Devilish Nature" (129).

Cary's furious, cruel Isabel has no counterpart in other accounts of Edward's reign. Her history greatly exaggerates the description of Spencer's punishment in Grafton's *Chronicle*, her primary source for this scene.[7] Grafton ascribes Spencer's humiliating treatment to a nobleman named Thomas Wage, and not, as Cary does, to Isabel. His text makes no reference to anger, vengeance, or hostility in the queen's character. Grafton depicts Isabel's victory as a blessing to a relieved people: "Queene Isabell conquered agayne all her estate and dignitie, and put unto execution her great enemies, to the great comfort and reioysing of the greatest parte of the realme" (213). By contrast, those who celebrate Isabel's victory in Cary's text sound like dogs: "A world of people do strain their wider throats to bid her welcome, with yelping cries that ecchoed with confusion" (128).[8]

Isabel ceases to be a virtuous, sympathetic figure when her efforts to reform Edward bring about a reversal of gender, marital, and political hierarchies. The model of subjection that has previously legitimized her actions and motives, and authorized some limited opposition, results in a direct challenge to male sovereign authority that is especially threatening because unintended. Isabel's story suggests that even the limited right to protect her interests and repair her marriage allowed to a wife in Cary's model can pose a danger to the entire system. Marital discontent culminates in the king's deposition, and this realization may be unsettling to a woman who, like Isabel or Cary, wants to "re-form" her situation while remaining obedient.

Cary's personal history may offer some parallels here. Her conversion to Catholicism, like Isabel's a virtuous motive, similarly placed her in direct conflict with her husband and Charles I, even though Cary also may not have meant to challenge male authority directly. She, too, was held responsible for events she had not intended: the public revelation of her conversion, the breakup of her family, the controversy surrounding her case at court. Initially attracted to Isabel's story by similarities in their situations, Cary may have discovered at the moment of Isabel's triumph where that attraction had taken her. The sharp change in Isabel's character evinces that recognition.

The subject's intentions, which in Cary's model distinguish certain acts of resistance from acts of rebellion, prove to be a less workable standard in Isabel's case than in the barons'. Like them, the queen has sought only Edward's reform, not his removal, but her conscious intentions are not determinative because other factors intervene. Isabel is held responsible for external events she did not plan (the Bishop's murder) and could not control (the momentum generated by popular support for her cause). Negative emotions such as anger, revenge, and pride erupt forcefully as soon as Isabel gains authority over Edward and "resolves to use it [the situation] to the best advantage" (127). These emotions produce behavior that "savour'd more of a savage, tyrannical disposition, than a judgment fit to command, or sway the Sword of Justice" (129), and that is also unforeseen when she captures Edward and Spencer. The line between justified resistance and rebellion becomes ambiguous when conscious intent is not the only, or even dominant, factor at work.

A victorious, morally good Isabel is not an option in Cary's text, not even momentarily. The queen is not allowed virtuously to act in her best interests ("to her best advantage") or virtuously to maximize the benefits of her new position. Instead, the history finds fault with (and a fault in) Isabel's character, censuring her behavior as soon as she gains control. The queen is criticized for displaying negative emotions, particularly anger and revenge, that were previously repressed or expressed indirectly, and that surface when she possesses power over those who have wronged her. Isabel is blamed severely for her lack of "Christian Piety, which is the Day-star that should direct and guide all humane Actions," for one's "heart should be as free from all that's cruel, as being too remiss in point of Justice" (129). The invocation of "Christian piety" (which also includes pity and empathy) as the standard for judging Isabel's conduct toward Spencer effectively closes off consideration of Isabel's injuries and the legitimacy of her anger. Calling on a basic Christian principle whose spiritual truth is undisputed, the text censures her actions and emotions simultaneously. As a result, there is no opportunity either to reflect on the causes and justness of her anger or to find her anger justifiable, but her conduct unacceptable.

Before Isabel yields to anger and its vengeful display, however, she is "seis'd . . . strongly" by ambition. This mention of ambition is curious, because the history has previously stressed Isabel's desire only to correct Edward. The wording of the passage complicates any sure sense of Isabel's agency, as she changes from being the *subject* who "resolves" to exercise her new authority "to the best advantage" to being the *object* of an ambition which then yields to "incensed passion."[9] The interplay of subjects and objects acting and being acted upon problematizes action itself precisely when Isabel has power to wield; it also suggests some ambivalence about Isabel's control over and responsibility for her emotions. Moreover, Isabel's ambition seems neither positive nor negative, but simply present momentarily before being replaced by anger, the dominant emotion ascribed to her. Ambition's brief appearance may highlight the intensity of an anger capable of overwhelming even strong ambition and thus indicate the depth of Isabel's feelings of injury and the force of her released anger. Even more than Isabel wants power for herself, then, she is angry and seeks revenge on Spencer. Alternately, anger may function to forestall exploration of Isabel's ambition and what it might entail, an inquiry that might cause more discomfort than dealing with anger, especially if female ambition is not rejected out of hand.

Isabel's anger, unlike that of the barons, undermines her character and actions. As we saw earlier, the noblemen are also angry: they feel "just Indignation," are "enraged" at Gaveston's recall, wield "angry Swords" and fight like "inraged Lions" against Edward's forces. Yet their anger is not inconsistent with their legitimate "defensive" resistance, and it does not override their reasonable demands for the king's reformation. They are presumed to act justly when they have the opportunity to punish Spencer ("it is clear, when they had him at their mercy, that they sought not blood, but reformation" (74)). Isabel's anger, on the other hand, disqualifies her from wielding her new authority judiciously and drives her to vengeful deeds unsuitable for "a Queen, a Woman, and a Victor" (129). Reason could have controlled her actions following Edward and Spencer's capture, as it does on an earlier occasion when Isabel's hoped for diplomatic mission to France is cancelled. Then, "[h]er heart so strongly fix'd upon this Journey, was torn as much with anger as with sorrow: Reason at length o'ercame her Sexes weakness, and bids her rather cure, than vent her Passion" (90). In this instance, anger does *not* override Isabel's reason or prevent her from acting virtuously or circumspectly; in fact, reason not only *masters* her anger and sorrow, but also *authorizes* her efforts to "cure" her present condition by engineering her own escape. This passage conveys a double message—that women are by nature more emotional than reasonable and that a woman's emotions need not prevail.

A slightly different conclusion appears in the account of the Earl of Arundel's execution, an event that immediately follows Spencer's execution in the text. Grafton's *Chronicle* states only the fact of Arundel's death, "And the Erle John of Arondell was put to death at Herforde within foure dayes after sir Hugh Spencer the sonne" (216). Cary's history, after remarking on the absence of explanations for Arundel's death in other accounts, invents its own: Arundel's fidelity to Edward. "It was then a very hard case, if it must be adjudged Treason to labour to defend his King and Soveraign, to whom he had sworn Faith and Obedience, suffering for preserving that Truth and Oath, which they had all treacherously broken, that were his Judges" (130). The good subject, Arundel proves his loyalty with his life and dies the victim of Isabel's anger and irrationality; "we may not properly expect Reason in Womens actions: It was enough the incensed Queen would have it [Arundel's execution] so, against which was no disputing" (130). It is significant that here, at a point in the historical narrative where a lack of information about Arundel's death invites speculation, Cary's history posits an unreasonable, irate Isabel and not, for instance, a culpable Arundel. The text invokes women's presumed natural irrationality not, as in the case of Isabel's trip, as conventional wisdom that Isabel's will disproves, but as the general expectation that her angry will fulfills. [That is, an angry Isabel wills unreasonable things.] The scene as a whole can be read as (re)affirming submission to male sovereign authority through Arundel by repudiating Isabel's conduct and anger.[10]

From the time Isabel captures Edward until the story ends, Cary's history displays considerable ambivalence about the queen's character. In her last scene, Isabel offers a number of reasoned arguments against Mortimer's plan to kill Edward, but Mortimer chooses to interpret her opposition as evidence of female "Weakness" and "tender pity" (153). Casting Isabel's unwillingness to consent as a personal rejection of him and his affection and as proof of her ingratitude, he threatens to leave: "Mortimer's resolv'd, since you refuse his judgment, you neither prize his safety, nor his service; and therefore he will seek some other refuge before it be too late, and too far hopeless" (153). Isabel quickly capitulates and accepts his view of women's inferiority: "Stay, gentle Mortimer, (quoth she) I am a Woman, fitter to hear and take advice, than to give it; think not I prize thee in so mean a fashion, as to despise thy Safety or thy Council" (153). She asks only not to know "the time, the means, the manner" of Edward's murder (154).

Cary's text passes a lenient sentence on Isabel, "guilty but in circumstance, and but an accessory to the Intention, not the Fact" (155), but on an Isabel who has ceded her belief in her own authority and judgment to Mortimer's view of women's natural weakness, and who is thus a very different figure from the cunning woman who earlier outwits a misogynistic Spencer. Cary leaves her finally in the "margent"—or margins—of the text: "[t]he Queen, who was guilty but in circumstance, and but an accessory to the Intention, not the Fact, tasted with a bitter time of Repentance, what it was but to be quoted in the Margent of such a Story" (155). This gesture may be an act of recontainment, the return to marginality of a female character who has come too close to the center of attention. Isabel has, through the history's increasing concern with her experience, arguably become Edward's historical *and* historiographic rival. The queen does not displace Edward, but she does dislodge his centrality, and as a result, it is difficult to determine final responsibility for Edward's fall.[11]

The lines above imply that if Isabel were more clearly evil, she might have remained within "such a Story," contained by a definite negative judgment of her, but the text's ambivalence toward Isabel prevents this possibility. From a reader's perspective, Cary's queen is ultimately both in the story *and* on the margins, both central *and* peripheral, and her rhetorical marginalization at the end calls attention to—and is symptomatic of—a disjunction in Isabel's characterization that first occurs when she captures Edward and wields his power for herself. The model of subjection that previously has authorized the barons' and queen's actions becomes significantly more complicated when Isabel's intentions result not in Edward's reformation but in her seizure of him and his power. Cary's history exhibits both an attraction and anxiety about female authority, as it points to the crucial work emotions can perform in the containment or invalidation of that authority.

Notes

An early version of this essay was presented at the Center for Twentieth Century Studies, University of Wisconsin, Milwaukee. My thanks to Virginia Chappell, Margaret Ferguson, Juliet Fleming, Alice Gillam, Janis Butler Holm, Carole Levin, Deirdre McCrystal, Phyllis Rackin, and Sandra Stark for their generous comments on various drafts of this essay.

1. The Afterward outlines my reasons for attributing *The History of The Life, Reign, and Death of Edward II* . . . (London: J. C. for C. Harper, S. Crouch, and T. Fox, 1680) (Wing F313) to Elizabeth Cary. Written in 1627, this text (hereafter *The History of Edward II*) is among the earliest historiographic writing by an Englishwoman. Elizabeth Cary (1585/6–1639) also wrote what may be the first drama by an Englishwoman, *The Tragedie of Mariam, The Faire Queene of Iewry* (publ. 1613), as well as sonnets to her sister-in-law and Queen Henrietta Maria, and an elegy on the Duke of Buckingham. She translated Abraham Ortelius's *Le Miroir du Monde* (unpublished) and a work of religious controversy, *The Reply of the Most Illustrious Cardinall of Perron* (Douay, 1630). A biography of Cary written by one of her daughters mentions other poems, translations, a verse play on Tamburlaine, and "one paper of controversy," *The Lady Falkland: Her Life: from a manuscript in the Imperial Archives at Lille*, ed. Richard Simpson (London: Catholic Publishing and Bookselling Co., 1861) p. 114. Cary had a lifelong interest in religious ideas, read widely, and taught herself French, Spanish, Italian, Latin, and Hebrew as a young woman. She was married to Henry Cary in 1602, but apparently he "did not care for his wife" and "married her only for being an heir" (7). Nine of their children lived to adulthood. In late 1626, Cary converted to Catholicism; some effects of this decision are discussed below. For biographical information, see Barry Weller and Margaret Ferguson, eds. *The Tragedy of Mariam, The Fair Queen of Jewry with The Lady Falkland: Her Life* (Berkeley: University of California Press, 1994) pp. 3–17 (their edition of *The Life*, unlike Simpson's, is a complete transcription of the original manuscript); and Elaine Beilin, *Redeeming Eve: Women Writers*

of the English Renaissance (Princeton: Princeton University Press, 1987), pp. 157–64.

Commentators on the text's genre include Betty Travitsky, "Husband-Murder and Petty Treason in English Renaissance Tragedy," *Renaissance Drama* 21 (1990), p. 172 ("protodrama"); Tina Krontiris, "Style and Gender in Elizabeth Cary's *The History of Edward II*," *The Renaissance Englishwoman in Print: Counterbalancing the Canon*, ed. Anne Haselkorn and Betty Travitsky (Amherst: University of Massachusetts Press, 1990), p. 137 ("play or biography"); Donald Stauffer, "A Deep and Sad Passion," *Essays in Dramatic Literature: The Parrott Presentation Volume*, ed. Hardin Craig (New York: Russell & Russell, 1967), p. 314 (marriage of genres); Margaret Ferguson and Barry Weller, ed. *Mariam and The Life* 12 ("biographical narrative"); Donald Foster, "Resurrecting the Author: Elizabeth Tanfield Cary," *Privileging Gender in Early Modern England*, ed. Jean Brink (Kirksville, MO: Sixteenth-Century Journal Publishers, 1994), p. 164 ("verse biography"); Elaine Beilin, *Redeeming Eve* p. 159 ("history"); and Barbara Lewalski, *Writing Women in Jacobean England* (Cambridge, MA: Harvard University Press, 1993), p. 179 ("history"). Long sections of Cary's history are in blank verse; frequent interpolated speeches produce a play-like feel, and there is considerable attention to character and motivation.

2. For discussions of the analogy in political and religious writings, see Gordon Schochet, *Patriarchalism in Political Thought* (Oxford: Basil Blackwell, 1975), J. P. Somerville, *Politics and Ideology in England 1603–1640* (London: Longman, 1986); Charles McIlwain, intro. *The Political Works of James I* (Cambridge, MA: Harvard University Press, 1918). For the analogy's use in domestic and marital writings, see Susan Amussen, *An Ordered Society: Gender and Class in Early Modern England* (London: Basil Blackwell, 1988), ch. 2; Catherine Belsey, *The Subject of Tragedy: Identity & Difference in Renaissance Drama* (London: Methuen, 1985), p. 149–63; Frances Dolan, *Dangerous Familiars: Representations of Domestic Crime in England, 1550–1700* (Ithaca: Cornell University Press, 1994). Cary's text is unusual in not addressing the wife's role in the context of her other domestic relationships, such as mother or mistress.

3. This is a severely abbreviated account of events. Richard Grafton's *This Chronicle of Briteyn, beginning at William the Conqueror, endeth wyth our moste dread and soveraigne Lady Queene Elizabeth* (London, 1569) is clearly a primary historiographic source for much of *The History of Edward II*. It is possible that Cary drew also from *Vita et mors Edwardii Secundi* by Geoffrey Baker, available in William Camden's *Anglica, Hibernica, Normannica, Cambrica . . .* (Frankfort, 1602). D. R. Woolf has identified this chronicle as a source for the mistaken information that Piers Gaveston was Italian. "The True Date and Authorship of Henry, Viscount Falkland's *History of The Life, Reign and Death of King Edward II*," *Bodleian Library Record* 12 (1988): 451. Cary's history states that "the Author whom I most credit and follow, speaks him [Gaveston] an *Italian*" (4).

For modern historical discussions of Edward II's reign, see Natalie Fryde, *The tyranny and fall of Edward II, 1321–1326* (Cambridge: Cambridge University Press, 1979); Caroline Bingham, *The Life and Times of Edward II* (London: Weidenfeld and Nicolson, 1973); Harold Hutchinson, *Edward II: the Pliant King* (London: Eyre and Spotiswoode, 1971); and Michael Prestwich, *The Three Edwards: war and state in England 1272–1377* (London: Weidenfield and Nicolson, 1980).

4. Her queen is a solitary, needy, and determined woman seeking help for her just cause. She is without money or a place to live and in an estranged relation from her husband, voluntary but necessary, that forces others to choose between them. She must defend herself before powerful male authorities, her brother and the Pope, against her husband's accusations and must demand the right to speak for herself. On parallels between Cary's situation and Isabel's, see Krontiris, "Style and Gender," pp. 137–38; and Foster, "Resurrecting," pp. 167–73.

5. James I also invokes transparency to express his accessibility to his subjects and to guarantee his veracity. In a 1607 speech, he asserts that "with the olde Philosophers, I would heartily wish my brest were a transparent glasse for you all to see through, that you might looke into my heart, and then would you be satisfied of my meaning," *The Political Works of James I*, p. 292. The importance of the visibility of sovereign virtue to subjects in Cary's history may underlie two suggestions that rulers hide their weaknesses from public sight and at least *appear* to be good (44, 139), although other comments admit that sovereigns, like everyone else, are not perfect (139–40).

6. This is not the first time that armed force is relegated to parentheses. Earlier the nobles send a "fair and humble" message to Edward "the more to justifie their Arms (which in the best construction seem'd to smatch of Rebellion" (55–56).

7. Krontiris reads this moment differently; she argues that Cary "strives to make Isabel as consistent a character as possible" (144), but is unable to reconcile her sources with her personal beliefs. Krontiris, "Style and Gender," pp. 144–46. To Krontiris, Cary could not sanction Isabel's cruelty, as depicted by other authors, and was forced to censure her character while defending her. I see less consistency in the text's attitude toward Isabel and argue instead that Cary actually *elaborates* Grafton's account, her main source for the queen's treatment of Spencer, in ways which magnify Isabel's cruelty and anger and emphasize her responsibility for his punishment.

8. As it does when the queen's cause gathers momentum, the text here undercuts Isabel's character and actions by aligning her with the thoughtless, easily swayed crowds. At this point, they enthusiastically celebrate her victory and Spencer's humiliation and death: "To see such a Monster [Spencer] so monstrously used, no question pleased the giddy Multitude, who scarcely

know the civil grounds of Reason: the recollected Judgement that beheld it, censur'd it was at best too great and deep a blemish to suit a Queen, a Woman, and a Victor" (129). This view of commoners as fickle, insatiable, and irrational is not unusual in Renaissance historiography. See Phyllis Rackin, *Stages of History: Shakespeare's English Chronicles* (Ithaca: Cornell University Press, 1990), ch. 5 for an excellent discussion of commoners in Shakespeare's history plays.

9. I am very grateful to Margaret Ferguson for calling my attention to the significance of the grammar here and to the peculiar place of ambition.

10. My reading of these lines thus generally agrees with Foster's, who uses them to illustrate his contention that in "the latter half of her narrative, Cary subtly (or timidly, or hastily) rewrites the Queen's revenge as springing, not from feminine subjection to irrational passions, but from a potent female will (notwithstanding the unchallenged sentiments about women's supposed unreasonability)." Foster, "Resurrecting," p. 169.

11. The history concludes by offering two perspectives. Although it may be true that Edward "fell by Infidelity and Treason" of "a Wife, and a Son which were the greatest Traytors," yet "had he not indeed been a Traytor to himself, they could not all have wronged him" (160).

Afterward

There is no critical consensus regarding the authorship and date of composition of *The History of The Life, Reign, and Death of Edward II*, the text discussed in this essay, or those of a second history, *The History of the most unfortunate Prince, King Edward II*. Margaret Ferguson and Barry Weller remain "agnostic" on the authorship question, and Elaine Beilin also withholds judgment. Donald Stauffer, Tina Krontiris, Betty Travitsky, Barbara Lewalski, and Donald Foster attribute *The History of Edward II* to Elizabeth Cary, but disagree about who wrote *The History of the most unfortunate Prince*. My reasons for attributing only *The History of Edward II* to Elizabeth Cary are outlined briefly here.

The History of The Life, Reign, and Death of Edward II. King of England, and Lord of Ireland. With the Rise and Fall of his great Favourites, Gaveston and the Spencers (London: J. C. for Charles Harper, Samuel Crouch, and Thomas Fox, 1680), a folio, is the longer text. It has an author's preface signed "E.F." and dated "20 Feb. 1627." The title page adds the claim, "Printed verbatim from the Original." The shorter octavo version, *The History of the most unfortunate Prince, King Edward II. With Choice Political Observations on Him and his unhappy Favourites, Gaveston & Spencer* (London: A. G. and J. P. for J. Playford, 1680), lacks the author's preface, initials, and date. Its title page claims that this text was "Found among the Papers of, and (supposed to be) Writ by the Right Honourable Henry Viscount Faulkland, Sometime Lord Deputy of Ireland."

The relationship between the two histories is uncertain. It seems likely that the author of the later one had the other version at hand when writing and used it extensively. Numerous verbal ties, some exact and others quite similar or close paraphrase, the nearly identical choice and ordering of events, and the presence of material not found in other sources (e.g., the discussion of Arundel's execution) all support this view. Like Foster and Lewalski, I believe the histories were written by different people. At several points, the texts differ in diction and word choice; they derive separate morals from Edward's career and contradict each other in some key respects. Many of the features that distinguish *The History of Edward II* from other accounts of Edward II's reign are either absent from the octavo or treated less extensively (Isabel's perspective, Edward's homoerotic desire, pro-Catholic sentiments). I am not as certain as Foster that the octavo predates the folio. At present, it seems to me more likely that Cary worked from Grafton's *Chronicle* (an important source for the folio), and someone else from her history, than that Cary revised the octavo, expanding it in light of Grafton's account, which she also rewrote. Close study of other sources, such as Geoffrey Baker's chronicle, may help determine the relationship between folio and octavo.

There is good evidence for attributing the folio to Elizabeth Cary. As several critics note, there are the initials E. F. (Elizabeth Falkland, Cary's signature after 1620), and *The Tragedie of Mariam* was printed with Cary's initials (E.C.). The author's preface to the folio history and prefatory material to Cary's Perron translation invoke their rapid composition as a disclaimer (both took a month to write). The octavo attribution to Henry Cary provides a link to Elizabeth Cary. According to the *Life*, her Perron translation was found "in his [Henry Cary's] closet after his death, all noted by him" (40). This remark raises the possibility that other works by Elizabeth also may have been among her husband's papers. It is tempting to speculate that "all noted by him" alludes to Henry's revisions or comments on Elizabeth's writing, and that the octavo, if a reworking of her folio text, might in fact be his. Foster also entertains the possibility that Henry Cary may have authored *The History of the most unfortunate Prince.*

Other support for Cary's authorship of *The History of Edward II* lies in similarities between her play and the folio history. Convincing biographical parallels can be drawn between Cary's life and each text. For a discussion of such parallels in *Mariam*, see Margaret Ferguson, "Running On with Almost Public Voice: The Case of E.C.," *Tradition and the Talents of Women*, ed. Florence Howe (Urbana: University of Illinois Press, 1991), pp. 37–67; and Beilin, *Redeeming Eve*, pp. 157–76. Stauffer, Krontiris, and Foster identify similarities between Cary's and Isabel's experiences. Like *Mariam*, *Edward II* extensively reworks a male-authored narrative and devotes extraordinary attention to its female characters. The *kind* of attention that each text pays its principal female character is quite similar. The marital relationship of a royal couple is central to both works. The queens are portrayed primarily as wives, with little or no reference to their other domestic roles. At issue in both texts are the grounds and limits of a good wife's duty of obedience to her husband, though the play emphasizes the wife's right to speak, and the history, her right to act. Anger complicates a reading of Mariam and Isabel as clearly virtuous wives. Both texts look for an alternative to an absolutist model of submission and interrogate a virtuous wife's duty of obedience to her less virtuous husband. Neither text is concerned with a wife's sexual obedience; Cary ignores evidence of Mariam's sexual withholding in Josephus and greatly downplays the significance of Isabel's adultery.

D. R. Woolf contends that the folio is a product of the Exclusion crisis, written near its date of publication in 1680. Although we concur that Henry Cary did not write *The History of Edward II*, Woolf fails to consider Elizabeth Cary as its possible author, a point Isobel Grundy raises in her response to Woolf's article, "Falkland's *History of . . . King Edward II*," *Bodleian Library Record* 13 (1988): 82–83. The anachronisms he offers as evidence of later composition are also appropriate to the late 1620s; certain remarks in the folio seem well suited to late Jacobean politics, such as the argument against prerogative (158), which would have particular relevance to Charles I's actions early in his reign. The association of Spencer with Buckingham makes the folio's author a harsh critic of the Jacobean favorite, an unlikely view for either Henry Cary (a protegé of Buckingham) or Elizabeth, who was helped after her conversion by Buckingham's wife. This point, as Weller and Ferguson observe, is difficult to answer, but it does not necessarily preclude Elizabeth Cary's authorship of the folio. For instance, the text's criticism of Spencer often moves from his person to a general indictment of court corruption, so that his negative portrayal is both specific and representative. Cary's experiences with court politics and officials following her conversion may have made her feel less charitably about that arena and to Buckingham/Spencer as its embodiment. In addition, the pattern of indirect criticism of male authority that structures both *Mariam* and *The History of Edward II* makes it plausible to suggest that Henry Cary or Charles I/Edward II are as much her targets as Buckingham/Spencer. For a recent, careful, and thorough discussion of these attribution issues, see Weller and Ferguson (12–17).

Wits, Whigs, and Women: Domestic Politics as Anti-Whig Rhetoric in Aphra Behn's Town Comedies

Arlen Feldwick

After centuries of neglect or outright hostility by critics,[1] Aphra Behn (1640–1689) has finally been recognized for the importance of her contributions to English literature. Although she published prose, poems, and translations, she was primarily known to her contemporaries as a dramatist, and revenue from plays was probably her main source of income. Behn was a prolific author. She wrote some nineteen plays in as many years,[2] a literary output that ranks second among her contemporaries only to Dryden.

Behn's "politics" (in the broadest sense) are not easy to discern. If one investigates her work, especially her so-called "Town Comedies,"[3] one finds a profound cleavage between two dimensions in her writing: her supposed feminism and her partisan political convictions. Up to the present, there has been no adequate explanation of the relationship between these two commitments. Indeed, it might be thought that no such reconciliation is possible, that her attitudes are simply incommensurable. The present paper suggests, however, that careful attention to the political rhetoric of her Town Comedies offers a solution to the apparent inconsistency within her politics.

Deciphering Behn's ambiguous politics is crucial to the development of a more general interpretation of her work. For Behn's current reputation as a playwright largely rests on one of two factors that are generally taken to be mutually exclusive. First, she was a woman successfully writing and staging her work in the almost exclusively male world of the London theater. Thus, Behn represented an anomaly,

and she was the object of repeated attempts to marginalize her personally as well as her work. Recent feminist criticism has identified both
her personal and dramatic disruption of male paradigms in the Restoration. As the first professional woman playwright, she is lauded as
a pioneering voice who created important precedents for female expression.[4] In support of this claim, Susan Carlson points to Behn's
"novel characterization of the female self, her feminist understanding
of sexuality, her direct eroticism, her rethinking of comic plot, and her
rethinking of stage representations of men and women."[5] On the feminist reading, Behn's work endorses a sexual politics, rooted in the
subversion of the expectations of gender and genre.

The second pillar of Behn's literary reputation stems from her
overtly political stance as an unabashed partisan of the cause of the
Stuart monarchy and an acknowledged favorite of Charles II. The years
1676 to 1683 mark Behn's most successful and industrious period as a
playwright.[6] But this was a time of intense political turmoil,[7] and her
plays contain significant commentary on current English affairs. The
political dimension of Behn's theater was not, as in the case of some
Restoration dramatists, simply a sop to an audience fascinated by the
machinations and conspiracies of court and country. Rather, she clearly
viewed the design of her comedies as overtly polemical. As Behn tes-
tifies in her dedication to the Earl of Rochester preceding *The Lucky
Chance*:

> [Plays] are secret Instructions to the People, in things that 'tis
> impossible to insinuate into them any other Way. 'Tis Example
> that prevails above Reason or DIVINE PRECEPTS. . . . I have
> my self known a Man, whom neither Conscience nor Religion
> cou'd perswade to Loyalty, who with beholdings in our The-
> atre a Modern Politician in all his Colours, was converted,
> renounc'd his opinion, and quitted the Party. . . . Plays have
> been ever held most important to the very Political Part of
> Government.[8]

One could hardly imagine a more explicit admission on the part of
any author of the rhetorical intentions of her literary production. Most
charitably, Behn encourages us to think of her theater as political
education; a more cynical reading would see her as a self-confessed
propagandist. Consequently, Lorrie Jean Snook speaks of Behn as a
"radical Royalist,"[9] while Mary Ann O'Donnell observes that she
"deeply loved the King."[10] Many commentators on the Town Comedies indeed concentrate almost exclusively upon their partisan con-

tents, employing the known personal sympathies of their author as the primary setting for the interpretation of her plays.[11]

It may seem incongruous that someone who evinces a deeply rooted aversion to patriarchy, particularly in the form of forced marriages and parental authority, could also be an avid supporter of a monarchy which depended upon patriarchal rhetoric,[12] as well as a dynasty noted for its libertine treatment of women.[13] As George Woodcock has observed,

> Aphra Behn . . . was a devoted personal supporter of Charles
> II and his brother James, but she evidently did not regard that
> kind of direct emotional loyalty as inconsistent with radical
> criticisms of social institutions that restricted the freedoms of
> individuals . . . Aphra added a collection of radical ideas and
> attitudes which seem at variance with her support of reaction-
> ary kings and politicians. She despised the life of court . . ., she
> attacked the institution of marriage, and declared that sexual
> unions should be based on spontaneous love and not hedged
> round with restrictions. She subverted the authority of parents
> and maintained that women should have equal opportunities
> with men.[14]

Woodcock believes that it is "illogical" for her to support the Royal cause so fervently in view of her feminist leanings. At best, the "inconsistencies of her attitude" simply reflect her love of Cavalier liberty, her upbringing, her Royalist friends and her "uncritical loyalty to the King and his brother."[15] In truth, he can think of no coherent explanation for her "odd jumble of emotional and unthinking loyalties towards men whose actions were too often those of would-be despots."[16] While other critics have on occasion recognized a similar tension in Behn, they have likewise been at a loss to account for it.[17]

It is possible, however, to integrate the disparate political dimensions of Behn's Town Comedies if we are more sensitive to the force of her rhetoric. I claim that her sexual politics and her partisan politics are joined at the level of her extreme aversion to the Whigs. Whigism for her embodied the zenith of personal and intellectual marginalization. (To explain this aversion either historically or psychobiographically would take us outside of the scope of the present paper. Possibly she feared the threat to her literary career that the Whigs represented—they had closed London's theaters prior to the Restoration; perhaps the evidence surrounding her early marriage to a Dutch merchant holds some clues.)[18] Consequently, Behn's Toryism was less than wholehearted. She maintained loyalty to the crown as a logical consequence of her revulsion at the moral and social corruption and hypocrisy of the Whigs, a party which in her mind stood for the convergence of Puritanism, commercial acquisitiveness, and republican politics. It is not that Behn found the Cavaliers' values or behavior to be laudatory or ideal;[19] instead, she regarded the Whig claim to rule and methods of rulership unpalatable and untenable. It is in order to make this point that she brings sexual politics to the fore. Her demonstration of the illegitimacy of the Whig cause relies upon her illustration of the cruelty and incompetence of Whig men as husbands and fathers. Gender roles are often reversed, and women frequently outwit men, because those men are quintessential Whigs. In the end, however, this does not lead Behn to favor the liberation of women from male bondage entirely. She remains bound by a version of the patriarchal thesis that men naturally rule and women are naturally ruled. It is simply that the claim of men to rule on grounds such as wealth or morals cannot be sustained.

This interpretation explains the centrality in the Town Comedies of the domestic realm, particularly of the Whig household. All the aforementioned plays portray what is now called the dysfunctional family. Behn's unhappy families are in themselves an anti-Whig statement. Rich old Whig men, such as Sir Patient Fancy, Francisco (*The False Count*), Lord Lambert (*The Roundheads*), Sir Timothy Treat-All (*The City Heiress*), Sir Cautious Fulbank (*The Lucky Chance*) and Sir Feeble Fainwou'd (*The Lucky Chance*), always stand in for the tyrannical father or husband. Cavalier men, who are frequently themselves children of dysfunctional Whig families, never head a household nor do they have families for which to provide. They are stereotypically rogue males. Bellmour (*The Lucky Chance*), Wittmore (*Sir Patient Fancy*), Freeman (*The Roundheads*), Loveless (*The Roundheads*) and Wilding (*The City Heiress*), for example, are young, most often in meagre financial straits, and without a binding allegiance (by which is primarily meant marriage) to anyone, or anything, other than to a distant and quasi-mythical royal figure.

Whig fathers and husbands personify patriarchy at its most extreme. They attempt to force their daughters into unwanted marriages for social and/or pecuniary reasons. *Sir Patient Fancy* opens with a discussion of the evils of oppressive parents and forced marriages. As Lucretia remarks, "These are the precious things our grave Parents still chuse to make us happy with, and all for a filthy Jointure, the undeniable argument for our Slavery to Fools." Sir Fancy's daughter, Isabella, concurs: "Custom is unkind to our Sex, not to allow us free Choice; but we above all creatures must be forced to endure the formal Recommendations of a Parent, and the more insupportable Addresses of an odious Fop."[20] In *The False Count*, Clara bemoans to her sister Julia a similar condition: "We are both unhappy to be match'd to those we cannot love."[21] By definition, it seems, Whigs are unlovable. Moreover, if these ladies have precontracted love relationships to gallants (for example, Julia to Carlos in *The False Count*), laying with their Whig husbands "is flat Adultery."[22] There are numerous similar examples of forced marriage throughout these plays, but none more pointed and poignant than the declarations of Leticia and Diana, respectively wife and daughter of Sir Feeble Fainwou'd in *The Lucky Chance*. Before planning to run off with Bellmour, Leticia reflects: "Old Man forgive me—thou the Agressor art, / Who rudely forc'd the Hand without the Heart. / She cannot from the Paths of Honour rove, / Whose Guide's Religion, and whose End is Love."[23] Diana, also preparing to flee from patriarchal oppression, proclaims: "Father, farewell—if you dislike my course, / Blame the old rigid Customs of your Force."[24] It is clear that the daughters and wives (who are themselves victims of either a forced or undesired match) are unwillingly subjected to Whig oppression. That these women seek to, or do, escape from this domestic tyranny (into the arms of Cavaliers) demonstrates Whig inability to control their private lives, even their women.

Not only do women not love Whigs, but Whig men, husbands in particular, are characterized as unloving (in a romantic sense), brutal and vulgar. Francisco from *The False Count* is a prime example. His unhappy young wife, Julia, is in love with her former fiance, Carlos, yet she tries to remain loyal to her vows. To Carlos, who is disguised as a Sultan, she avers: "[I] wou'd not break my Marriage Vows to him."[25] Francisco habitually attacks Julia's honor. She says in her defense: "Which Virtue, before I'll lose, I'll die a thousand Deaths."[26] Francisco, on the other hand, easily exchanges her honor for his life. Knowing that his bride was coerced by her father into marrying him, he is obsessed with a fear of being cuckolded.[27] Francisco is an unpleasant character, not least because of his misogynistic cant: "A Man had better have a Mule to his wife than a Woman, and 'twere easier govern'd . . . my opinion is, my Wife's my Slave."[28] In addition, he not only expresses an intention to beat his wife,[29] but also threatens to murder her.[30]

The other Whig husbands fare little better by comparison. Sir Patient Fancy, a hypocritical, pious Puritan places no value on love within marriage. "Tell me not of lovers, my Lady *Fancy*; with Reverence to your good Ladyship, I value not whether there be Love between 'em or not. Pious Wedlock is my Business."[31] Lady Knowell, a learned bluestocking widow, pities Lady Fancy for demands made on her by her husband. Sir Fancy has turned his wife into "a Slave, a very Houshold Drudge."[32] His unwanted forceful attentions and childlike name-calling ("Ape's Face," "Monky-Face," "Fool's Face," "refractory Baggage," "Harlot," "Mungrel") ill-disguise the threat of violence if she is not compliant.[33] The behavior of Sir Cautious Fulbank is perhaps even more reprehensible. Without his wife's consent or knowledge, he gambles away a night with her rather than lose three hundred pounds at dice.[34] Sir Cautious not only has the audacity to ask Julia, his wife, to judge the contest but also responds to her innocent question, "What has my Husband lost?" with the cryptic answer: "Only a small parcel of Ware that lay dead on my hands, sweetheart."[35] Given these examples of Whig husbands, it is perhaps not surprising that Diana in *The City Heiress* expresses a certain lack of joy before her marriage to Sir Timothy Treat-All: "Marriage is a sort of Hanging, Sir; and I was only making a short prayer before Execution."[36]

Perhaps the least likely condition into which Behn's women will fall, if they remain faithful to their Whig husbands, is pregnancy. Whig men are characterized as old, lacking in virility, and frequently impotent. Sir Timothy Treat-All (whom Montague Summers identifies as the arch Whig "Lord Shaftesbury almost without disguise")[37] is said by the Cavalier Wilding to be "so visibly and undeniably impotent."[38] Gayman, the gallant of *The False Count*, observes that "neither Youth nor Beauty can grind his [Sir Feeble Fainwou'd's] Dudgeon to an edge."[39] To highlight Whig inadequacies, direct comparison is frequently made between their sexual inadequacy and Cavalier desires and desirability. In *The City Heiress*, Diana calls Sir Timothy a "Beast," an "old Dotard." She compares his "hollow Pair of thin blue withered lips" to "Tom's warm kisses." Tom Wilding, the gallant she loves, is "so young, so handsom, and so soft a Lover."[40] Behn's Whig men, unlike the Cavaliers, cannot win their women by charm, youth, or good looks. Instead they acquire and hold onto them by force and economic servitude.

Whig ineptness in the bedroom points to a problem of inheritance. In Behn's plays, Whigs appear physically unable to produce heirs. As Douglas Canfield has observed, it is ironic that disenfranchised young

Cavaliers such as Wilding in *The City Heiress* actually risk ousting themselves from the line of inheritance by cuckolding Whig men and impregnating their wives with possible successors.[41] Wilding's cast-off mistress, Diana, plans this as an act of revenge on him for being discarded. As a "trick" it is a wonderful gesture of patralineal subversion. As an improvement in the position of the woman involved (or as a subversive act for women in general), however, it has little to recommend it. Indeed, if an act of revenge, or lust, means "a Cradle full of Noise and Mischief, with a Pack of Repentence at my Back,"[42] one could argue that a woman might very well be better off declining the opportunity.

Behn's Whig men share many common characteristics. They are city merchants ("cits"), country squires, aldermen, and politicians, and are conventionally portrayed as rich, old fools who are invariably duped by women and cuckolded by young Cavalier gallants. Lucia maintains in *Sir Patient Fancy*: "At Games of Love Husbands to cheat is fair."[43] Indeed, she revels in her skill at deluding puritanical hypocrites like her husband, Sir Patient Fancy. She crows to her lover, Wittmore, "There's nothing so comical as to hear me cant, and even cheat those Knaves, the Preachers themselves, that delude the ignorant rabble."[44] Behn's Whigs are made *so* incompetent and contemptible that women can fool and control them. This reflects a clear inversion of the "proper" order, according to which women are subservient to men. In her view, the Whigs are *deserving* of manipulation at the hands of women, because they pretend to an authority on which they have no valid claim.

The disordered condition of Whig society is clearly revealed in *The Roundheads*, where Lady Lambert runs rings around her husband who is himself vying for leadership of the country. Lady Lambert informs her old lady-in-waiting: "She is not worthy of Intrigues of Love, that cannot manage a silly Husband as she pleases."[45] Freeman, the Lady's Royalist beau, petitions Sir Lambert through his wife: "We knew, my Lord, the Influence your Ladies have over you."[46] Indeed, Lord Lambert confesses to his wife: "I owe all my good fortune to thee."[47] She is the power behind the "throne" and has delusions of grandeur herself: she hopes to be (Whig) Queen.[48] Only toward the end of the play does she return to the royalist fold,[49] thus restoring the "natural" order. In a clear allusion to the Restoration, the Whigs fall from power and once again women are (happily?) under the control of Cavalier men.

Behn's condemnation of Whigs plays heavily upon her rejection of their crass materialistic and commercial values. The Whigs in the Tory

Comedies usually hold the purse strings, and employ wealth to justify their pretensions to power and status. As Janet Todd explains, Behn had a "distaste for the commercial classes and the parliamentary Whigs who, she felt, put a price on everything."[50] Isabella's tirade against the mercantile class in *The False Count* perhaps best reflects Behn's own sentiment.

> Merchant! a pretty Character! a Woman of my Beauty, and five Thousand Pound, marry a Merchant—a little, petty, dirty-heel'd Merchant; faugh, I'd rather live a Maid all the days of my life, or be sent to a Nunnery, and that's Plague enough I'm sure.[51]

Isabella is herself the daughter of a merchant. Indeed, her father, old Francisco, who now calls himself a "gentleman," was once a leather-seller.[52] Yet even she recognizes that commercial wealth is a poor substitute for personal happiness.

Behn's Whigs tend to abuse their economic advantage, which they use to maintain control over their women, as well as to bring into line young male dependents or potential rivals. Behn has a noted aversion to forced marriages, particularly unions based on money.[53] Behn's very first production was called *The Forced Marriage* (1671); it introduced a theme that is to be found in most of her plays, including the Town Comedies. Leticia in *The Lucky Chance* and Julia in *The False Count* are but two examples of women forced into undesirable marriages to Whigs. In Behn's plays, *forced* marriages are invariably to Whigs. Given her negative presentation of marriages to Whigs, one might be tempted to conclude that Behn views matrimony ultimately as a corrupting force.[54] But Susan Carlson argues that such a view is too simplistic: "Behn's portrait of marriage is complex, with the institution simultaneously romanticized and vilified."[55] Behn vilifies marriage when it is to a Whig, and romanticizes it when it is to a Cavalier. Yet, as shall be seen, relationships between her women and their Cavalier lovers are seldom more satisfying.

In consequence of Behn's concentration upon Whig marriage, her female characters are often objects of economic exchange. Drawing on the criticism of French feminist Luce Irigaray, Lorrie Jean Snook observes that "the economy only exchanges women, . . . men are always in control."[56] In "Women in the Market," Irigaray had argued that "women's bodies—through their use, consumption, and circulation—provide for the condition making social life and culture possible."[57] As we have already discovered, the rate of exchange for Sir Cautious Fulbank's wife is three hundred pounds. Francisco would rather have his wife Julia killed than pay her ransom.[58] Lord Lambert trades on Lady Lambert's attractiveness to other men. He turns a blind eye to, if not encourages, Cromwell to sleep with his wife in order to serve his own political ambitions.[59] It becomes apparent that a man's "worth," his power to trade socially and economically, is ultimately determined by his fortune, while patralineal concerns require a woman's "worth" to be her virtue. In effect, a woman's virtue is just another commodity. At birth a woman's "honour" belongs to her father. He may then trade it (advantageously) to a prospective husband. The woman never really possesses the power of exchange. Behn's Whigs are portrayed as the archetypical practitioners of the "traffic in women." Sir Patient Fancy, for instance, discovers that his daughter Isabella has been covertly seeing a young Cavalier. Incensed, he questions her closely. "Tell me Minion—private meeting . . . when? where? how? and how often? Oh, she's debauched!—her Reputation ruin'd, and she'll need a double Portion."[60] In taking charge of her own sexuality, Isabella has transgressed the boundaries of patriarchy. Her father is incensed not because she may have lost her virtue, but because "used goods" raise the bride price. Cavaliers, by contrast, are portrayed as neither fathers nor husbands, thus never actively taking part in the traffic in women.

And so in the plays themselves, as Susan Carlson observes, Whig men like "Sir Feeble Fainwou'd and Sir Cautious Fulbank have money and status, enough that they serve as city alderman and carry sway through their money."[61] Behn reveals the flawed nature of this equation of finances with political power. For her, the *right* to rule is not determined by the strength of the pocket book. The right to govern, domestically and publicly, is something other than financial tyranny. Whig inability to manage household affairs, their wives, daughters, and money, in the domestic realm is a microcosmic demonstration of their inability to govern in the macrocosm of the public realm. Behn's purpose is didactic. Whigs are fools, easily parted from their money and their women. She encourages her audience to conclude that they would be (and were during the Commonwealth) equally inept in governing the country.[62] For want of an alternative option, the political plays register that the rule of the King, of the Cavalier gallants, is preferable, but only by default.

Here one encounters a cogent explanation for the strong and exceptional women whom scholars have found in Behn's plays. The conduct of these women conveys a profound political message. Female characters such as Leticia in *The Lucky Chance* and Julia in *The False Count* are assertive, or particularly clever, in order to reveal the foolishness of the Whigs whom they trick or against whom they scheme. One is probably correct in thinking, then, that trumping one of Behn's Whigs is ultimately not particularly liberating for women.[63]

On the surface, marriage (or extra-marital union) to a Cavalier is what Behn's women desire. As Maundy, Lady Fancy's "Woman," wryly puts it, "There's no reason she should languish with an old Man when a Young Man may be had."[64] Cavalier charm and good looks are intoxicating to Behn's women. Witness Lady Lambert's effusive praise of Loveless to Lady Desbro:

> Lady Lam. I want Words to describe him; not tall, nor short; well made, and such a Face— / Love, Wit and Beauty revel'd in his Eyes; / From whence he shot a thousand winged Darts / That pierced quite through my Soul.
>
> Lady Des. Seem'd he a Gentleman?
>
> Lady Lam. A God! altho his outside were but mean; / But he shone thro like Lightning from a Cloud, / And he shot more piercing Rays.

Indeed, Lady Lambert is so besotted that she exclaims, "I had almost forgot all Decency."[65] For "sure 'tis the mode to love 'em—I cannot blame 'em."[66] It is not surprising, therefore, that these plays usually end in a round of marriages; Whigs, aldermen and merchants willingly (even joyfully) relinquishing their wives and daughters to their Cavalier rivals. Sir Patient Fancy, described by Behn in the "Dramatis Personae" as "an old rich Alderman," forgives all those who have transgressed against him, hands over his wife to Wittmore, intends to keep a mistress and turn "Spark."[67] Likewise, Francisco declares to his wife Julia that he "was an old Fool,"[68] and bids Carlos to "take her and rid me of one Plague."[69] Similar scenes conclude the other three plays under consideration.[70]

Finally, it seems, the misguided Whigs are converted. Misrule naturally gives way to correct rule. The plays, then, reveal that the Whig world is disordered domestically as well as publicly. The women invariably loathe their Whig partners and love (or at least are drawn to) their Cavalier beaus. As Susan Carlson concludes, "Arranged marriages must make way for marriage by consent."[71] As the plays draw to a close, the natural order appears to (re) assert itself with the implication that the women are (or soon will be) "happily" under Cavalier "rule." But once again it is a choice by default. The women do not choose Cavaliers so much as reject Whigs.

This conclusion is supported by the failure of these unions to achieve closure. The future happiness of couples such as Leticia and Bellmour, Lady Fulbank and Gayman, Lucia and Wittmore, Carlos and Julia and especially, Lady Galliard and Sir Charles Merriwell, and Wilding and his city heiress, remains tenuous and uncertain. Behn's plays tend to reinforce the view that Cavalier gentlemen do not necessarily make good and/or faithful husbands or partners. As Angeline Goreau remarks, "Marriage was anathema to the Restoration gallant."[72] Considering that most of the women in these plays are eventually matched with Cavalier men, Behn's resolutions remain open-ended for women. While there are many examples of problematic relationships between women and Cavaliers in the political plays, the events of *Sir Patient Fancy* may stand as a representative case. Wittmore, who is supposedly devoted to Lady Fancy, has constantly to check himself to remain faithful to her. Lady Fancy, apparently aware of his weaknesses, had previously cautioned him: "But take heed, dear Wittmore, whilst you only design to feign a Courtship, you do it not in good earnest."[73] Lady Fancy's fears are borne out; her young step-daughter, the pretty Isabella, sorely tempts him. He says:

> What an insensible Dog shall I be counted to refuse the Enjoyment of so fair, so new a creature, and who is like to be thrown into my Arms whether I will or not?—but Conscience and My Vows to the fair Mother: No, I will be honest.—Madam,—as Gad shall save me, . . . if you are not the most Belle person I ever saw.[74]

In turn, Lodwick loves Isabella, yet is visibly attracted to Lady Fancy. He exclaims: "Death! wou'd I had the consoling her, 'tis a charming Woman!"[75] His captivation is underscored by the stage direction: "To L. Fancy. gazing on her, goes out."[76] In the end Lodwick takes advantage of a confused situation and succeeds in sleeping with Lady Fancy."[77] Generally speaking, it would seem that Cavaliers do not expect, or intend, to maintain marital fidelity even if one were to marry for love. For instance, Isabella argues with Wittmore that she will make him a cuckold if they were to marry against her wishes. He responds cynically: "So wou'd you had you lov'd me, in a year or two."[78] Leander attempts to avert a match to Lady Knowell by saying: "I am that wild Extravagant, my Uncle rendered me, *and cannot live confin'd*."[79] His words summarize the very heart of the Cavalier creed.[80]

In addition, the future of these unions in society at large is frequently set into question. *The Lucky Chance*, for example, closes with

Lucia and Wittmore united but marginalized. As Douglas Canfield points out, they remain "excluded from the dominant patriarchal political economy . . . they may amass some wealth, may consequently garner some independence. But they cannot engender a legitimate heir, cannot create a place and a space of their own which is enduring, transmittable."[81] The women in Behn's comedies beat arranged marriage through consensual marriage. But, one might note, to be united with a Cavalier is *not* the road to wedded bliss, judging either by Behn's standards or our own. Hence, it seems wholly implausible to ascribe to Behn "a nostalgic invocation of *Cavalier unity*, the myth of an idyllic past before the divisiveness of civil war."[82] Her Town Comedies hold little promise that the Restoration constitutes a "return" to some blessed order that was upset by the Whig-dominated Interregnum. Although Whigs represent misrule, it would be a *non sequitur* to say that Behn believed Cavaliers to embody correct rule. If Behn subscribes to any ideal standard at all, or evinces any nostalgic longing, it is perhaps captured by the pre-lapsarian age of innocence, prior to the creation of kings, which she invokes in her poetic paraphrase, "The Golden Age," published around the same time as the Town Comedies. In this poem, it is the conventionally masculine virtue of honor that is made responsible for the Fall and for its aftermath.[83] And the restoration of the golden age is said to demand the replacement of honor with love, which is precisely the quality that neither Whigs nor Cavaliers seem able to display in Behn's plays.

Behn's evocation of a golden age, in conjunction with the lack of closure in her political plays, perhaps indicates that she looked outside her own period for solution to the dilemmas of domestic as well as partisan politics. Yet such unfocused desire for the recovery of a distant past is not sufficient to constitute a genuine subversion of the patriarchal conditions of her time. One should not be blinded to this fact by the singular quality of Behn's own career. Behn tried to live without male support and indeed there were times when she was financially secure. Nevertheless, she died reviled and in poverty.[84] As Angeline Goreau argues, "The choice was limited: one could become a wife or a mistress . . . there was little possibility, financial or social, of a single woman's surviving on her own."[85] No less than Behn's life, the questionable future happiness she gives her female characters is testimony to Goreau's claim. It might appear a paradox that Behn's plays seethe with anti-matrimonial sentiment yet end with a "round of marriages." However, these unions, as has been seen, are in themselves problematic. It is difficult to dispute Susan Carlson's conclusion that "at best she [Behn] raises questions about what else may be possible; she cannot define a new course of action."[86] Women such as Julia, Lucia, and Leticia may come up against the conventional comic ending but, like their creator, they are unable to break free from male paradigms or male (both Whig *and* Cavalier) control of their sexuality. For Behn, as for her ostensively "transgressive" female characters, an existence beyond male economic, sexual and social control falls outside the realm of possibility, if not quite imagination.

Here the limitations of domestic politics once again coincide with the circumstances of public partisan conflicts. Behn's women might be able to escape from the worst abuses (social as well as physical) of their Whig husbands, yet just in order to be delivered into the dubious protection of Cavalier lovers. This reinforces the general impression of the halfhearted quality of her royalism. Without doubt, the crown was preferable for Behn to a Whiggish parliament as a source of authority; but both were so embedded in a patriarchal order that neither could permit the realization of genuine female autonomy. The predicament of the Restoration woman, even one as transgressive as Behn, was unequivocal: the ultimate female reality was marginalization.

Notes

The author is grateful to Cary Nederman for lending invaluable support in the course of writing this essay, as well as to Doug Canfield for his many helpful comments and suggestions.

1. For a sampling of the critical reception of Behn by her contemporaries and later generations, see Sara Heller Mendelson, *The Mental World of Stuart Women: Three Studies* (Amherst: University of Massachusetts Press, 1987), pp. 176–77; Dale Spender, *Women of Ideas and What Men Have Done to Them* (London: Routledge, 1982), pp. 32–43; and Angeline Goreau, *Reconstructing Aphra: A Social Biography of Aphra Behn* (New York: Dial Press, 1980), pp. 14–16.

2. Jacqueline Pearson, *The Prostituted Muse: Images of Women and Women Dramatists 1642–1737* (New York: Harvester, 1988), p. 145.

3. Behn's "Town Comedies" (or sometimes "Tory Comedies") comprise *Sir Patient Fancy* (1678), *The Roundheads* (1681), *The False Count* (1681 or 1682), *The City Heiress* (1682), and *The Lucky Chance* (1686).

4. In this vein, see J. Douglas Canfield, "Woman's Wit: Subversive Women Tricksters in Restoration Comedy," unpublished manuscript; Lorrie Jean Snook, "The Performance of Sexual and Economic Politics in the Plays of Aphra Behn" (Ph.D. diss., Department of English, University of Arizona, 1992); Robert

Markley, " 'Be impudent, be saucey, forward, bold, touzing and lewd': The Politics of Masculine Sexuality and Feminine Desire in Aphra Behn's Tory Comedies," unpublished manuscript; Catherine Gallagher, "Who was that masked woman? The Prostitute and the Playwright in the Comedies of Aphra Behn" *Women's Studies* 15 (1988): 23–42; Cheri Davis Langdell, "Aphra Behn and Sexual Politics: A Dramatist's Discourse with her Audience," in *Drama, Sex and Politics*, J. Redmond, ed. (Cambridge: Cambridge University Press, 1985), pp. 109–26; Judith K. Gardiner, "Aphra Behn: Sexuality and Self-Respect," *Women's Studies* 7 (1980): 67–78; Mendelson, *Mental World*; Laura Brown, *English Dramatic Form: 1600–1760* (New Haven: Yale University Press, 1981); Dale Spender, *Mothers of the Novel* (London: Routledge, 1986), pp. 47–66; Pearson, *Prostituted Muse*; Rose Zimbardo, *A Mirror to Nature: Transformations in Drama and Aesthetics, 1660–1732* (Lexington: University of Kentucky Press, 1986).

5. Susan Carlson, *Women and Comedy: Rewriting the British Theatrical Tradition* (Ann Arbor: University of Michigan Press, 1991), p. 128.

6. For reasons that are still unclear, Behn ceased to produce plays for four years after the production of *The False Count* in 1682. She wrote few comedies after this hiatus. Of the few she did write, the *Lucky Chance*, produced in 1687, is generally considered to be the most outstanding. For one interpretation of Behn's silence, see George Woodcock, *Aphra Behn: The English Sappho* (Montreal: Black Rose Books, 1989), pp. 164–174.

7. Those interested in a general account of the historical background may consult Christopher Hill, *Century of Revolution, 1603–1714* (Edinburgh: Thomas Nelson, 1961).

8. Aphra Behn, *The Works of Aphra Behn*, Montague Summers, ed. vol. 3 (New York: Benjamin Blom, 1967 [1913]), p. 183. (A new edition of Behn's collected works, under the editorship of Janet Todd, has begun to appear from Ohio State University Press; unfortunately, the volumes containing her plays have yet to be published as of the completion of this essay.)

9. Snook, "Sexual and Economic Politics," p. 172.

10. Mary Ann O'Donnell, *Aprha Behn: An Annotated Bibliography of Primary and Secondary Sources* (New York: Garland, 1986), p. 5.

11. See, for example, George Guffey, "Aphra Behn's *Oroonoko*: Occasion and Accomplishment," in George Guffey and Andrew Wright, *Two English Novelists* (Los Angeles: Clark Library, 1975), pp. 8–15; Edward Burns, *Restoration Comedy: Crises of Desire and Identity* (London: Macmillan, 1987), pp. 136–40; Goreau, *Reconstructing Aphra*, pp. 236–61; Maureen Duffy, *The Passionate Shepherdess: Aphra Behn 1640–89* (London: Cape, 1977), pp. 174–83, 160–75; and Janet Todd, *The Sign of Angelica: Women, Writing and Fiction 1660–1800* (London: Virago, 1989), pp. 39, 72–3.

12. On the widespread adherence to patriarchal ideology in the seventeenth century, see Gordon Schochet, *Patriarchalism in Political Thought* (New York: Basic Books, 1975), pp. 54–114.

13. Goreau, *Reconstructing Aphra*, p. 166.

14. Woodcock, *Behn*, pp. xv, 151.

15. Woodcock, *Behn*, pp. 151–52.

16. Woodcock, *Behn*, p. 151.

17. For example, see Goreau, *Reconstructing Aphra*, pp. 252, 272–73; William R. Hersey, *A Critical Old Spelling Edition of Aphra Behn's The City Heiress* (New York: Garland Press, 1987), pp. 85–118; and Gardiner, "Aphra Behn," p. 69.

18. Details and speculation about Behn's marriage are examined by Mary Ann O'Donnell, "Alphra Behn: Tory Wit and Unconventional Woman," in K. M. Wilson and F. J. Warnke, eds., *Women Writers of the Seventeenth Century* (Athens: University of Georgia Press, 1989), p. 343.

19. Take, for example, these lines from her poem "The Golden Age," where she posits a paradisiacal past without kings or queens: "Then no rough sounds of Wars Alarms, / Had taught the World the needless use of Arms: / Monarchs were uncreated then, / Those Arbitrary Rulers over men: / Kings that made Laws first broke 'em" (6: 139).

20. Behn, *Works*, 4: 11.

21. Behn, *Works*, 3: 119.

22. Behn, *Works*, 3: 107.

23. Behn, *Works*, 3: 230.

24. Behn, *Works*, 3: 260.

25. Behn, *Works*, 3: 158.

26. Behn, *Works*, 3: 165.

27. For example, see Behn, *Works*, 3: 109–11 and passim.

28. Behn, *Works*, 3: 110–11.

29. Behn, *Works*, 3: 125.

30. Behn, *Works*, 3: 126.

31. Behn, *Works*, 4: 74.

32. Behn, *Works*, 4: 45.

33. Behn, *Works*, 4: 84–85.

34. Behn, *Works*, 3: 255–59.

35. Behn, *Works*, 3: 358.

36. Behn, *Works*, 2: 287.

37. Behn, *Works*, 2: 198.

38. Behn, *Works*, 2: 232.

39. Behn, *Works*, 3: 194.

40. Behn, *Works*, 2: 286.

41. Canfield, "Woman's Wit."

42. Behn, *Works*, 1: 101.

43. Behn, *Works*, 4: 44.

44. Behn, *Works*, 4: 26.

45. Behn, *Works*, 1: 410.

46. Behn, *Works*, 1: 372.

47. Behn, *Works*, 1: 355.

48. Behn, *Works*, 1: 359, 400.

49. Behn, *Works*, 1: 412–13.

50. Todd, *Sign of Angellica*, p. 72.

51. Behn, *Works*, 3: 115. For similar sentiments, see Behn, *Works*, 3: 115–16, 136.

52. Behn, *Works*, 3: 175.

53. As observed by Goreau, *Reconstructing Aphra*, pp. 86–7, 229.

54. The view of Goreau, *Reconstructing Aphra*, p. 287.

55. Carlson, *Women and Comedy*, p. 149.

56. Snook, "Sexual and Economic Politics," p. 82.

57. Luce Irigaray, *This Sex Which Is Not One*, trans. Catherine Porter (Ithaca: Cornell University Press, 1985), p. 171.

58. Behn, *Works*, 3: 149.

59. Behn, *Works*, 1: 403.

60. Behn, *Works*, 4: 81.

61. Carlson, *Women and Comedy*, p. 133.

62. *The Roundheads*, especially the epilogue (1: 424–5), is obviously Behn's clearest statement of Whig incapacity to rule—in the past, in the future, and certainly in the present.

63. Among the primary examples of Whigs tricked by women, see *Sir Patient Fancy*, 4: 51, 55–58, 69, 112–114; *The False Count*, 3: 119; *The Roundheads*, 1: 401–5; and *The City Heiress*, 2: 287, 297–8. For a more detailed analysis of female tricksters and subverters in Behn's plays, see Canfield, "Woman's Wit" and idem, "Female Rebels and Patriarchal Paradigms in Some Neoclassical Works," in John W. Yolton and Laura E. Brown, eds., *Studies in Eighteenth-Century Culture*, vol. 18 (Madison: Univ. of Wisconsin Press, 1988).

64. Behn, *Works*, 4: 49.

65. Behn, *Works*, 1: 350.

66. Behn, *Works*, 1: 415.

67. Behn, *Works*, 4: 114–15.

68. Behn, *Works*, 3: 171.

69. Behn, *Works*, 3: 175.

70. See Behn, *Works*, 1: 416–25 (*The Roundheads*); ibid., 2: 297–98 (*The City Heiress*); and ibid., 3: 275–78 (*The Lucky Chance*). In this connection, comparison should be drawn between *The City Heiress* and Thomas Middleton's *Mad World, My Masters*. Behn lifted many scenes with little variation (for instance, the robbery scene) from Middleton's play yet she chose to change the ending. *Mad World, My Master* concludes with the Whig character Sir Bounteous Progress proclaiming the gulliblity of his nephew, Follywit. The young gentleman has been tricked into marrying his uncle's mistress believing her to be a gentlewoman. Sir Bounteous closes the play by saying: "Who lives by cunning, mark it, his fate's cast; / When he has gull'd all, then is himself the last" (Thomas Middleton, *A Mad World, My Masters*, S. Henning, ed. [Lincoln: University of Nebraska Press, 1967], p. 102). That a Whig should triumph must have been anathema to Behn. Her version, not surprisingly, inverts Middleton's outcome. Sir Timothy Treat-All, "an old seditious Knight" (remember that he is a caricature of the Whig leader Shaftesbury), is tricked by Diana into marriage by her claim to be a "city heiress." In truth, Diana is the cast-off mistress of Wilding, a Cavalier who is also Sir Timothy's "discarded nephew." Detailed comparison may be found in Marston S. Blach, *Thomas Middleton's "A Trick to Catch the Old One: A Mad World, My Masters" and Aphra Behn's "The City Heiress"* (Salzburg: Institut für Anglistik und Amerikanistik, 1981).

71. Carlson, *Women and Comedy*, p. 137.

72. Goreau, *Reconstructing Aphra*, p. 173.

73. Behn, *Works*, 4: 32.

74. Behn, *Works*, 4: 33–4.

75. Behn, *Works*, 4: 45.

76. Behn, *Works*, 4: 46.

77. Behn, *Works*, 4: 50–1.

78. Behn, *Works*, 4: 90.

79. Behn, *Works*, 4: 94 (my emphasis).

80. Restoration Wits promoted a lifestyle which advocated what might be called today "free love." Thus, to be bound to one woman in marriage was undesirable unless economic necessity demanded it. In real life, of course, not only Whigs but also Cavaliers took part in arranged marriages and they too wed for "interest." For example, Goreau, *Reconstructing Aphra*, p. 228 tells us that "the Earl of Rochester, having been left with a sadly reduced estate by his improvident father, sought to repair his fortune by choosing to pursue one of the richest heiresses in England—at the King's suggestion. . . . Once in possession of the fortune, he left her to the isolation of the country while entertaining mistresses in London." We might image that, in doing so, the Restoration gallants not only freed themselves from observation by their wives, but also protected their rights of primogeniture. With their spouses shut up in country estates they were less likely to be cuckolded. It was not always the case that marriages were "forced" by economic paucity or reasons of social advancement. In these instances, Goreau maintains: Wit "objections to marriage might be seen, then, in the most unfavourable light, as reluctance to be tied to any woman who could not be as easily discarded as a whore or a mistress and who might even believe he had some responsibility to her" (Behn, *Works*, 229).

81. Canfield, "Woman's Wit."

82. Markley, " 'Be impudent . . .' "

83. Behn, *Works*, 6: 140–42.

84. Goreau, *Reconstructing Aphra*, pp. 291–92.

85. Goreau, *Reconstructing Aphra*, p. 175.

86. Carlson, *Women and Comedy*, p. 151.

WILHELMUS REX & MARIA REGINA.

The Coronation of William and Mary. Reproduced by permission of the British Museum.

Queen Mary II: Image and Substance During the Glorious Revolution

W. M. Spellman

In the large body of recent literature published around the occasion of the tercentenary of the Glorious Revolution, little attention has been devoted to the role of one of the partners in the unprecedented joint monarchy of William and Mary. Curiously, the six-year reign of Mary II (1689–1695) has elicited scant scholarly interest over the centuries, particularly when one considers the central place occupied by the Revolution in the constitutional and religious history of early modern England. Both in terms of biography and political analysis, the focus of attention has most often been on the new king and his struggles with the rival parties in Parliament and with Louis XIV on the Continent.[1] By way of explanation for the omission, we are assured that the queen's printed advice to members of her own sex, that "women should not meddle in government" is sufficient evidence of her apolitical nature and intense deference to her husband.[2] Twenty-six years of age at her accession and completely lacking in the knowledge of state affairs, Mary's arrival after the flight of her father had been essential solely in winning the support of Tory politicians who stuck at the question of legitimacy and hereditary principle in the removal of James II. The youthful and politically naive queen, we are told, could in no respect be compared to another, more illustrious female monarch who had ascended the English throne at the age of twenty-five. Points of comparison with the exceptional age of Elizabeth were entirely misplaced, mere wishful thinking on the part of those who refused to recognize the hard fact of William's primacy in the awkward joint monarchy.

The main problem with this picture is that it fails to come to terms with the fact that for virtually one-half of the period between the Revolution of 1688–89 and Mary's premature death from smallpox in December 1695, the king was outside the country and executive authority rested with the queen. During these thirty-six months the stereotype of Mary as merely obedient and submissive, a woman whose husband, in the words of one recent scholar, "was forced to lay upon her a greater burden than she was able to bear," simply does not square with the record of her activity as ruler during the king's protracted absences.[3] A reassessment, it seems, is long overdue, and in recent years some preliminary work in this area has been undertaken.

Between June and September of 1690 William was away with an army in Ireland, and before his departure Parliament passed a special Regency Bill that placed the administration of the kingdom in Mary's hands. The powers granted to the queen under that Bill came into force again between January and September 1691, March and October 1692 and again during the same months in 1693, and between May and November of 1694, while the king was otherwise engaged on the Continent. For this first regularly absent monarch since Henry V, and for the often divided council appointed by William to advise the queen while he was out of the country, the Regency Bill was, if nothing else, a clear affirmation of the integrity and the intelligence of a woman whose partnership in administration, while perhaps unenthusiastic, was in no sense either ceremonial or perfunctory. This essay will explore some of the reasons for this partiality in the historical literature and close with a look at one recent, and altogether more satisfying portrait of the queen and her place in the Revolution settlement. Finally, I shall offer some additional observations on Mary's significance for the religious life of the official Church during the eighteenth-century "Age of Reason," a period which scholars have more often than not associated with the decline of traditional teaching and practice within the Church of England.

Two main interpretations of Mary's character and performance as Queen of England after 1688 dominated the partisan contemporary literature. An explicitly hostile viewpoint was put forward by the Jacobite opponents of the Glorious Revolution, those individuals who for a variety of personal, constitutional, and religious reasons undertook to maintain their allegiance to the exiled James II and who refused to cooperate with the newly installed regime of Mary and William.[4] The Jacobite offensive against the new monarchs took the form of personal, and often scurrilous, attacks on the motives and the ambitions of Mary and William. According to this perspective the Revolution of 1688 had shamefully legitimized the principle that might makes right in the matter of succession, and Mary's betrayal of her father was extended to charges of marital infidelity and adultery, charges which had some grounding with respect to the king but were without foundation when lodged against Mary. In other words, Jacobite attacks were designed to impugn the personal morality of a "usurping" princess on the assumption that a woman who lacks even a modicum of loyalty to her own parents would not hesitate to engage in promiscuous sexual conduct. In one Jacobite calumny, the queen, princess Anne, and king William all receive equally derisive treatment as sexual libertines:

> In a court full of vice may Shrewsbury lay Molly on
> Whilst Nanny enjoys her episcopal Stallion
> And Billy with Benting does play the Italian[5]

The numerous Jacobite epitaphs on the occasion of the queen's death in 1694 stress the disgrace of familial disloyalty:

> Here ends, notwithstanding, her specious pretenses,
> The undutiful child of the kindest of princes;
> Well, here let her lie, for by this time she knows,
> What it is such a father and king to depose;
> Between vice and virtue, she parted her life,
> She was too bad a daughter, and too good a wife.[6]

This criticism of the joint monarchs' ambitions was not of a temporary nature either. Even in the late eighteenth-century, such a well-known champion of democratic political revolution as Thomas Paine could write that "The characters of William and Mary have always appeared to me as detestable; the one seeking to destroy his uncle, and the other her father, to get possession of power themselves."[7] William, it must be said, provided the Jacobite opposition, not to mention Whig and Tory supporters of the Revolution, adequate cause for disillusionment with his rule. Cold, taciturn, uncomfortable with his English advisors, and an indifferent leader of the State Church, William's unpopularity with his English subjects made it all the more essential that the queen cultivate her image for propriety and devotion to the Church of England, images of most concern to her friendly contemporaries.[8]

The second important interpretive convention was employed by the queen's ardent supporters. They adopted a eulogistic narrative structure when discussing the daughter of James II and almost always avoided treatment of Mary's political and administrative abilities. One of the earliest evaluations of the queen's overall character—and perhaps one reason for the subsequent lopsided interest in Mary's comportment as a symbol of female virtue—comes from one of her closest advisors, Gilbert Burnet, Bishop of Salisbury after the Glorious Revolution and author of the enormously influential *History of My Own Time*. Burnet was a strong supporter of William's enterprise against James II and was elevated to the see of Salisbury soon after the Revolution. "She was the glory of her sex," wrote Burnet in a representative outpouring in 1695, "the darling of human nature and the wonder of all that knew her."[9] Like so many other backers of Mary and William, Burnet assuredly equated the "glory" of women with unrestricted support for their husband's wishes, a willingness to defer private advancement for the good of a male-dominated political agenda. And this outlook was not confined to representatives of Mary's own State Church. Even dissenters from the Church of England who had benefited from the Toleration Act were, not surprisingly, prepared to acknowledge the late queen's salutary impact on the moral life of an otherwise dissolute court.

Actually, both supporters and detractors of the new monarchy assumed, almost instinctively, that the proper sphere for a female ruler, even one who shared in an unprecedented joint monarchy, was to serve her husband's interests and to improve the moral tone of the court. While Burnet applauded Mary for being "so entirely resigned to the king's judgment, and so constantly determined by it," he simultaneously celebrated the fact that while "the female part of the court had been in former reigns subject to much censure," the present queen "used all possible methods for reforming whatever was amiss."[10] Nineteenth-century biographers would repeat these glib attributions. According to Agnes Strickland, the queen "had no feelings, but as they were reflected from the mind of her husband."[11] Interested solely in those aspects of the queen's life which supported the eulogistic convention, Burnet and other contemporaries felt no pressing need to address Mary's role in the formal government of the realm.[12]

Contemporary supporters of the queen like Burnet were not only obliged to defend the new monarchs from the aspersions cast by the Jacobites, for they also found themselves responding to a more principled opposition after 1689: the non-juring clergy. One of the more controversial aspects of the 1689 settlement involved the displacement of the nonjurors—those ordained members of the Church of England who refused to abjure their oath of obedience to James II even in light of his schemes to advance the interests of Roman Catholicism.[13] The majority of the Episcopal bench was deeply troubled by James's flight and many were uneasy about the new oaths required by William and Mary, but in the end the fear of James's catholicizing schemes reconciled the bulk of the clergy to the new regime.[14] The nonjurors, on the other hand, believed that consistency in the matter of oaths transcended the danger to the Church of England represented by James. Led by the Archbishop of Canterbury, William Sancroft, and six other bishops, including four who along with Sancroft had resisted James's call for a general indulgence for all dissenters, the nonjurors placed William and Mary in the awkward position of removing some two hundred popular clerics in 1691, thereby effectively creating a new schism in the Church soon after the bill for toleration of dissenters had been passed by Parliament. One illustration of the repeated attempts by nonjurors to claim the moral high ground involves an exchange between Thomas Ken, nonjuring Bishop of Bath and Wells, and Mary's chaplain during the early years of her marriage in Holland, and Thomas Tenison, Mary and William's second Archbishop of Canterbury. After the queen's death Ken reproached Tenison for his "failure" to demand that the dying queen seek repentance for her sins against her father, clearly implying that the whole Revolution had been tantamount to rebellion against God.[15]

Mary's undeserved reputation for familial insensitivity and political immaturity was established soon after the arrival of the new queen from Holland in February 1689. The diarist John Evelyn's sardonic description of the princess's jovial behavior at Whitehall so soon after the expulsion of her father has captured the imagination of almost all subsequent writers. Upon her arrival in the capital so recently vacated by her father, Evelyn observed, the Princess "came into W-hall as to a Wedding, raint & jolly, so as seeming to be quite Transported."[16] Even Burnet expressed dismay at the queen's actions in this instance.[17] The great nineteenth-century Whig historian Lord Macaulay, building upon Evelyn's description, magnified this deprecation of Mary's stature. His picture of her entry into Whitehall did nothing to allay the image of immaturity: "A young woman, placed by a destiny as mournful and awful as that which brooded over the fabled houses of Labdacus and Pelops, in such a situation that she could not, without violating her duty to her God, her husband, refuse to take her seat on the throne from which her father had just been hurled, should have been sad, or at least serious. Mary was not merely in high, but in extravagant spirits. She entered Whitehall, it was asserted, with a girlish delight at being mistress of so fine a house, ran about the rooms, peeped into the closets, and examined the quilt of the state bed, without seeming to remember by whom those magnificent apartments had last been occupied."[18]

In fairness to Macaulay it should be said that he went on to explain how this seeming frivolity, behavior which had cost the queen even the opinion of some whom she valued, was in fact a contrivance designed to dispel any hint that the queen was displeased with her husband for ousting her father. The entire episode, we learn, was just additional proof of Mary's unswerving loyalty to her husband, "of that perfect disinterestedness and self-devotion of which man seems to be incapable, but which is sometimes found in women."[19] Clearly Macaulay was imposing his own nineteenth-century gender attitudes regarding the proper sphere for women who exhibit the appropriate characteristics. But if we put aside Macaulay's tendentious assumptions, we are left with one of the central themes in studies of Mary: conjugal devotion and moral rectitude. The trivial Whitehall episode has been repeated, albeit with less color than the imaginative Macaulay, by a number of twentieth-century popular biographers whose focus remains on the examination of appropriate gender roles in late seventeenth-century England.[20] Hester Chapman, for example, thought that Mary's initial appearance at Whitehall was a disappointment to all since the princess was expected to introduce not only the "warmth and friendliness" missing in her husband's demeanor at Court, but more importantly "the feminine sensibility and the gentle self-abnegation" which was essential to a general public "looking forward to a display of beauty, pleasant manners and fine feeling."[21] This image of the queen has effectively reduced her stature in the eyes of most historians to one of court ornament, a woman without a mind of her own on the events of the day, events which directly affected her family—particularly her estranged father—and the nation as a whole.

Happily, this older view of the queen, informed as it was by the heated political debates of the day and by gender assumptions which we no longer share, is beginning to be replaced by a more balanced perspective, although the new scholarship is only recently underway. An article by W. A. Speck in one of the new books on the Glorious Revolution has begun the work of redefining Mary's contribution to those crucial years of political and religious change after 1688, and one certainly looks forward to more scholarship of this type.[22] Interestingly enough, Speck develops a number of suggestions made by Agnes Strickland in her mid-nineteenth century study *Lives of the Queens of England*.[23]

Speck firmly establishes the significance of Mary's actions during those many months when the king was engaged outside England. The Regency Bill, he argues, created two basic problems, one constitutional and the second political. The earlier Bill of Rights had established a joint monarchy, but lodged sole executive authority with the king. The Regency Bill was designed to make a special exception of this earlier arrangement. However, the Bill left undefined the constitutional powers to be exercised by the king while outside the country, especially in the event that Mary should disagree with him. Since the queen was eager to insure that her decisions echoed William's overall position, the constitutional ambiguity did not pose any immediate difficulties. But the political problem, which in brief centered around the fact that many politicians—Whig and Tory alike—did not trust Mary to administer the government, could only be resolved by the queen's assertion of her authority in council and by her attention to a host of broad social and religious issues.

Speck examines the performance of the queen during William's absences, and while agreeing that she often sought the advice of her husband on a variety of matters, when events demanded immediate action, as when the fleet was defeated by the French at Beachy Head in June 1690, the queen took the decision to imprison the Admiral responsible for the disaster, Arthur Herbert, earl of Torrington, pending a full judicial investigation of the affair. Mary's letters to William during this juncture are not, as the contributor to the *Dictionary of National Biography* would have us believe, the "pathetic" outpourings of a woman who was able to do her duty solely as a result of her "piety and affection for her husband."[74] Rather they indicate that the queen was critical of the council which had been established to assist her, and it is obvious from the correspondence that she was not about to let either Whig or Tory advisors dominate her administration. Cabinet minutes reveal that while routine matters were handled without the queen's assent, she was present at twenty-one of the thirty-four meetings in 1690 and fifty-five of fifty-nine meetings in 1691. By 1692, her position began to decline as more and more matters were referred to the king, but by this juncture her importance as an advocate of social and religious reform and personal integrity at Court contributed enormously to the continued support that the monarchy—and the revolution settlement—received from both Whigs and Tories.

Perhaps more importantly, Speck argues that had William been the sole ruler after the successful invasion, he would have quickly faced a situation in which one half of the English nation opposed him.

That the Jacobites were small in number and influence was due to the tireless work of the queen as the older daughter of James II who based her claim to the throne of the direct providence of God in rescuing the English nation from Catholic tyranny. In addition, Mary was able to reconcile many Tories to the new regime despite the disdain they felt for the king and his upstart foreign advisors. She effectively presented the humane and communicative side of the monarchy. Obviously, she was also English, and to a population which had not forgotten the fact that two wars had been fought against the Dutch since the 1650s, Mary's origins were no small matter of comfort to a political class distrustful of her soldier husband.

Speck, I believe, admirably puts aside preconceived notions about the appropriate role of women in seventeenth-century court culture and attempts to evaluate her contribution on the basis of her political activity. Clearly, we need additional work in other aspects of her administration in order to round out the picture. In one other central area, for example, I believe that Mary's role has been sadly underestimated. The vacancies created by the removal of the nonjurors, particularly at the Episcopal level, were filled by a number of divines who were called by their critics "latitudinarians." This rather clumsy term of derision was first used after the Restoration to describe churchmen at Cambridge who had, allegedly, found little spiritual difficulty in adjusting to the requirements of the Cromwellian regime.[25]

By the 1680s, the informal leader of the group was John Tillotson, Tuesday lecturer at St. Lawrence Jewry, Dean of Canterbury since 1672, and Dean of St. Paul's after the accession of the new monarchs. Mary and William had first met Tillotson in 1677 when the newly married couple were on their way to Holland. Tillotson was Dean of Canterbury at the time and had assisted the prince and princess out of some financial difficulties. The friendship continued over the years, and despite Bishop of London Henry Compton's ardent support for William in 1688, Tillotson was chosen to succeed Archbishop Sancroft at Canterbury while fellow latitudinarians Gilbert Burnet, Simon Patrick, Edward Stillingfleet, and Edward Fowler were elevated to Salisbury, Ely, Gloucester, and Worcester respectively. Compton had been the only bishop to sign the invitation asking William to invade in 1688, presided at Convocation in 1689, and had officiated at the coronation ceremony after Sancroft refused to participate. His disappointment at being passed over for Tillotson was obvious enough, but Mary and William both felt that the Dean of St. Paul's, whose consistent efforts to achieve a more comprehensive Church of England through his emphasis on the importance of behavior over belief in the life of the Church spoke to the deepest inclinations of the new monarchy.

Mary's role in these crucial Episcopal appointments has, in my view, been consistently underestimated.[26] The king had little interest in Church of England affairs, and beyond making appointments to sees vacated by the death of an incumbent, William left the sensitive issues of replacing many of the nonjurors in his wife's trust. Perhaps the king's mishandling of the proposed bills for comprehension and toleration during the Parliament of 1689 cooled his interest in the politics of Church of England affairs. Whatever the case may have been, the queen spent much of her time during William's absence in 1691 "filling the Bishoprics."[27] The deprivation of the nonjuring bishops, all of whom still resided at their sees although they had been denied actual power, was an issue bound to further undermine an already divided Church. The actual deprivations were carried out while the king was away in 1691, leaving Mary to wrestle with the inevitable fallout. Tillotson was appointed archbishop of Canterbury on 31 May 1691, and the queen was obliged to issue a mandate requiring the aged Sancroft to vacate Lambeth Palace within ten days. And while her friend Tillotson was archbishop for only three-and-a-half years before the burdens of office and a torrent of nonjuror abuse hastened his own death, this powerful preacher's overall impact on the eighteenth-century Church of England was enormous. As the late G. V. Bennett pointed out, Tillotson's rational and unenthusiastic approach to religion, his urbane and rational sermons before London congregations, and his sympathy for the plight of dissenters exemplified the best spirit of the Age of Reason.[28] His entire public life had been devoted to reconciling all shades of Protestant opinion to a broad-based communion where theological orthodoxy was combined with a call to works and personal reformation.[29] Mary's friendship with both Burnet and Tillotson, together with her deep concern for conduct over dogma as illustrated in her support for the Societies for the Reformation of Manners and Thomas Bray's Society for Promoting Christian Knowledge, suggests that her impress upon the shape of the late seventeenth-century Church—both in England and in the American colonies—was not insignificant. Her strong opposition to nonresidence and pluralities, although certainly of little immediate impact, nonetheless reflected the reformist tone of the latitudinarian movement. Unfortunately, it has been concern with the queen's personal piety in the context of court culture that has too often obscured her important influence on the character of the episcopate after the Glorious Revolution.

Although the sources have not expanded markedly over the last century, new work on the period of the Revolution and its aftermath will doubtless take greater account of the Mary's role in the unique joint monarchy. It is perhaps not insignificant that the unofficial *apologia* for the Revolution of 1688, John Locke's *Two Treatises of Government*, should begin with a sustained attack upon Robert Filmer's *Patriarcha*, a work which had attempted to draw an analogy between the power of the king with the authority of the father in the private family. As Lawrence Stone has argued, Locke's repudiation of Filmer essentially redefined both relationships, public and private, to the point where passive obedience was discredited as a viable model for personal and political interaction.[30] Marriage, like government, had now become a matter of contract, a contract which even extended to the power of the parents over their children. Locke's efforts to reshape ideas about state power ultimately, albeit very slowly, transformed power relations within the family, and in particular in relations between the adult partners. Domestic patriarchy had been called into question by the very theory which legitimized the accession of the joint monarchs, and patriarchal relations could not be maintained in their old form so long as the king was engaged outside of England. Locke's decision to return to England after six years of exile was made largely on the basis of his friendship with Mary and William, and it may have been more than coincidence which placed him on the same ship as Mary when he arrived at Greenwich in February 1689.

I think that it is fair to assume that neither Mary nor William were much interested in their friend Locke's surreptitious challenge to the centuries-old patriarchal model. And no one is calling for a revision of the fact that the queen did in fact disdain politics and the party struggle which made its way into the council while her husband was overseas. Nor is it any more acceptable to discount the strong role played by the queen in those areas of Court reform that appear so central in the estimation of earlier historians. But the very fact that the author of a popular text in British history could, as recently as 1992, repeat contemporary descriptions of the queen as "ignorant of history, politics, science, mathematics," and possessed of a mind "as sluggish as an island river" should tell us more than a little about the strength of older interpretations.[31] Surely we can no longer accept the value of works built upon biographical conventions common to the late seventeenth century, conventions that do little more than transform Mary into an intellectual cipher of her partner. To do so would be an unfortunate distortion of an especially rich and varied period in constitutional and religious history. It would be to resign ourselves to an exploration of revolution solely from the perspective of an elite who had scant interest in, or appreciation for, the contributions of those outside the traditional intellectual world of male dominated power politics.

Notes

1. Two of the better new offerings include Lois G. Schwoerer, ed., *The Revolution of 1688–1689: Changing Perspectives* (Cambridge: Cambridge University Press, 1992); and David Israel, ed., *From Persecution to Toleration* (Oxford: Clarendon Press, 1989). Current popular textbooks that do not cover Mary's contribution to the Revolution Settlement include Clayton Roberts and David Roberts, *A History of England* 2 vols. (Englewood Cliffs, N.J.: Prentice Hall, 1991); Lacey Baldwin Smith, *This Realm of England* (Lexington, MA: D.C. Heath and Co., 1992); and Barry Coward, *The Stuart Age* (New York: Longman, 1980).

2. R. Doebner, ed., *Memoirs of Mary Queen of England* (London: D. Nutt, 1886), p. 23.

3. Quoting Hester Chapman, *Mary II Queen of England* (1953. reprint. Westport, CT.: Greenwood Press, 1976), p. 168.

4. On the Jacobites, see Geoffrey Holmes, *Politics, Religion, and Society in England, 1679–1742* (London: Hambledon Press, 1986); and Gordon Rupp, *Religion in England, 1688–1791* (Oxford: Oxford University Press, 1986).

5. George deF. Lord, ed., *Poems on Affairs of State*, vol. 5 (London: Yale University Press, 1963–75), p. 221, as quoted in W. A. Speck, "William—and Mary?" in Schwoerer, ed., *The Revolution of 1688–1689*. As will become apparent, I am indebted to Professor Speck for the argument of much of this essay.

6. Anonymous Jacobite epitaph quoted in Agnes Strickland, *Lives of the Queens of England*, vol. 5 (1852. reprint. London: John W. Lovell, Co., n.d.), p. 341.

7. Thomas Paine, *The Rights of Man* in *The Life and Works of Thomas Paine* vol. 7 (New York: Thomas Paine National Historical Association, 1925), p. 43.

8. Lucile Pinkham, *William III and the Respectable Revolution* (n.p.: Archon Books, 1969), p. 219; and Maurice Asheley, *The Glorious Revolution of 1688* (New York: Charles Scribner's Sons, 1966), pp. 187–188.

9. Burnet, *Essay on the Memory of the late Queen* (London, 1695), p. 96.

10. Gilbert Burnet, *History of His Own Time* vol. 4 (Oxford: Oxford University Press, 1833), pp. 239–240.

11. Strickland, *Lives of the Queens of England*, vol. 5, p. 167; Leopold von Ranke, *A History of England Principally in the Seventeenth Century*, vol. 5 (1875. reprint. New York: AMS Press, 1955), p. 86.

12. Funeral sermons published on the occasion of the Queen's death also stressed the same deferential themes. See, for example, Andrew Barnett, *A Just Lamentation* (London: Thomas Parkhurst, 1695); and White Kennett, *The Righteous Taken Away from the Evil to Come* (Oxford: Leonard Litchfield, 1695).

13. On the nonjurors see L. M. Hawkins, *Allegiance in Church and State: The Problem of the Nonjurors* (London: Routledge and Sons, 1928); and G. V. Bennett, *The Tory Crisis in Church and State* (Oxford: Clarendon Press, 1975).

14. Gerald Straka, *Anglican Reaction to the Revolution of 1688* (Madison, WI: State Historical Society, 1962), offers the best coverage.

15. Strickland, *Lives of the Queens*, vol. 5, p. 342.

16. John Evelyn, *The Diary of John Evelyn*, E. S. De Beer, ed., vol. 4 (Oxford: Oxford University Press, 1955), p. 624.

17. Burnet, *History*, vol. 3, p. 406.

18. Macaulay, *History of England from the Accession of James II*, (London: Longmans, 1873), I, p. 650.

19. Macauley, *History*, I, p. 651.

20. Elizabeth Hamilton, *William's Mary* (New York: Taplinger Publishing Company, 1972), p. 208; Henri and Barbara Van Der Zee, *William and Mary* (New York: Alfred A. Knopf, 1973), p. 275; Hester W. Chapman, *Mary II, Queen of England* (London: Jonathan Cape, 1953), pp. 164–166.

21. Chapman, *Mary II, Queen of England*, pp. 163–164.

22. W. A. Speck, "William—and Mary?" in Schwoerer, ed., *The Revolution of 1688–89*, pp. 131–146.

23. Strickland, *Lives of the Queens*, vol. 5, p. 243.

24. *Dictionary of National Biography*, 12:1246 (article by Adolphus Wood).

25. On the Latitudinarians see W. M. Spellman, *The Latitudinarians and the Church of England, 1660–1700* (Athens: University of Georgia Press, 1993).

26. The one important exception to this misreading of the latitudinarians is G. V. Bennett, "William III and the Episcopate," in G. V. Bennett and J. D. Walsh, eds., *Essays in Modern English Church History* (New York: Oxford University Press, 1966), pp. 104–131.

27. Doebner, ed., *Memoirs*, p. 37.

28. G. V. Bennett, *To the Church of England* (Worthing: Churchman Publishing, 1988), p. 75.

29. An excellent new treatment of Tillotson's theology is G. R. Reedy, "Interpreting Tillotson" forthcoming in *Harvard Theological Review*. See also Spellman, "Archbishop John Tillotson and the Meaning of Moralism" *Anglican and Episcopal History* 56 (1987): 404–422.

30. Lawrence Stone, *The Family, Sex and Marriage in England, 1500–1800* (New York: Harper Torchbooks, 1979), p. 164.

31. Lacey Baldwin Smith, *This Realm of England*, p. 314.

"Typus Gramatio" [Lady Grammar] from Gregor Reisch, *Margarita Philosophica* (Frieburg, 1503), reproduced from the Collections of the Library of Congress.

The Politics of Renaissance Rhetorical Theory by Women

Jane Donawerth

Women who published rhetorical theory in seventeenth century France and England were appropriating the Renaissance for their own use.[1] In particular, they used the myth of a renaissance as a discursive strategy to disguise, through nostalgia for the past, the radical goals of their proposals: women's right to education and women's right to speak. In the process, they also revised classical rhetorical theory to include the politics of gender, creating a tradition of women's rhetoric. In this essay I shall be offering analysis of this new rhetorical theory in seventeenth-century works by Madeleine de Scudéry, Margaret Cavendish Duchess of Newcastle, Margaret Fell, Bathsua Makin, and Mary Astell, discussing these theorists' manipulations of the cultural myth of a renaissance, a rebirth of learning, to support women's right to speak.[2]

Examining the deterioration of women's property rights and opportunities for power in fifteenth-century Italy and France, Joan Kelly simply denies that women had a Renaissance. But if the Renaissance is defined as a rebirth of classical rhetorical education, as many historians define it, then these seventeenth-century women theorists who argued for rhetorical education of women are appropriating the Renaissance, although two centuries later than the period Kelly examines.[3]

These women appropriate the Renaissance in another way, as well: they see that the Renaissance is a myth, a discursive strategy that had enabled middle class and newly aristocratic men to consolidate or even achieve rise in their social status, a discursive strategy that could be used for women's own ends. Thus, these women argue for women's rights to education and speech as if these rights formerly existed, with only a Renaissance needed for women to reclaim them.

The aristocrat Madeleine de Scudéry, in works spanning 1642 to 1684, formulated a new rhetoric for women in French salon society. Carolyn Lougee has argued, in *Le Paradis des Femmes*, that the salon of seventeenth-century France centered on women and provided a means of social mobility: the salon assimilated the new nobility and some bourgeois members into aristocratic French society by facilitating marriage across class lines and by redefining nobility as behavior not bloodlines. Addressed to women as an audience, and published in 1642 under her brother's name, Madeleine de Scudéry's *Les Femmes Illustres or the Heroick Harangues of Illustrious Women*, promotes women's education rather than beauty and marriage as a means of social mobility. Thus, it justifies for French women their participation in literary culture, especially as writers.[4]

De Scudéry's *Les Femmes Illustres* disguises the radical nature of its proposal by appropriating the central tenet of the Renaissance: a return to classical literature. In "Sapho to Erinna," the final speech in *Les Femmes Illustres*, the older poet Sapho acts as mentor to the younger aspirant Erinna, urging her to acquire an education and to write: "They who say that beauty is the portion of women; And that fine arts, good learning, and all the . . . eminent sciences, are of the domination of men, without our having power to pretend to any part of them; Are equalie differing from justice and vertue" (sig. V6^v); for "our Sex is capable of every thing that it would undertake" (sig. X2^v). De Scudéry identifies herself with this radical proposal for women's education and right to a voice, since she was called "Sapho" in *précieuse* salon circles where participants chose classical names for themselves. She sees women's roles as socially constructed; women must resist not only men's expectations, but also their own interiorization of those roles: "*Erinna*, I must this day overcome in your mynd that distrust of your self, and that falie shame, that hinders you from employing your mind with things which it is capable of" (sig. V6^r).[5] The larger text, however, disguises the radical nature of this proposal by presenting itself as a traditionally Renaissance text: a recovery of antiquity for contemporary Europe. The volume presents twenty fictional speeches by women of classical antiquity, including Cleopatra, Mariamne, and Volumnia, as well as Sappho. By 1642, since men's philosophy is being shaped by Cartesian rationalism and empiricism, this recovery of the classics for women appears safely nostalgic to the public, representing a past that men have moved beyond.

But de Scudéry's goal is not conservative: through the return to classical principles, she aims to appropriate rhetoric for women as a means of political power—the right to speak and, thus, to influence others. In the preface to *Les Femmes Illustres*, generally attributed to her brother Georges but expressing the attitudes of Madeleine, the de Scudérys argue that eloquence is natural to women: "Certainlie . . . the Ancients . . . always said that you [women] possesse Eloquence, without art, without Labour, and without Pains, and that nature gives liberallie to you, that which studie sells to us [men] at a dear rate: . . . facilitie of speaking well is naturall to you, in place of being acquired by us" (sig. A2ʳ). Reworking the stereotype that women talk too much, the de Scudérys argue that women have always been naturally good at speaking, and that the ancients recognized and promoted this quality as a virtue in women. It is in this sense that their use of the Renaissance is mythic, since ancient Greece and Rome were notably misogynistic and did not freely offer rhetorical educations to women.

In *Conversations*, a collection of dialogues, Madeleine de Scudéry continues her appropriation of the myth of the Renaissance as a means of promoting education and a voice for women. Her dialogue form imitates classical rhetorical theory (as in Plato's *Phaedrus* or Cicero's *De Oratore*), although instead of settling a debate through the male authority of a Socrates or Crassus, her dialogues generally reach a consensus through a female speaker, a Valeria or Euridamia. The dialogues cover "Conversation," "The Art of Speaking," "Raillery," "Invention," and "The Manner of Writing Letters." Her content also appropriates classical rhetorical theory, adapting ideas from Cicero, Quintilian, and Aristotle on the five divisions of oratory, diction, wit, debates on imitations *vs.* practice and art *vs.* nature, and the division of sophistries into those based on words and those based on matter—all to conversation.[6] The mimicry of the classical past in de Scudéry's form includes Greek and Roman names for the speakers, and Roman place names for settings. Such details, although not developed in a novelistic fashion, indicate her political strategy: a nostalgic creation of an idealized past where women were educated and had the right to speak, even to pronounce the rules for speech. If the Renaissance creates the values of its present by giving rebirth to its past, then de Scudéry will create a history justifying the ideal of one who "speaks as becomes a rational Woman to speak" (*Conversations* sig. F7ᵛ).

Margaret Cavendish's appropriation of the men's Renaissance is more hesitant than de Scudéry's confident takeover. An English royalist in exile on the continent, Cavendish is one of the most prolific English women writers of the seventeenth century. In *The Worlds Olio*, published during the Interregnum, Cavendish claims the encyclopedia as an enterprise for women, that eclectic form dear to the hearts of second generation male humanists a century before Cavendish, who wanted to bring all of classical knowledge into the vernacular. "All of classical knowledge" centered on rhetoric, since the Roman tradition that influenced the Renaissance made rhetoric the architectonic art organizing other arts (see n3). So also with Cavendish's encyclopedia, *The Worlds Olio*: rhetoric is an informing principle, beginning the work, and recurring throughout, as demonstrated in entry titles like "Of Eloquence, art and speculation," "What discourses are enemies to Society," and "Of speaking much or little." Rhetoric is interwoven with other subjects as disparate as "desire," "tyrannical government," and "to cry on one's wedding day": this is an eccentric encyclopedia. Cavendish scatters her rhetorical theory throughout the encyclopedia, but nevertheless covers invention, levels of style, nature *vs.* art in eloquence, discourse as promoting society, and the dangers of words over things. Influenced by Bacon and other seventeenth-century theorists who turn rhetoric into a science, Cavendish outlines a physiology of speech in several passages (fols. D1^v, D2, D4^v -E1^r), introduces the empiricists' concepts of the mind as a *tabula rasa* or blank slate on which experience makes impressions (fol. E4^r), and presents words as marks of things rather than thoughts (fol. D4^r). She combines this contemporary empiricism with the sophistic conceptions of *kairos* or timeliness of speech (fol. D2^r) and of language as the bond of human society (fols. C4^r, D2^r, and D4^r).[7]

Unlike de Scudéry, who is putting one over on her audience by borrowing the myth of the Renaissance to promote women's rights, Cavendish seems to be putting one over on herself, on the surface accepting the misogyny of the classical rhetorical tradition and writing to a male audience, but in asides defending herself and other women against such charges. In one entry in *The Worlds Olio*, Cavendish suggests that "All Women are a kind of Mountebanks; for they would make the World believe they are better than they are. . . . For a Womans onely delight is to be flatter'd of Men" (fol. M1^r). Cavendish thus dissembles her takeover of rhetoric. Cavendish's is a "double-voiced discourse," as Sue Lanser and Evi Beck define that concept for feminist theory, and she even gives names to the voice of the tradition *vs.* the voice of the text: her husband the Duke and herself.[8]

In a long passage in the epistle to Book II of *Worlds of Olio*, Cavendish sorts out the relative strengths and weaknesses of speaking much and speaking little—a tongue less apt to falter, *vs.* time to gather one's wit and invent something worth listening to. But having spoken with authority, Cavendish then questions her own authority to write: "but it is very probable, my readers will at this discourse condemn me, saying I take upon me to instruct, as if I thought my self a master, when I am but a novice, and fitter to learn" (fol. E3ᵛ). Cavendish answers the objection to women's speech by dividing herself into two voices: her husband, the master, who has taught her what she knows but thinks women inferior to men, and her self, the novice, who admires her husband and men's learning, but who speaks "though I do not speak so well as I wish I could, yet it is civility to speak" (fol. E4ʳ). While Cavendish's answer does bring about the radical instability of woman as subject that Catherine Belsey has identified as characteristic of seventeenth-century discourses,[9] Cavendish has also managed to put her husband in the position of the facile speaker whose tongue is less apt to falter, and herself in the position of the contemplative speaker who has time to invent something worth listening to. Double-voiced, Cavendish both succumbs to the patriarch's power in her obeisance to her husband's learning, and resists that power with her argument of civil responsibility supporting women's right to speak.

Unlike de Scudéry and Cavendish, who appropriate the secular myth of the Renaissance, Margaret Fell takes over the religious myth of the Renaissance, the Reformation—religion reborn out of the ancient church as learning was reborn out of the ancient world. An early Quaker convert and influential "preacher," Margaret Fell wrote *Women's Speaking Justified* while she was in prison in 1667.[10] Offering an argument in favor of women's preaching and prophesying, Fell is appropriating for women the tradition of sermon rhetorics. Rather than organizing her pamphlet as a classic rhetorical defense, she adopts the ecstatic voice of a sectarian preacher, interweaving biblical quotations and imitating the Bible in her style: "And such hath the Lord chosen, even *the weak things of the world to confound the things which are mighty* . . . I. Cor. i. And God hath put no such difference between the Male and Female as men would make" (3). Her form, then, makes a claim to inspired text that renders Fell's female gender no longer a mark of inferiority.

Fell's argument that women's preaching is a recovery of early church tradition (thus a seventeenth-century Renaissance of earlier godly custom, or a reformation) begins with her title page: "Womens Speaking Justified, Proved and Allowed of by the Scriptures. . . . And how WOMEN were the first that preached the Tidings of the

Resurrection of Jesus, and were sent by CHRISTS Own Command." The body of her text is a series of reflections on those passages in the Bible—the Reformation "fountain of authority"—where women preach or prophesy. She thus recuperates the Bible as an ally rather than an obstruction in the cause of women's preaching, citing as examples Mary Magdalene, Mary the mother of James (7), Aquila and Priscilla (8), Hannah (13), Queen Esther (15–16), Deborah (18), and others. She constructs a tradition of women preaching based on scriptural authority, a tradition that she may refer to in order to reform her contemporary English church.

Many misognynist pamphlets in the Renaissance had invoked St. Paul in favor of women's silence in church.[11] An important section of Fell's pamphlet refutes these Pauline injunctions against women's speaking in church (in 1 Cor. 14, and 1 Tim. 2), arguing that the apostle means not *all* women, but only women under the old law, who were not yet moved by their Inner Light (8–12). To do so, she must establish as a hermeneutic principle that scriptures must be interpreted according to the intent and context of the speaker (5). Fell carefully distinguishes between women who were not yet educated in the use of their Inner Light, and who should not speak, from those who were full participants and might preach.[12] In re-visioning the Bible as an ancient source documenting women's right to preach, Fell also feminizes the church as the True Wife of Christ, a "free woman," a feminine place where "Daughters Prophesie" (17).

In a postscript, she points out that the very Anglican priests who deny women the right to speak get some of their best sermon material from women: from Elizabeth, Ruth, Esther, and Judith in the Bible. These "blind priests" "make a Trade of Womens words to get money by . . . and still cry out, Women must not speak, Women must be silent" (16). Fell asserts that the custom of women's silence in church originates not in the Bible, but in the darkness of the years in apostacy under the Roman Catholic Church (10, 13–19).[13] This argument, like Fell's overall strategy, links her pamphlet to the Reformation: contemporary Christians need to return to the early church and the fountains of the scriptures because Catholic oral tradition has corrupted Christianity in intervening centuries. It is not contemporary Quaker men who wish to prohibit women from their rightful voice in the church; it is the "hungry Priests that denyes Women's Speaking [but] makes a trade of her words for a livelyhood" (18). Conflating the practices of Catholic and Anglican priests, Fell tries to win the English lay audience she addresses away from the religious authorities who stand most adamantly against women's preaching and the Quaker religion in general. Rather than rejecting women's words as outside the category of preaching, Fell appropriates the Reformation as a strategy for redefining the category of preaching to include women.

Bathsua Reginald Makin, by 1640 known as the most learned woman in England, published *An Essay to Revive the Antient Education of Gentlewomen* in 1673, as an advertisement for her school. Whereas de Scudéry's and Fell's arguments for women's rights are direct, Makin's is subversive. Makin's middle-class standing (in comparison to de Scudéry's and Fell's aristocratic status) possibly motivated her to take a more conciliatory rhetorical strategy. In her introduction to Makin's essay, Paula Barbour describes it as a "plea that England revive the sixteenth-century experiment in the rigorous education of women." But in doing so, Barbour is taken in by Makin's subversive strategy.[14] Most women in sixteenth-century England were not rigorously educated, certainly not women of Makin's class. Thus, Makin appropriates the myth of a Renaissance to argue for the creation of what had never been: women's right to education.

Makin early states her case: "Women were formerly Educated in the knowledge of Arts and Tongues. . . . Were Women thus Educated now, . . . Women would have Honour and Pleasure, . . . and the whole Nation Advantage" (3–4). Like Fell, Makin begins with biblical women (8), calling on the resonance of the return *ad fontes*, especially when arguing that because apostate Christians keep women ignorant, Anglicans must take it as "a piece of the Reformation to correct it" (23). Unlike Fell, however, Makin extends the myth to include a secular return to the classics, offering a history of classical and Tudor women with rhetorical educations, including Sappho, Aspasia, Cornelia, Lady Jane Grey, and Queen Elizabeth (9–14). In recalling earlier women's education, in invoking the myth of a Renaissance, her main aim is to shift her argument from a refutation of women's innate vices—her nature—to an examination of socially constructed education for women—custom: "Custom . . . hath a mighty influence: The Barbarous custom to breed Women low . . . hath prevailed so far, that it is . . . believed . . . that Women are not endued with such Reason, as Men" (3).

But Makin's *Essay* is also a defense of women's right to speak; it may be read as a rhetoric of the politics of gender in speaking. Makin begins her subversion by cross-dressing as a male narrator, posing as one reasonable man willing to give up the privilege of rhetorical education as restricted to men. Her defense of speech for women centers on their political position: with almost no financial or political power, women need the resources of persuasion—"The Tongue is the only Weapon Women have to defend themselves with, and they had need to use it dextrously" (11). Listing classical and Renaissance women who have excelled in each art and science, Makin ties each discipline to her defense of women speaking. Female orators demonstrate that "Women have not been meer Talkers: but . . . have known how to use Languages, when they have had them" (12). Female logicians show that women are not simply "naturally disposed to be talkative," but also share "solid Jugment or depth of Reason" (13). This defense of women's speech, then, becomes also the main supporting argument for moving the entire grounds of discussion from women's innate weakness (her nature) to women's faulty education (social custom). Makin's defense thus counters the misogynistic derogation of women's speech that occurred during the Renaissance and that Jardine, Belsey, and Ferguson have examined. Clearly Makin sees herself within a tradition of classical female teachers of rhetoric like Aspasia and Arete.[15] Makin's strategy shows clearly her awareness that the Renaissance is re-iterable, a strategy that may be repeated for the benfit of women: women of antiquity once had rights to education and speech, but lost them; Renaissance women regained them; women of Makin's time may foment their own Renaissance for women again.

Mary Astell, from the lower gentry, published in 1694 *A Serious Proposal to the Ladies* arguing that women like men should receive a humanist education, and *Part II* in 1697, detailing a curriculum, including an art of rhetoric.[16] Like Margaret Fell, Astell proposes a "Reformation" that will restore to women their spiritual potential (5, 37). Drawing on nostalgia for past times, the myth of a Renaissance for women, Mary Astell calls her plan for a women's college a "Monastery" or a "Religious Retirement" for women (14, 30). She argues that women are inferior mentally to men neither through God nor through nature, but only through "the mistakes of our Education" (6). As a corrective she offers a retreat from the world that would also prepare women to serve in the world (14). More cautious (and more Anglican) than Fell, Astell reassures her audience that she does not intend that women should teach in church (20); yet she follows her denial of women's right to preach with the biblical example of Priscilla who "catechized" Apollos—an example cited by both Fell and Makin. Like Makin, Astell draws upon the secular Renaissance, citing Tudor England, when women knew Greek and Latin and read Plato and Aristotle.

But beyond these versions of mythic Renaissances, Astell evokes a utopian nostalgia for women's religious communities when she names her design a "Monastery" (14). In this utopian world, women will reproduce themselves intellectually and spiritually, if not physically, without the help of men, thus serving as a "Seminary to stock the Kingdom with pious and prudent Ladies, whose good example will so influence the rest of their Sex, that Women may no longer pass for those little useless and impertinent Animals, which the ill conduct of too many has caus'd 'em to be mistaken for" (17). She quite consciously manipulates this nostalgia: "You are therefore Ladies, invited into a place, where you shall suffer no other confinement, but to be kept out of the road of sin" (15). Astell, then, draws on the myth of a Renaissance in the specific form of the Catholic Counter-Reformation, with its reliance on the reform of monastic institutions, hoping to accomplish through the English Anglican church a growth of female education similar to that in progress in seventeenth-century France. In *Part II*, we see that Astell incorporates as a central subject the art of rhetoric into the curriculum of her college. Influenced by the Port-Royal rhetoric, and Augustine, she treats method, arrangement, imitation, style, self-criticism, ornament, and sophistry, creating an entire rhetorical curriculum for women.[17]

Astell imagines a utopian place that will be "such a *Paradise* as your Mother *Eve* forfeited" (15), "delicious Gardens" (16) offering the "fruits of Paradise" (34), with "no Serpents to deceive you" (16). (We later learn that deceivers are male.) Rather than the "True Wife" that Fell imagines the church to be, Astell imagines her a "Holy Mother" (21) nurturing an "Amicable Society" (16). Astell slyly introduces women's education not as the main point of her college but, instead, as a necessary foundation for a house of religious retirement (17). Because she underestimated anti-Catholic sentiment in England, Astell's strategy was not immediately successful. It was rumored, in fact, that a lady, about to donate the funds to establish Astell's college, was dissuaded by an Anglican bishop. But Astell's strategy did work eventually, for her ideas were strongly influential on the pamphlet and fiction writing that argued throughout the eighteenth century in favor of women's education (by writers like Judith Drake, Mary Lee Lady Chudleigh, and Sarah Scott).[18]

My conclusion, then, is that women appropriated rhetorical theory and so the Renaissance in the seventeenth century when the men were pretty much through with it. Because of the gender role assigned to women in Renaissance Europe, though, appropriating rhetoric was a particularly radical thing to do. The ideal woman was "chaste, silent, and obedient," to the point that she did not study the art of rhetoric. According to Joan Gibson's analysis of Renaissance educational treatises, she was instead limited to grammar. If we look at the early Renaissance illustrations of Gregor Reisch's encyclopedia, *Margarita Philosophica*, we can see depicted this cultural restriction: Lady Grammar, in the first illustration (Figure 1), is a modest womanly figure, with her hair done up under a cap, and a sober gown up to her neck; she holds the key to the house of grammar, wherein the famous scholars of grammar—Donatus, Priscian, and others—are studying; she is the sort of woman humanists would like their daughters to grow up to be. Logic, in the second illustration in *Margarita Philosophica* (not shown here), is so inappropriate to women that it is represented by a man, a hunter with his hounds. Lady Rhetoric, in the third illustration (Figure 2), is not an appropriate model for daughters: her hair is waved and flowing loose over her shoulders, her low-necked gown is made of extravagant patterned brocade, and the circle of famous rhetors surrounding her openly admire her theatricality; she is anything but modest. As Lisa Jardine, Peter Stallybrass, and Margaret Ferguson have explored, conservatives feared education for women, because, they thought, if a woman opened her mind and opened her mouth, she might very well choose to open herself in other ways.[19] The Rhetorica of the illustrations in Reisch's *Margarita Philosophica* looks like medieval depictions of Fortuna, a loose woman ready to give her favors to whatever man is handy.

All of the seventeenth-century theorists needed to negotiate these cultural anxieties about rhetoric. Yet we may still call them feminists, as Hilda Smith does, not in any modern sense of the term, but because of their advocacy of women's rights to education and to speech.[20] Their strategy of appropriation worked, sometimes in little, sometimes on a grand scale. De Scudéry and Astell supported themselves through their writing. Women developed schools for women: Makin ran one, Astell ran one, Astell's friend Lady Elizabeth Hastings ran one. There is a great deal of power to be gained by one who "speaks as becomes a rational Woman to speak."

Notes

1. As Susan Sniader Lanser and Evelyn Torton Beck point out in "[Why] Are There No Great Women Critics?" "patriarchal culture . . . continues to resist, denigrate, and mistrust woman as critic, theory-builder, or judge"; see *The*

Prism of Sex: Essays in the Sociology of Knowledge, ed. Julie A. Sherman and Evelyn Torton Beck (Madison: University of Wisconsin Press, 1979), p. 79. The standard histories of rhetorical theory include almost no women. Standard histories that do not mention female teachers of rhetoric or women rhetorical theorists include Warren Guthrie, "The Development of Rhetorical Theory in America, 1635–1850," *Speech Monographs* 15 (1948): 61–71; Wilbur Samuel Howell, *Eighteenth-Century British Logic and Rhetoric* (Princeton: Princeton University Press, 1971); Nan Johnson, *Nineteenth-Century Rhetoric in America* (Carbondale: Southern Illinois University Press, 1991); George Kennedy, *The Art of Rhetoric in the Roman World 300 B.C.–300 A.D.* (Princeton: Princeton University Press, 1972), and *Classical Rhetoric and Its Christian and Secular Tradition from Ancient to Modern Times* (Chapel Hill, NC: University of North Carolina Press, 1980); James J. Murphy, ed., *A Synoptic History of Classical Rhetoric* (New York: Random House, 1972), *Rhetoric in the Middle Ages* (Berkley: University of California Press, 1974), and *Medieval Rhetoric: A Select Bibliography,* 2nd ed. (Toronto: University of Toronto Press, 1989). Standard histories that mention only one woman theorist include James Berlin, *Writing Instruction in Nineteenth-century American Colleges* (Carbondale: Southern Illinois University Press, 1984), p. 80 on Gertrude Buck; Wilbur Samuel Howell, *Logic and Rhetoric in England 1500–1700* (1956; New York: Russell & Russell, 1961), pp. 166–67 on Mary Queen of Scots; George Kennedy, *The Art of Persuasion in Greece* (Princeton: Princeton University Press, 1963), pp. 158–64 on Aspasia, and *Greek Rhetoric Under Christian Emperors* (Princeton: Princeton University Press, 1983), pp. 301–302 on Anna Comnena. A recent anthology, *The Rhetorical Tradition: Readings from Classical Times to Present,* ed. Patricia Bizzell and Bruce Herzberg (Boston: Bedford, 1990), finally includes a few women before 1900: Christine de Pisan, Laura Cereta, Margaret Fell, and Sarah Grimke. In order to include women, we must redefine rhetorical theory to cover areas other than the kinds of speech that men historically made to each other in the public business of law, government, and preaching, where women were excluded; recent calls for a revision of the history of rhetorical theory include John Schilb, "The History of Rhetoric and the Rhetoric of History," *PrefText* 7 (1986): 11–34; Jane Donawerth, "Transforming the History of Rhetorical Theory," *Feminist Teacher* 7 (1992): 35–39; and Carole Blair, "Contested Histories of Rhetoric: The Politics of Preservation, Progress, and Chance," *Quarterly Journal of Speech* 78 (1992): 403–428.

2. These seventeenth-century women were not the first women rhetorical theorists: Aspasia is recorded by Plato, Cicero, and Quintilian as having taught rhetoric in fifth-century B.C. Athens; Arete, who lived about the time of Plato, and whose father and son were famous philosophers and teachers of rhetoric (both named Aristippus), probably ran her own school or salon of sophistic rhetoric; Ban Zhao (or Pan Chao) taught eloquence at the first-century Chinese court and wrote *Lessons for Women,* a book that includes advice on "women's words"; Sosipatra taught sophistic rhetoric and philosophy during the fourth century A.D. near Ephesus; Christine de Pizan, who

earned her living through writing in fourteenth-century France, is included as
a rhetorical theorist in Bizzell and Herzog; in the thirteenth century, Bettisia
Bezzidini was an Italian professor of rhetoric; and Beatrix Galindo, who taught
Catharine of Aragon, was a professor of rhetoric at the University of Salamanca.
On Aspasia, see Plato, *Menexenus*, trans. R. G. Bury (1929; Cambridge, MA:
Harvard University Press, 1961), pp. 329–381; Cicero, *De Inventione*, trans. H.
M. Hubbell (1949; Cambridge, MA: Harvard University Press, 1968), pp. 92–
95 (I.xxxi.51–53); and Quintilian, *Institutio Oratoria*, trans. H. E. Butler, (1921;
Cambridge, MA: Harvard University Press, 1966), vol. 2, pp. 286–289 (V.xi.27–
29). On Arete, see Guy Cromwell Field, "Aristippus," *The Oxford Classical
Dictionary*, 2nd ed., ed. N. G. L. Hammond and H. H. Scullard (1970; Oxford:
Clarendon Press, 1976), p. 111; and Bathsua Makin, *An Essay to Revive the
Antient Education of Gentlewomen* (1673; rpt. Los Angeles: William Andrews
Clark Memorial Library, 1980), p. 14. On Ban Zhao, see Nancy Lee Swann, *Pan
Chao: Foremost Woman Scholar of China, First Century* A.D. (1932; New York:
Russell & Russell, 1968), esp. pp. 82–99. On Sosipatra, see Eunapius, *Lives of
the Philosophers and Sophists*, trans. Wilmer Cave Wright (1921; Cambridge,
MA: Harvard University Press, 1961), pp. 399–419. On Christine de Pizan, see
Bizzell and Herzberg. On Beatrix Galindo, see Susan Bassnett, *Elizabeth I: A
Feminist Perspective* (1988; Oxford: Berg, 1989), p. 21. For help in finding these
theorists, I wish to thank Richard Fravel, Ana Kothe, Shirley Logan, Marc
Mirrell, and many graduate students in my courses on the history of rhetorical
theory at the University of Maryland at College Park.

3. See Joan Kelly, "Did Women Have a Renaissance?" in *Women, History & Theory: The Essays of Joan Kelly* (Chicago: University of Chicago Press,
1984); for a good summary of arguments since Kelly that women did not
participate in the Renaissance, see Joan Gibson, "Educating for Silence,"
Hypatia 4 (Spring 1989): 9. On defining the Renaissance as a rebirth of classical rhetorical education, see especially Paul Oscar Kirsteller, *Renaissance
Thought: The Classic, Scholastic, and Humanist Strains* (1955; New York: Harper
& Row, 1961); see also Madeleine Doran, *Endeavors of Art: A Study of Form
in Elizabethan Drama* (Madison: University of Wisconsin Press, 1954), esp.
p. 26: "To the Renaissance, rhetoric . . . formed the central core of humanistic
education"; W. S. Howell, *Logic and Rhetoric in England*; Nancy S. Struever,
*The Language of History in the Renaissance; Rhetoric and Historical Consciousness
in Florentine Humanism* (Princeton: Princeton University Press, 1970); Richard Lanham, *The Motives of Eloquence: Literary Rhetoric in the Renaissance* (New
Haven: Yale University Press, 1976); Stephen Greenblatt, *Renaissance Self-
Fashioning From More to Shakespeare* (Chicago: University of Chicago Press,
1980), esp. p. 162: "The chief intellectual and linguistic tool in this creation
[of the self and the state as works of art in the Renaissance] was rhetoric";
and Gary Waller, *English Poetry of the Sixteenth Century* (New York: Longman,
1986), pp. 48–59. For further information on ideas about language and communication in this age in which education is centered on rhetoric, see my

Shakespeare and the Sixteenth-Century Study of Language (Urbana: University of Illinois Press, 1984).

4. See Carolyn Lougee, *Le Paradis des Femmes: Women, Salons, and Social Stratification in Seventeenth-Century France* (Princeton: Princeton University Press, 1976); see also Domna C. Stanton, *The Aristocrat as Art: A Study of the Honnête Homme and the Dandy in Seventeenth-Century French Literature* (New York: Columbia University Press, 1980). I quote Madeleine de Scudéry's 1650 *Les Femmes Illustres* in its seventeenth-century English translation, *Les Femmes Illustres or the Heroick Harangues of the Illustrious Women*, trans. James Innes (London, 1681). For further information on de Scudéry's life, see Nicole Aronson, *Mademoiselle de Scudéry*, trans. Stuart R. Aronson (Boston: G. K. Hall & Co., 1978), p. 13. For a reading that places de Scudéry's *Conversations* in a seventeenth-century context, see Elizabeth Goldsmith, *"Exclusive Conversations": The Art of Interaction in Seventeenth-Century France* (Philadelphia: University of Pennsylvania Press, 1988).

5. Is "falie" a misprint for "false" or a Scottish spelling of foolish? From other constructions in the translation, I would guess the translator to be Scots.

6. For all the dialogues except "The Manner of Writing Letters," I quote from the seventeenth-century English translation of de Scudéry's 1680 *Conversations Sur Divers Sujets, Conversations Upon Several Subjects*, trans. Ferrand Spence (London, 1683). For *"Conversation de la manière d'écrire des lettres,"* I have worked out my own translation from *Conversations Nouvelles sur Divers Sujets, Dedié'es Au Roy* (La Haye, 1685). For contemporary feminist rejection of argument and debate in favor of community and consensus as goals of writing, see Sally Miller Gearhart, "The Womanization of Rhetoric," *Women's Studies International Quarterly* 2 (1979): 195–201. De Scudéry adapts the influential Roman five divisions of oratory, probably from Cicero, to conversation (*Conversations upon Diverse Subjects* I: sig. F7^v); Quintilian's advice on diction (I: sig. F3^v); Cicero's dicta on wit (II: sigs. D5^v and D9^v); Cicero's and Quintilian's summaries of the debates on imitation *vs.* practice and art *vs.* nature in the ideal speaker (I: sig. F9^r and II: sig. D9^v); and Aristotle's division of sophistries into those based on words and those based on matter (sig. F?)

7. Margaret Cavendish, Duchess of Newcastle, *The Worlds Olio* (London, 1655). Although Cavendish echoes Montaigne's encyclopedic form and the title of Montaigne's essay, "Of Ready or Slow Speech," she does not seem influenced by his ideas on speech; see Michel de Montaigne, *Essays*, trans. John Florio (London: Nonesuch Press, 1931): Vol. I, pp. 37–39. Compare Cavendish's use of sophistic rhetorical theory to Susan Jarratt's present-day adaptation of sophistry to feminist composition theory, in *Rereading the Sophists: Classical Rhetoric Refigured* (Carbondale: Southern Illinois University Press, 1991).

8. See Lanser and Beck, p. 86: "Androcentric thinking—which in our day usually masquerades as scientific objectivity—is rewarded in the woman

scholar, while thinking within a gynocentric frame of reference is dismissed as emotional, subjective, specialized, or intuitive—that is, not scholarly as the patriarchs have defined the term. As a result, many female thinkers have been reduced to parroting the patriarchy or remaining silent. The writings of women who are struggling to define themselves but have not yet given up a patriarchal frame of reference may betray a tension so strong as to produce a virtually 'double-voiced' discourse."

9. See Catherine Belsey, *The Subject of Tragedy* (London: Methuen, 1985), especially chapter 6, "Silence and Speech," pp. 149–191.

10. All references to the pamphlet will be to Margaret Fell, *Women's Speaking Justified* (1667; rpt. Los Angeles: William Andrews Clark Memorial Library, 1979). On Fell's career as a preacher and Quaker organizer, see Isabel Ross, *Margaret Fell, Mother of Quakerism* (London: Longman, Green and Co., 1949).

11. See, for example, Belsey, *Subject*, p. 178; Elaine Hobby, *Virtue of Necessity: English Women's Writing 1649–1688* (London: Virago Press, 1988), p. 6; and Constance Jordan, *Renaissance Feminism: Literary Texts and Political Models* (Ithaca: Cornell University Press, 1990), pp. 25, 63, 129.

12. Perhaps Fell is so careful to distinguish between appropriate and inappropriate speaking by women because the London Quaker meetings during 1655 to 1657 had been disrupted by Martha Simmonds, Hannah Stranger, and other women using "Ranter" tactics in favor of James Naylor against George Fox (whom Fell supported); see Ross, *Margaret Fell*, pp. 101–114.

13. I am indebted to an unpublished paper on "Margaret Fell" by Will Stofega, who points out that Fell's inclusion of the "dark Priests, that are so mad against Women's Speaking" (Fell 18), "gives her text a 'villain' of sorts who is responsible for silencing women," and allows her to attack those who misinterpret the Bible, rather than the Bible itself (Stofega 4).

14. Paula L. Barbour, "Introduction" to Bathsua Makin, *An Essay To Revive the Antient Education of Gentlewomen*, p. iii. All quotations from Makin are taken from this edition. Hilda Smith also thinks of Makin as "conservative"; see *Reason's Disciples: Seventeenth-Century English Feminists* (Urbana: University of Illinois Press, 1982), p. 13. I am greatly indebted to Smith's argument that seventeenth–century rationalism allowed women to reformulate the terms under which they combatted their inferior position. For new information on Makin's identity and an explanation for my use of "Reginald" rather than the off-repeated "Pell" as Makin's maiden name, see Frances Teague, "The Identity of Bathsua Makin," *Biography* 16.1 (Winter 1993): 1–17.

15. Indeed, I know that Arete was a teacher of rhetoric not from histories of classical rhetoric, who never mention her, but from Makin. On the Renaissance derogation of women's speech, see Belsey (above n9); Lisa Jardine,

"Shrewd or Shrewish? When the Disorderly Woman has her Head," *Still Harping on Daughters: Women and Drama in the Age of Shakespeare* (Totowa, NJ: Barnes & Noble Books, 1983), pp. 103–140; and Margaret Ferguson, "A Room Not Their Own: Renaissance Women as Readers and Writers," in *The Comparative Perspective on Literature*, eds. Clayton Koelb and Susan Noakes (Ithaca: Cornell University Press, 1988), pp. 93–116. Paula Barbour ("Introduction," p. iv) suggests that Makin derives much of the argument of her treatise from Anna Maria van Schurman. Makin's treatise shares with Schurman's treatise, *Amica dissertatio . . . de capacitate ingenii muliebris ad scientias* (Paris, 1638), rpt. as *De ingenii muliebris ad doctrinam et meliores litteras aptitudine* (Leyden, 1641), and translated into English by John Redmayne as *The Learned Maid; or, Whether a Maid may be a Scholar? A Logick Exercise* (London, 1659), the thesis that women with enough time, wealth, and intelligence should receive a humanist education, and the qualification that women not use their education for public office. But Makin's treatise gradually extends the franchise of education to all classes of women, whereas Schurman's does not, and Schurman does not support her argument about education with Makin's analysis of the politics of speech.

16. All quotations from Mary Astell's treatise are to *A Serious Proposal to the Ladies, Part I* and *Part II*, 4th ed. (1701; rpt. New York: Source Book Press, 1970).

17. I think that a major model for Astell's college was Madame de Maintenon's Saint-Cyr, a school for girls, founded in 1686, that attempted "to counter the social processes at work in polite society" (Lougee 173). Although Lougee sees Saint-Cyr as conservative and anti-feminist as compared to French salon society, Astell seems to have used this model to double ends: conservative in the sense of protecting young women from what Astell saw as the trivialities of English society, and radical in providing a place where women could gather to educate themselves (see Lougee, *Le Paradis des Femmes*, pp. 172–195). English society did not in general provide the intellectual advantages for women that French salon society did (although Katherine Philips had earlier tried to imitate the salon society—see Harriet Andreadis, "The Sapphic-Platonics of Katherine Philips, 1632–1664," *Signs* 15 [1989]: 34–60). Ruth Perry offers a useful summary of the influence of Antoine Arnauld's *Art de Penser*, the Port-Royal logic in her biography of Astell, pp. 84–87; see also Christine Mason Sutherland, "Outside the Rhetorical Tradition: Mary Astell's Advice to Women in Seventeenth-Century England," *Rhetorica* 9.2 (Spring 1991): 147–163, for further information on the influences of Augustine, Arnauld, and Bernard Lamy's Port-Royal *The Art of Speaking*.

18. On the influences of Astell's *Serious Proposal*, see Ruth Perry, *The Celebrated Mary Astell* (Chicago: University of Chicago Press, 1986), esp. pp. 103–105, and ch. 8.

19. Gregor Reisch, *Margarita Philosophica* (Freiburg, 1503). On fears about women's education, see Gibson, "Educating for Silence," esp. pp. 10–12, 16, and 18–20; Jardine, *Still Harping*, esp. pp. 121–133; Peter Stallybrass, "Patriarchal Territories: The Body Enclosed," from *Rewriting the Renaissance*, ed. Margaret Ferguson, Maureen Quilligan, and Nancy J. Vickers (Chicago: University of Chicago Press, 1986), esp. pp. 126–127; and Margaret Ferguson, "A Room Not Their Own: Renaissance Women as Readers and Writers," esp. pp. 99–102.

20. See Smith, *Reason's Disciples*, p. 5: "Seventeenth-century feminists fitted these two major points—intellectual restriction and domestic subordination— into a general system of protest against men's total control of the public and private institutions of English society. These women desired to change the sexual balance of power. They did not simply criticize women's position in society, but saw social change as necessary to restoring women's rightful opportunities."

Democratic Congresswomen. By permission of
Stephen Crowley/NYT Pictures.

Women and Political Communication: From the Margins to the Center

Patricia A. Sullivan and Carole Levin

Just as a constellation of circumstances brought political power to women in the Renaissance, a number of factors coalesced to politically empower United States women in 1992. During the Renaissance, accidents of female birth and male death, as well as a religious reformation and changes in political structure, led to new opportunities for women. For contemporary women in the United States, the Thomas-Hill Hearings, as well as voter interest in change due to disgust with "politics as usual," fostered a favorable climate for women seeking elected offices.[1] Media coverage of 1992 campaign victories declared that "the year of the woman" had arrived, although women remain underrepresented in Congress. More women, including one African-American woman, serve in the United States Senate than ever before —now there are seven, rather than two, out of 100— but they continue to exist on the margins of political discourse.[2] The recognition of women—at least a small number of women—as viable political candidates in 1992 prompted a writer for *Time* to observe: "It is now thinkable that someday women candidates for public office will be simply taken for granted."[3] The most visible woman on the current United States political scene, however, was not elected to serve in public office. Hillary Rodham Clinton, in her role as chair of the health-reform task force, "is solidifying her position as the power beside, rather than behind, the throne."[4] Barbara Bush's press secretary, Anna Perez, claims that if Rodham Clinton succeeds, she "will have designed a new paradigm for First Ladies."[5] Her efforts to revision the role of First Lady calls to mind Elizabeth I's determination to redefine queenship by ruling alone. Elizabeth succeeded in demonstrating that a queen could exercise political power without benefit of a king beside her.

As Hillary Rodham Clinton follows in the steps of her foremothers and becomes a powerful figure on the political scene, people may forget questions about her that emerged during Campaign 1992. A *Time* cover asked, "The Hillary Factor: Is she helping or hurting her husband?"[6] When Republicans escalated their attacks on Rodham Clinton, some reporters wondered whether she would become the " 'Willary Horton' for the '92 campaign" and "an emblem for all that is wrong with family values, working mothers, and modern women in general."[7]

The misogynistic attacks—centering on questions of female authority—on Rodham Clinton were reminiscent of charges against Catherine de Médicis, Isabel, and Mary II. Floyd Brown, founder of ClintonWatch, called Rodham Clinton "a broom-riding political virago," suggesting both witch and monstrous queen.[8] Unlike her foremothers in the Renaissance, however, Rodham Clinton is *acknowledged* as a positive political force. After she testified on health-care reform before the House Ways and Means Committee, Representative Dan Rostenkowski, chair of the powerful committee, gushed: "I think in the very near future the President will be known as your husband. Who's that fella? That's Hillary's husband?"[9] Of course, such a remark must be greeted with ambivalence by observers charting the progress of women in the political realm. The committee chair's comments reflected discomfort with changing gender roles and implied that powerful women emasculate their husbands.

Although, as Rostenkowski's comments suggested, Rodham Clinton's successes in transforming the role of First Lady must be viewed with some skepticism, her strategies as a rhetorician in transforming her public persona deserve scrutiny. Her rhetorical strategies parallel those developed by Renaissance women included in this collection. Lena Cowen Orlin's essay in this collection examines Elizabeth I's use of familial tropes; future essays may examine Rodham Clinton's use of familial tropes. An analysis of Rodham Clinton's rhetoric will prompt the following questions. How did Hillary Rodham Clinton emerge as an accepted and powerful figure on Capitol Hill? How did her image evolve from "Wicked Witch of the West Wing" to "respected policy wonk?" How did she overcome a concerted Republican effort to cast her "as a lawsuit-mongering feminist who likened marriage to slavery and encouraged children to sue their parents?"[10] How did she recast the image created during primary season when she remarked, "I suppose I could have stayed home, baked cookies and had teas."[11] During one of her most serious gaffes in primary season, she was entrapped by a sound bite that suggested she disparaged women who had chosen to stay home to take care of their children. As a reporter noted, few news sources reported the rest of her statement: "The work that I have done as a professional, a public advocate, has been aimed . . . to assure that women can make choices . . . whether it's full-time career, full-time motherhood or some combination."[12]

Throughout her journey in Campaign 1992, Hillary Rodham Clinton expressed sadness concerning the distortions of her views; however, she adjusted her rhetoric—verbally and nonverbally—to respond to "radical feminist" charges mounted by critics such as Marilyn Quayle, Pat Robertson, and Pat Buchanan. Her efforts were assisted by a changing climate for women in the United States, as well as by Republicans who created a rhetorical situation that invited "backlash" concerning their "meanspirited attacks." They seemed to be attacking all "good mothers"—mothers trying to do their best under difficult circumstances.[13] In adjusting her rhetoric to suit the political climate, Rodham Clinton suggested that she was less powerful than her adversaries proposed. Just as Mary II was a powerful figure in her own right, but presented herself as a devoted wife, so did Rodham Clinton.

An examination of Hillary Rodham Clinton's rhetorical strategies reveals a number of transformations from Spring 1992 to Fall 1993. Throughout Campaign 1992, for example, she was known as Hillary Clinton; however, after her husband was inaugurated, her office made it clear that she wanted to be referred to as Hillary Rodham Clinton. She increased photo opportunities with her daughter, Chelsea, and engaged in the "great chocolate chip cookie bake-off" with Barbara Bush.[14]

Just as Elizabeth I recognized the constraints she faced as a woman seeking power in a patriarchal world and adjusted her rhetoric accordingly, so did Hillary Rodham Clinton. Through familial tropes, Elizabeth I rhetorically reassured her subjects that she had maternal qualities—wife to the kingdom, mother of the people, cousin to the nobility, and sister to foreign princes. Rodham Clinton's rhetoric—including verbal and nonverbal strategies—also reassured the public that she inhabited two worlds—the traditional realm of the First Lady and the policy realm of the Presidency. Stories circulated that she rejected an offer of help from a White House steward when she was preparing scrambled eggs for Chelsea—Chelsea was ill and the eggs had to be prepared in a particular way by her mother. Furthermore, a political consultant declared that she "mothers" the staff, and noted: "I've never seen her lose her temper, and you can tell her anything." She "presses coffee and bagels on the staff and frequently sends them home to bed [if ill] and for holidays."[15] She benefited from "a public image softened by Easter egg rolls on the South Lawn."[16]

From her first week in the White House, Rodham Clinton communicated that she could do it all—serve as traditional First Lady and policy adviser. She adopted Elizabeth I's approach and insisted that she could play a number of roles—from mother to her people to their stern ruler. Two front-page photos of Rodham Clinton in *The New York Times* captured the essence of her reassuring rhetoric. On February 2, 1993, she was shown—clad in a black bare-shouldered evening dress—making final arrangements for the Clintons' first state dinner. The accompanying article assured readers that she had supervised the menu and flower arrangements.[17] She recognized that, just as pageantry was important for Queens in Shakespeare's time, it is also important for First Ladies. Her choice of the bare-shouldered evening dress also revealed that she, along with Anne Boleyn, was willing to exploit her sexual appeal. Three days later, in her other role as health-reform task force director, Rodham Clinton appeared on the front page of *The New York Times* meeting with George J. Mitchell, Senate Majority Leader. The photo of her appearance—in a suit—on Capitol Hill signalled that this First Lady's roles would go beyond planning menus and flower arrangements.

The First Lady's efforts to recast her public image were particularly apparent during her testimonies on health-care reform before powerful Congressional committees. As she presented sophisticated policy proposals, she softened her messages by citing personal experiences to support her claims. She seemed to be reminding the committees that she "is a woman"—even though she is engaged in political decision-making. In her pathbraking efforts to define women as political decision-makers, she navigated careful rhetorical terrain. As one reporter noted, "During the campaign, Mrs. Clinton was surprised to learn from polls that many Americans did not picture her in a maternal way and did not even know that she had a daughter."[18] When she addressed committees on Capitol Hill, "she was careful to lace her testimony with personal references, beginning in the morning by telling the Ways and Means Committee that she was 'here as a mother, a wife, a daughter, a sister, a woman.' "[19] She emphasized that health-care reform must pass the " 'mother test,'—that is, whether mothers would feel the changes were in their interests."[20] When she spoke about death with dignity, unmarred by the intervention of extraordinary medical technology, she mentioned her own experience with a dying father.[21] Furthermore, she showed deference for members of the committees and "filigreed her answers with those ingratiating clauses that members of Congress hold dear."[22] She sprinkled her testimony with phrases such as, "Which you know better than I" and "as you have pointed out."[23] When scholars of rhetoric and history prepare accounts of Rodham Clinton as First Lady, they will confront the same issues Elizabeth Cary faced in writing about Isabel. Cary acknowledged that Isabel was a powerful figure in her royal household, but also addressed the limits of female authority. The limits of female authority for a woman holding the unelected office of First Lady will occupy those who chronicle Rodham Clinton's life in the White House. A reporter for *Time* foreshadowed the issues that will engage scholars and observed: "Hillary functions in the White House rather like the queen on a chessboard. Her power comes from her unrestricted movement; but the risk of capture is great, and a player without a queen is at a fatal disadvantage. Clinton's presidency would be severely disabled by a direct hit to his wife."[24]

Although Rodham Clinton has more power than her Renaissance predecessors, however, her conservative critics continue to cast her as a witch. A cover of *The American Spectator* featured a caricature of Rodham Clinton as "the Wicked Witch of the West" astride an airplane.[25] Furthermore, she is patronized by powerful patriarchs. Members of Congress might not agree with Knox that "the Regiment of a Woman" is "monstrous," but their treatment of the First Lady during health plan hearings indicate that they wanted to view her as an anomaly—the type of witness they will not necessarily hear from in the future. As members of Congressional committees lauded her capabilities and, in some cases, credited her with engineering health-care reform, a subtext crept into their discourse. They seemed to be saying, "Hillary Rodham Clinton is an *unusual woman*. Future First Ladies will not follow her path." To her credit, Rodham Clinton refused to acknowledge the accolades and implied that her testimony constituted "business as usual." She seemed to understand the line of reasoning of her audience—as did Protestant martyr Anne Askew—and used that reasoning to forward her agenda.

Hillary Rodham Clinton is an acknowledged force on Capitol Hill, but she is not the President of the United States. Eleanor Smeal,

President of The National Organization for Women (NOW), praised the First Lady as a role model for young girls. She said, "Can you imagine how many girls saw her testify about the health-care plan, who are now saying, 'I want to be a lawyer when I grow up?' "[26] A reporter for *The New York Times* noted that "some young girls might get the message that they should try to marry the President."[27] The same reporter observed that Rodham Clinton's rhetorical strategies—particularly her efforts "not to offend"—"leaves her sounding a little bit like a Miss America contestant, looking for an answer bland enough to please everyone."[28] Are we really so far from the Renaissance and women, such as Catherine de Médicis, Isabel, and Mary II who exercised power indirectly?

Although a number of essays in this collection chronicle the rhetorical strategies of Renaissance women who were on the "margins of discourse," we must remember that contemporary American women continue to communicate on the margins of discourse. Just as Madeleine de Scudéry, Margaret Cavendish, Margaret Fell, Bathsua Makin, and Mary Astell used the myth of the Renaissance to their advantage, contemporary female political figures may use disenchantment with "politics as usual" to their advantage. Maybe the next generation of women will be able to move beyond the "spooky"—anomalous and deferential—"picture-perfect performances" of Rodham Clinton.[29] The next generation of women may test Dale Spender's hypothesis concerning women and naming power. Spender proposes: "It is my belief that if women were to gain a public voice, they would in many instances supply very different meanings from those which have been provided and legitimated, by males."[30]

Hillary Rodham Clinton—with the blending of the personal and the political—may be proposing alternatives to "politics as usual" and questioning meanings legitimated by men. She may be strategizing rhetorically to solidify her power in a changing United States society just as Elizabeth I strategized to solidify her rule in the face of Knox's challenges to Queenship. Although women of the Renaissance faced even greater constraints than contemporary women in entering the world of politics, we must remember that histories of both periods must be viewed as gendered.

Retha Warnicke argues that the unsympathetic history and representation of Anne Boleyn by her contemporaries—and later patriarchal historians—must be questioned. When historians look back on the contributions of Hillary Rodham Clinton, a similar caution will be in order. As contemporaries write the history of her role on the political stage—and as historians interpret that role—gendered biases will inform their accounts. We wonder how historians will respond to the First Lady described in the following manner by one reporter. Tamar Lewin, a reporter for *The New York Times* said: "Few women in American public life have so publicly and so seamlessly incorporated the disarming charm once called 'feminine' with the steely confidence associated with powerful and persuasive men."[31] In this characterization, we find echoes of the Renaissance and the voices and representations of Christine de Pizan, Anne Boleyn, Elizabeth I, Catherine de Médicis, Anne Askew, Aphra Behn, Mary II, Madeleine de Scudéry, Margaret Cavendish, Margaret Fell, Bathsua Makin, and Mary II.

Notes

1. Jill Smolowe, "Politics: The Feminist Machine," *Time*, 4 May 1992: 34.

2. The seven include: Barbara Boxer (Democrat-California); Dianne Feinstein (Democrat-California); Kay Bailey Hutchison (Republican-Texas); Nancy Kassebaum (Republican-Kansas); Barbara Mikulski (Democrat-Maryland); and Patty Murray (Democrat-Washington).

3. Smolowe, "Politics," p. 35.

4. Gwen Ifill, "Role in Health Expands Hillary Clinton's Power," *The New York Times*, 22 September 1993, sec. A, p. 24.

5. Quoted in Ifill, sec. A, p. 24.

6. *Time* [cover], 14 September 1992.

7. Margaret Carlson, "All Eyes on Hillary," *Time*, 14 September 1992: 28.

8. Quoted in "Conservatives say first lady may be a fund-raising gold mine," *The Norman (Okla.) Transcript*, 30 April 1993, sec. A, p. 5. Our thanks to Martha Skeeters for this reference.

9. Maureen Dowd, "Witness Works Hill and Ends an Era," *The New York Times*, 29 September 1993, sec. A, p. 19.

10. Carlson, "All Eyes," p. 30.

11. Carlson, p. 30.

12. Carlson, p. 30.

13. Carlson, p. 32 and Susan Chira, "New Realities Fight Old Images of Mother," *The New York Times*, 4 October 1992, sec. A, p. 1.

14. Sally Quinn, "Look Out, It's Superwoman: The main problem with Hillary is, she's like us," *Time*, 15 February 1993, pp. 24–25.

15. Carlson, "All Eyes," p. 34.

16. Ifill, sec. A, p. 24.

17. Marian Burros, "Hillary Clinton's New Home: Broccoli's In, Smoking's Out," *The New York Times*, 2 February 1993, sec. A, pp. 1, 12.

18. Dowd, "Witness Works Hill," sec. A, p. 19.

19. Dowd, sec. A, p. 19.

20. Tamar Lewin, "A Feminism That Speaks for Itself," *The New York Times*, 3 October 1993, sec. E, p. 3.

21. Lewin, "A Feminism," sec. E, p. 3.

22. Dowd, "Witness Works Hill," sec. A, p. 19.

23. Dowd, sec. A, p. 19.

24. Nancy Gibbs, "The Trials of Hillary," *Time*, 21 March 1994, p. 33.

25. *The American Spectator* [cover], June 1994.

26. Quoted in Lewin, "A Feminism," sec. E, p. 3.

27. Lewin, sec. E, p. 3.

28. Lewin, sec. E, p. 3.

29. Lewin, sec. E, p. 3.

30. Dale Spender, *Man Made Language* (1980; reprint ed., Glasgow: Harper Collins, 1992), p. 78.

31. Lewin, "A Feminism," sec. E, p. 3.

NOTES ON CONTRIBUTORS

Ilona Bell is Professor of English at Williams College. She has written numerous articles on English Renaissance literature and is currently completing a manuscript on the poetry and practice of Elizabethan courtship.

Jo Eldridge Carney is Assistant Professor of English at Trenton State College. She received her Ph.D. from the University of Iowa. Her articles have appeared in such collections as *Sexuality and Politics in Renaissance Drama* and *Historical Dictionary of Stuart England*.

Jane L. Donawerth, Associate Professor of English and Affiliate Faculty in Women's Studies at the University of Maryland at College Park, has published a book on Shakespeare and language, and articles on pedagogy, science fiction by women, the history of rhetorical theory, ad Renaissance women writers. She has co-edited with Carol Kolmerton a collection of essays on *Utopian and Science Fiction By Women* (New York: Syracuse University Press, 1994), and is finishing a book on contemporary science fiction by women, as well as beginning an anthology of rhetorical theory by women before 1900. Her children, Donnie and Kate, are six and eight years old, and are learning piano and sign language.

Arlen Feldwick is a graduate student and teaching assistant in the Department of English at the University of Arizona. She coauthored an article on John of Salisbury in *Journal of Medieval and Renaissance Studies* and has published a critical bibliography on multiculturalism in Australia, New Zealand and the South Pacific.

Daniel Kempton is Assistant Professor in the Department of English at SUNY at New Paltz where he teaches medieval literature. He has published several articles on Chaucer's *Canterbury Tales* and on language theory.

Gwynne Kennedy is an Assistant Professor of English at the University of Wisconsin, Milwaukee. She has written on Elizabeth Cary and Mary Wroth and is currently working on a book that examines representations of female anger in texts by early modern English women writers.

Elaine Kruse, Associate Professor of History at Nebraska Wesleyan University, received her Ph.D. from the University of Iowa. She has published articles on women and the family in Early Modern France.

Carole Levin is Professor of History at SUNY at New Paltz. She is the author of *"The Heart and Stomach of a King"*: *Elizabeth I and the Politics of Sex and Power* (1994) and *Propaganda in the English Reformation: Heroic and Villainous Images of King John* (1988) as well as the editor (with Jeanie Watson) of *Ambiguous Realities: Women in the Middle Ages and Renaissance* (1987) and (with Karen Robertson) of *Sexuality and Politics in Renaissance Drama* (1991). She has also published articles on Elizabethan cultural history in such journals as *Albion, Examplaria,* and *The Sixteenth Century Journal.*

Elizabeth Mazzola received her Ph.D. from New York University in 1991. She is Assistant Professor of English at City College of CUNY where she teaches Renaissance literature. In addition to several articles on Shakespeare and Spenser, she has completed a book on Spenser's *Faerie Queene.* She is now working on a study of the evolution of privacy within the changing literary designs of romance.

Dennis Moore is Associate Professor in the Department of Rhetoric at the University of Iowa, where he works with Renaissance and modern arts of language. His writings include *The Politics of Spenser's "Complaints" and Sidney's Philisides Poems.* His study in this volume is part of a series on the Tudor-Stuart queenship controversy.

Lena Cowen Orlin Is Executive Director of the Folger Institute at the Folger Shakespeare Library. She is the author of *Private Matters and Public Culture in Post-Reformation England* (1994) and a co-editor of *The Fashioning and Functioning of the British Country House* (1989).

W. M. Spellman is Associate Professor of History at the University of North Carolina, Asheville. He is the author of *John Locke and the Problem of Depravity* (Oxford, 1988) and *The Latitudinarians and the Church of England, 1660–1700* (Georgia, 1993). He has contributed articles to *The Harvard Theological Review, The Journal of Religion, Anglican and Episcopal History,* and *Revue Internationale De Philosophie.*

Patricia A. Sullivan is Assistant Professor in the Department of Communication at SUNY at New Paltz. Current research interests include: women's political discourse and feminist approaches to human communication ethics. She is writing a book (with Lynn H. Turner) on contemporary women and political communication and has published in journals such as *The Quarterly Journal of Speech, Communication Quarterly,* and *The Western Journal of Communication.*

Retha M. Warnicke earned her Ph.D. at Harvard University and has been Professor of History at Arizona State University since 1984. She is the author of three books including *Women of the English Renaissance and Reformation* (Greenwood Press, 1983) and *The Rise and Fall of Anne Boleyn: Family Politics at the Court of Henry VIII* (Cambridge University Press, 1989). Her articles on women's history have appeared in such journals as *English Historical Review, Historical Journal, Albion,* and *Sixteenth Century Journal.*

INDEX